Venice: Extraordinary Maintenance

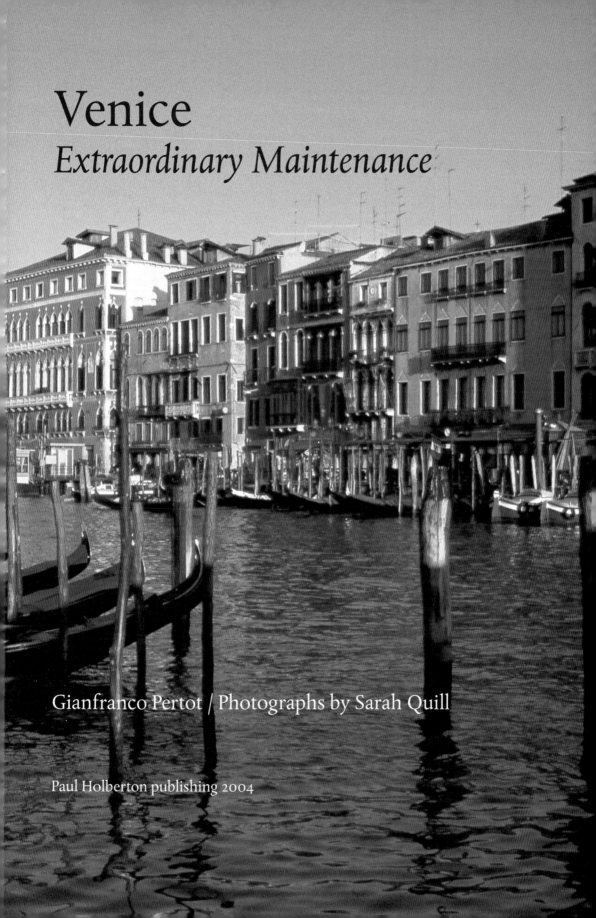

Venice
Extraordinary Maintenance

Gianfranco Pertot / Photographs by Sarah Quill

Paul Holberton publishing 2004

A history of the restoration, conservation,
destruction and adulteration of the fabric of the
city of Venice from the Fall of the Republic to the present

First published 2004

Text © 2004 Gianfranco Pertot and Paul Holberton
publishing
Colour photographs © 2004 Sarah Quill
(unless otherwise specified)
Archival photographs have been supplied by the
author, acknowledging the following sources::
Archivio Naya-Böhm, Venice
Fondazione Giorgio Cini, Venice

Translated from the Italian by Christine Donougher

ISBN 1 903470 12 9

British Library Cataloguing in Publication Data
A catalogue record for this book is available from the
British Library

Produced by Paul Holberton publishing,
37 Snowsfields, London SE1 3SU
www.paul-holberton.net

Designed by Roger Davies
daviesdesign@onetel.net

Printed in Italy

Cover image: Venice, gondolas, the Doge's Palace,
St Mark's Campanile (and, inset, the Campanile after
its collapse in 1902)

Frontispieces: (*half title*) Old and new: a modern
drainpipe kinks and modern rendering is cut away in
order to make visible stones carved perhaps a
millennium ago; this house at San Silvestro has
recently been restored, see p. 218;

(*pp. 2–3*) Up the Grand Canal, towards the Rialto
Bridge: all these palaces have been rebuilt or radically
restored since the Fall of the Republic. Ruskin
commented on entering the Grand Canal in
September 1845: "... two thirds of the palaces are under
repair – we know what that means ..." (full quotation
on pages 221–22);

(*pp. 4–5*) Campo San Giovanni in Bragora (Bandiera e
Moro), in one of the more 'working-class' areas of the
city, near the Arsenale; the palace in the background is
the Gritti-Badoer. The palace has been subject to a
new restoration (since this photograph) in 2004, with
what appear to be dubious results.

Contents

Author's Acknowledgements

If I were to repeat my thanks to the many individuals and institutions who made possible the Italian edition, by facilitating my investigations, my research or my access to various places, the list would be far too long; and I hope that over the past sixteen years I have demonstrated my gratitude to them fittingly.

However, it remains my pleasant obligation to mention and thank Marco Dezzi Bardeschi, lecturer on architectural conservation at the *Politecnico di Milano* and President of the Italian committee of ICOMOS (International Council on Monuments and Sites), who was the inspiration for this book, who contributed many insights and precious advice during its preparation, and who made its initial publication possible; the publisher Franco Angeli of Milan, who kindly granted the rights for the English language edition; the Italian section of UNESCO; the Boards of Directors and Staff of the Committees for Venice, contacted in their offices and through their websites, who have provided information and documentation, in particular Jill Weinreich of Save Venice, and the Venice in Peril Fund.

Merely to thank Christine Donougher, Sarah Quill and Paul Holberton (who initiated, encouraged and personally handled the preparation and publication of the English version) is hardly enough: *grazie di cuore!*

This book is dedicated, with a touch of envy, to children of every age, and especially to my son Giovanni. My dedication is of a wishful nature: in their eyes Venice is still, despite everything, an amazing and magical surprise. May it ever remain so.

Gianfranco Pertot

Publisher's Acknowledgements

I owe many thanks to Sarah Quill not just for her photographs (which speak for themselves) but also for her passion, interest and care for the text and the purpose of the book, and all the time and knowledge of Venice that has involved. I thank Gianfranco above all for his patience (for the editing and preparation of the English edition took longer than anticipated), and his care and attention, too. My guide and friend in many of these difficult matters has been the *unico* Giorgio (Nubar) Gianighian (whose tireless work for Venice the author properly acknowledges in the notes to Chapter 11). Further thanks to John Millerchip, who was kind enough to look over the script, and to all those who, directly or indirectly, helped me write the captions.

Paul Holberton

Preface

This book was first published sixteen years ago, in 1988. The original title was *Venezia 'restaurata'* (Venice 'restored'). The inverted commas round the word 'restored' were intended to suggest how vain was the ambition to restore the works we loved to their desired integrity and to an original state, and how false, falsifying and alienating were, in most cases, the results obtained.

In the last few years, research into the history of the restoration and repair of monuments has made it possible to examine the vicissitudes of many that have been subjected, in the name of restoration, to extensive redefinition, to reconstructions that were often pastiches based on value judgements (often aesthetic judgement alone), to cleaning up, purging, renovation, *ripristino* (a term which will recur in this book) or a kind of archaeological re-composition.

All these operations, which, regrettably, account for by far the greater part of works done on existing buildings, have in common that they damage or destroy, by substitution and abrasive cleaning, the physical surface in which the history of the buildings and of the men who have lived in them is inscribed and leaves its daily record. I believe that within our culture it is now accepted that it is precisely in its stratification, its complexity, its multiple traces of constructive and destructive deeds, even in its signs of degradation, that the identity of a building can be fully understood. This variegated and irregular physical territory, where difference is more important that homogeneity, patina more important than newness, has always been regarded by 'restorers' as a damaged, defective, ailing world to be put right again, made whole and cured, no matter what the cost.

Thus Venice 'restored' was born of the conviction that even a world icon of art such as Venice now represents an architectural landscape more consistent with the advertised image of itself than with its own actual history. It has been at once fascinating and complicated to identify the reasons for this slow but continuous construction of a one-dimensional image of Venice – reasons that extend over a long period, going back to the very beginnings of the discipline of restoration in the first half of the nineteenth century. My task was not merely a question of locating and identifying case by case the boundary between true (original and genuine, not affected by restoration) and false (redone, renovated, reconstructed, invented; in other words, restored) but above all of establishing the many reasons for what happened, the cultural implications, the expectations, the reception. The first part of the book in particular should be read in these terms; it gives, I hope, an overview of events that are to be understood in the context of the cultural life of those years, often highlighted by the work of particular individuals. But serious misgivings should also arise as to the reasons why those works and those results have been accepted by our age, without any attempt to see them as historical phenomena, and why we continue to permit methods of operation that are certainly at odds with the highest level of the current cultural debate on the conservation of remnants of the past.

This research sparked curiosity about another set of events and considerations, and their economic, political or cultural causes, which often seem to conform to a typically Italian or Venetian tradition of governing, legislating and applying laws and regulations. In recent times Venice has ever more frequently got into serious difficulties: as an entity it is too uncommon (a city on water; a former world economic power; the biggest open-air and indoor theatre-museum in the world, then as now); its physiology is too unpredictable (its lagoon, its water that rises and falls four times a day); its anatomy is too peculiar (houses on water, 'elastic' buildings constructed with techniques that in any other part of Europe would seem absurd); and the image generally held of the city, with its inherent expectations, is too rigid and simple not to be upset in a crisis.

And crises there have been, and they continue: industrial Marghera, *acqua alta* (exceptionally high tides); legislation that was at first inoperable and paralysing, then surprisingly permissive; grandiose plans and no action taken; fires, concerts, special funding and then an inability to spend the funds collected throughout the world; the exodus of Venetians from Venice and the daily invasion of mass tourism.

When one rounds up the most recent developments, an inescapable conclusion emerges: all this has been, is now and will be, every day and in every instance, on the blocks of stone brought from Istria and on the *masegni* quarried from the Veneto hinterland that pave the streets and squares; on the marble panels that for centuries the Serenissima found, pillaged or bought from the four corners of the known world, attracting and developing the very best artists and craftsmen to give shape and glory to houses, churches, squares, extraordinary warships and even more extraordinary boats for life on the lagoon; working with wood, stone, enamels and metals to produce that miracle of acrobatics, intelligence and technical knowledge that every Venetian building and house represents.

In all of our homes there is at least one book, postcard or photograph of Venice. These images are inseparable from the fabric of the city, the stones of Venice, which must, above all, be safeguarded and preserved, even from restoration.

Sixteen years on, the intentions and objectives that led to the writing of this book are still the same, of course. However, other more rigorous pieces of research have been published in the meantime, and there has been progress in the historiography of restoration, as indeed in the debate about the handling of heritage architecture, both in relation to new technologies available and owing to growth and ever greater sophistication in the discipline of conservation. However, I have not thought it advisable to change the structure of my original text. I have limited myself to clarifying the narrative, correcting a few inaccuracies and expanding a few details. A new, brief concluding chapter attempts to bring the situation up to date with a concise account of recent developments.

Sources and references, which in the Italian edition were footnoted, are here noted or summarized at the end of each chapter. I have not provided a complete bibliography of the works consulted or used in my research, which were almost solely in Italian. The illustrative material has, however, been enriched by some unpublished historical pictures that I have managed to trace in recent years, and above all by the photographic images taken by Sarah Quill.

Postscript. Just as I was completing my work on this English edition, the umpteenth incident of destruction amid the destruction befell the city. The *Molino Stucky* (Stucky flour mill), constructed on the Giudecca for Giovanni Stucky by Ernst Wullekopf at the end of the nineteenth century, was burnt down. Another fire, like that at the *Teatro La Fenice* (1996), again on a restoration site, and perhaps another case of arson. As the Molino's crenellations collapsed and the metal scaffolding surrounding the great mass of the building melted, one could not but reflect how the stones of Venice were being recast in familiar roles and pursued again by phantoms seen so many times before – the long neglect of a building (the mill had been empty since 1955) on the periphery of the lagoon city; a recent project to convert the site into a luxury conference hotel of 32,000 m² (in the main building), together with 138 apartments (on the outer, western side) and a commercial centre (the apartments have been sold at a price agreed with the *Comune* (Municipality) of Venice, only three of them to Venetian citizens). Thus tourism, once again, is practically the sole reference for Venetian life; and then there are the mistakes, the accusations, perhaps the negligence, and the delays: it should have been finished in 2000, then 2005–06, now, who knows. Finally, there rise the protestations of the day after: rebuild immediately, reconstruct, exorcise 'Death in Venice', eliminate all traces of it – *come era e dove era* (as it was, and where it was).

Milan, April 2004

1 | The Roots of Venice's Modern Crisis

1.1 The loss of political autonomy,
the decline in the economy and the break in
continuity, 1797–1866

What Venice is today is in many crucial ways a consequence of the events of the early years of the nineteenth century, of the brief but intensely active period of Napoleonic rule following the fall of the Republic (1797) and of the three successive periods of Austrian rule, which prevailed until 1866. Without warning or preparation, these events deprived the city of all continuity in the political and economic role it had hitherto exercised, following its own traditions, for hundreds of years.

The Fall of the Republic not only brought an end to the political autonomy Venice had enjoyed for some thousand years, but also precipitated an economic decline, with all its attendant demographic, social and environmental implications, from which there has been no recovery. In addition, the city was forced into new relationships with continental states alien to its unique physiology and its own particular needs. The vast majority of the decisions, projects and initiatives that have followed since the Fall of the Republic have as their context this eternal 'crisis', which stems directly from the city's deprivation of a role and an identity, its reduction to a monument of the past, its loss of an active, organic existence.

The negative repercussions of Venice's new and alienated situation became immediately evident after the Treaty of Campoformio (in which Venice was ceded to Austria) and the first period of Austrian rule (1797–1806). However, the Napoleonic administration that succeeded it, when Venice became part of the Kingdom of Italy (1806–1814), made innovative and radical attempts to confront the city's problems, entrusting the city's leading technical experts with the design of projects of ambition and scope. As in the capital of the Kingdom, Milan, so in Venice a *Commissione di Ornato* (Commission for architectural and decorative design) was set

Fig. 1
Of the church of Sant'Antonio Abate only this solitary arch, part of the Lando Chapel designed by Michele Sanmicheli in the mid sixteenth century, was preserved when four convents – Sant'Antonio Abate, San Domenico, San Nicola di Bari and the convent of the Capuchins – and other buildings, too, were appropriated and demolished under the powers of the Napoleonic special law of 1807. In their place the *Giardini Pubblici* (Public gardens) were laid out – now best known and most often frequented as the site of the various national pavilions of the Venice Biennale. Except during the Biennales, these vegetatively and picturesquely uninteresting spaces, imposed after a kind of Neoclassical 'Lustgarten' model, are best suitable for the exercise and relief of household dogs.

Fig. 2

The eastern end of the city, which, apart from its convents (demolished by the second Napoleonic administration) was dominated by boatyards and the unsightly sprawl of marine industry (see, for example, fig. 14, p. 32), was an early target of the new authorities' new broom. The solid *banchina* of the Riva dei Sette Martiri on the right is a development of the very early twentieth century, intended to provide for modern tourist boats, but the Via Garibaldi on the left, formerly – before the formation of the Italian state – Via Eugenia, was a Napoleonic initiative, created by the filling-in of an earlier, conveniently straight, canal. Connecting to the *Giardini Pubblici* through the Viale Garibaldi down to the right, the Via Eugenia imposed a monumental route – of a kind that the city was felt keenly in the nineteenth century to lack – through to the city's former cathedral, San Pietro in Castello. These new foci of the city bore a political message, imparting modernity and secular civility to a proletarian district and providing an alternative gathering place to that of the Piazza outside the Doge's Palace and St Mark's.

All over modern Venice there are such pavemented areas, *rio terà*, substituting for Venice's original watery thoroughfares. In the nineteenth century Venice became a pedestrian city in a manner previously unthinkable to Venetians.

The house wedged in the angle between the two walkways had been, until the 1930s, typically plain, the Istrian stone lining its windows and doors constituting its only decoration. It was made to look more picturesquely 'Venetian' in the 1930s, by the introduction especially of Gothic windows and of 'Carpaccio' chimneys.

up, with responsibilities to oversee the treatment of buildings fronting on public thorough-fares, to safeguard monuments, to advise on public projects and above all to draw up a *Piano regolatore* (General town plan) for the city. The plan for Milan, the so-called *Piano dei rettifili* (Rectification plan) was comprehensive and highly specific, while the one for Venice was less coherent but no less radical. It was conceived by a specially appointed commission and developed in detail by the *Commissione di Ornato*, headed by the Secretary of the *Accademia di Belle Arti* (Academy of fine arts), Antonio Diedo, and including on its board Giannantonio Selva.

The Venetian *Piano regolatore*, financed by a Napoleonic special law, was passed by decree on 7 December 1807, and implemented immediately, at least in part. It involved the creation of new gardens, notably those in Castello, the work of Selva – and much criticized, for he demolished four large convents and their dependent churches, as well as some other buildings of merit, to make way for them. Canals were filled in and new pedestrian routes opened up: Selva's new via Eugenia (now via Garibaldi) in Castello was a leading example. Obsolete buildings, for the most part Gothic and Early Renaissance, were demolished; enormous areas of ecclesiastical property were expropriated (under the decrees of 1806 and 1807, some twenty-six convent complexes and dependent churches and some four thousand houses belonging to suppressed monastic orders, in Venice alone), not only for public use but also simply for sale. A *catasto* or city land registry was compiled (1808–11). Perhaps the best-known and most visible result of the Napoleonic programme was the restructuring of the civic buildings in the Piazza, with the demolition of the church of San Geminiano and the construction in its place of the Procuratie Nuovissime (or Ala Napoleonica, erected between 1810 and 1814). Here the royal apartments and the seat of government were established.

All this activity did not, however, do anything to improve the condition of the city as a whole or of its architectural heritage in particular. Criticism of the management of the city's buildings and infrastructure was already being voiced during the Napoleonic period, and is well summarized in twelve paragraphs in a valuable document dating from 1814, the *Relazione dello stato materiale di Venezia recercata da un Amico assente dall'Italia* (Account of the material state of Venice conducted by a friend absent from Italy). Its author, Gaetano Pinali, indicted the "destruction inflicted entirely gratuitously on Venice, both on its public and on its private buildings". He accused as responsible not only the city's administrators but the generation of architects inspired by the Academicians Giannantonio Selva and Leopoldo Cicognara, and above all Giuseppe Mezzani, director of works on the controversial Procuratie Nuovissime.

Although, after 1815, the returning Austrian administration took over most of the Napoleonic plan, continuing to put into effect its main elements, the Austrians seriously neglected the need for revitalizing Venice's commercial, manufacturing and port economy: these, by contrast, the Kingdom of Italy had supported and attempted to re-invigorate. They were severely hit by the British naval blockade of 1813–14, and declined still further while the Austrians refused to concede, until 1830, customs-free status to the port of Venice, to the great

Figs. 3, 4

At the opposite end of the Piazza to St Mark's Basilica, the church of San Geminiano (seen at the centre of this painting by Canaletto) was equally old, even though it had been rebuilt and provided with a modern façade by Jacopo Sansovino in the 1550s. Its demolition and substitution with the so-called Ala Napoleonica subtly but radically altered the nature of the city's historic centre. It signalled very obviously the new order, since the Ala Napoleonica, housing the royal state rooms, was the seat of the new authority; the new powers would not re-occupy the Doge's Palace, but put up in the south (left) Procuratie offices until the new building was ready. Among the monuments destroyed in the city's reorganization San Geminiano was the one most lamented by the populace. Giovanni Antolini, who had previously planned the redevelopment of Milan in Neoclassical style, was brought in to build the new wing, but cries that his style was too insensitive to the surrroundings were heard, he was dismissed, and eventually a design that blended better with the Procuratie around it was built.

All the offices of government in the city have remained displaced. The *Comune* or municipality and even institutions that survived the Republic, such as the *Magistrato alle Acque* or Water authority, occupy for the most part former private palaces along the Grand Canal.

Thus the Piazza was transformed from the political and religious heart of the city to the 'drawing room' of Europe (an epithet alleged to go back to Napoleon himself), in which the rest of the world took up chairs in cafés to admire the view – even at night, following the introduction of a lighting system by the Napoleonic régime. Half willingly – in collaboration with the régime– and half painfully, Venice was adapting and becoming a modern city.

Antonio Canaletto, *The Piazza San Marco looking West*, The Wallace Collection, London, inv. P505; by kind permission of the Trustees of the Wallace Collection

advantage of nearby Pula and, in particular, Trieste, on the opposite coast of the Adriatic. Trieste had the benefit of a ruling elite that was profoundly pro-Austrian; a free port since the eighteenth century, it was the home of shipbuilders of Greek or Dalmatian origin who actively promoted its potential.

As a direct consequence of Venice's annexation to the Austro-Hungarian empire, its economy collapsed. The administration had no interest in adapting its economic policy to the needs of Venice, which, in terms of the empire, was a peripheral city, and in any case one that was politically hostile and potentially an enemy. Certainly its new rulers lacked the will to alter the decision-making processes and incentives of the existing system in order to respond to the city's particular circumstances; instead they merely absorbed it into the workings of government in the vast empire to which it now belonged.

In his valuable book *Venezia Ottocento* Giandomenico Romanelli pictures the city's dismal situation: "These early years of Austrian rule saw the beginning of an administrative pressure completely new to the lagoon city: the interminable bureaucratic procedures – applications for permission, for finance, for approval – that had to be made to a distant central government (often indifferent, ill-informed and hostile when it came to Venetian matters) were another of the many factors that contributed to the establishment of a climate of apathy and weariness, of general demoralization in the way lives were conducted in a city that had outlived itself."

It is true that any attempt to protect Venetian commercial interests would have been at the expense of the ports, trading centres and cities that had long been of key importance to Habsburg economic policy. It was inconceivable that the complex economic, administrative and legislative system which the Venetian judicial authorities had enjoyed for centuries could be reinstated. Metaphorically speaking, Mercury, patron of merchants, whom Jacopo de' Barbari depicted as a tutelary deity (together with Neptune, god of the seas) in his splendid view of Venice in 1500, now vanished from the city's horizons. In his place came a new deity, that of tourism, which was encouraged by the opening of museums and sustained by the spread of commercial activities directed towards the reception of visitors, especially from the third decade of the nineteenth century onwards.

During the period of the Kingdom of Italy (a political entity of rather more limited extent territorially) Venice had enjoyed both a degree of prominence and the favour of its rulers, but when it became part of the Austro-Hungarian empire it was forced to submit to a crushing change of status. Venice had for centuries had far-flung commercial and strategic interests, but a very small territorial sovereignty: in fact all the power and wealth of the Serenissima had been concentrated in the lagoon islands, which formed a vital, complex and wealthy nerve-centre of an importance out of all proportion to its size. Governed hitherto by methods and procedures entirely of its own making, it now became a kind of discarded limb manipulated slowly and impersonally from a remote source. Venice ceased to be herself, but became merely the physical symbol of her former self – the physical manifestation of an aborted enterprise. In the eyes of her Austrian rulers the city was difficult to manage, problematic and in many senses redundant, even though, for cultural reasons, it was impossible not to pay lip service to the protection of the city.

In this state of affairs the Austrian authorities naturally took the less adventurous and less demanding course of action: they regarded Venice as a city like any other, a normal city. No attempt was made to revive the manufacturing activities that underpinned the lagoon's local economy, and, as we have seen, its port was virtually repressed. Venice was to be kept alive from the outside, preserving appearances, since very little was to be done to save its intrinsic identity. The solutions that were to be found for the problems of Venice were solutions of the kind customary for other cities, even though these might be conceived for completely different circumstances and not particularly well adapted to the dynamics of the lagoon.

The consequences of Venice's 'fall', which occurred not in any gradual way but almost at a stroke, extend right up to the present day. Hence it is that Venice is seen as an 'impossible' city, 'not modern', 'problematic', an outmoded cultural jewel, in effect useless, visitable but uninhabitable. It was during these early years of the nineteenth century that the premises were established for the development of the stereotype of the 'museum city', a stereotype which threatens ever more insistently to smother the infinitely richer, more complex and vital reality of Venice.

Fig. 5

Venice seen from the air in a mid-nineteenth-
century steel engraving has taken on a 'Disney'
quality: it is portrayed not as a present living city
but as a phantasm from the past. This is indeed an
image taken from a history of Venice, L. Galimbert's
Histoire de la Republique de Venise, Paris 1855, one
among many studies driven by a fascination with
the Venice that had been lost but in harness to a
desire to moralize. The engraver, E. Rouargue, also
produced illustrations for contemporary travellers'
books, such as *Voyage pittoresque en Italie*, 1856.

The distortions to the topography and the
unusual viewpoint serve to bring into prominence
the city's 'iconic' monuments, lining up on a central
axis the Doge's Palace, St Mark's Basilica and the
Rialto Bridge.

Museo Correr, Venice, 854 leg. Vianello, photo M32645bis

1.2 The loss of population and of identity

The demographic crisis brought about by its economic and political nullification is one from which the city has never recovered: certainly in this respect the 'modern' fate of Venice, its endemic state of crisis, begins in the second decade of the nineteenth century, when the return of the Austrians forced the city towards what would now be called tertiarization, induced by the collapse of its port and industries. There was a simultaneous steep drop in the resident population in the islands, falling to about 100,000 from a number that during the preceding centuries had always been around 200,000 to 300,000.

The state to which the city was suddenly reduced in the nineteenth century is noted in two valuable documents presented by contemporary observers to the Austrian emperor Francis I: the *Ricorso ...* (Appeal) which the Patriarch of Venice Ladislaw Pyrker personally delivered to the sovereign in 1825, and the *Rapporto* (Report) sent to the monarch in 1830 by the patrician Nicolò Priuli and the merchant Pietro Du Bois. In the latter the authors record how from the beginning of Napoleonic rule "… repairs were neglected. Time hastened [the city's] destruction, and before long many ancient buildings, left abandoned or in want of the necessary repairs, were collapsing in various parts of the city. Their unfortunate owners had no alternative but to demolish their houses in order to sell the building materials at the lowest prices. This demolition continues daily" – despite the fact that from 1816 there existed, in addition to the *Commissione di Ornato*, a *Commissione civica per le case rovinose* (Municipal commission for dilapidated housing) and a *Commissione alla sopraveglianza delle Procuratie Vecchie ed altre fabbriche private nella gran Piazza di Venezia* (Commission for the overseeing of the Procuratie Vecchie and other private buildings in the Gran Piazza of Venice).

To complete the circle of cause and effect thus established, local financial and governing structures that had survived the political upheavals no longer had any reason or means to survive, and were replaced by a complex bureaucracy that shifted the balance still further to tertiary activities. The trend continued after the revolutionary moment of 1848–49, and even between 1859 and 1864 exports to the mainland fell by 54.5%, exports by sea fell by 37%, and imports by sea rose 42%. Indeed the political repression of the 1850s, following the rebellion of 1848–49, was implemented through economic sanctions: punitive measures made still worse the decline of the port and manufacturing, forcing the city into ever greater dependence on external aid and on tourism, vitiating its traditions and its physical and historical characteristics.

While it is true that Venice's decline, its 'normalization', its deprivation or denial of identity was mainly initiated by the policies of the Austrian empire, it is also true that a similar approach has consistently been taken by those who have subsequently found themselves with the power of administration over the lagoon. In surveying the modern history of Venice we are confronted by a series of initiatives, undoubtedly with different objectives and methods – but in so many of these, whether they involve the creation of the causeway linking Venice to the mainland, or the restoration of the Fondaco dei Turchi (see pp. 51–59), or the industrial zone at Marghera and Mestre, or the provision of seven *Leggi speciali* (Special laws) since the Second World War, we can identify a vacuum, a kind of missing link, a credibility gap. This is the disjunction between the theoretical basis and the reality of the object with which the project is concerned, in other words the presumption to reduce the object – Venice – to models, typologies and statistics, disregarding and underestimating its rich uniqueness.

1.3 Venice's 'Copernican Revolution': the railway
bridge, the pedestrian thoroughfares

Once the goal had become the 'normalization' of the Venetian economy, attention turned to the 'normalization' of the city's physical form, and above all its infrastructure. The administration set itself two objectives, which were pursued with remarkable tenacity: the construction of a bridge linking Venice to the mainland and the creation of a network of pedestrian thoroughfares alongside, or replacing, that of the canals, which was deemed obsolete – and so indeed it had become, from 1800 onwards.

The railway bridge was constructed between 1841 and 1846 and finally completed about 1857. At a time when the creation of rapid and stable rail links seemed revolutionary, the Milan–Venice line, the *Ferdinandea*, connected, both literally and symbolically, the Lombard capital (where industrial development was in full swing) with the lagoon city, and also linked these cities, as the railway continued past Venice and the ports of Venezia Giulia, to Trieste. At Trieste the *Ferdinandea* connected with the Trieste–Vienna line and thus the innermost regions of the empire.

The completion of the railway line and of the bridge signalled the arrival of the new machine age: the enthusiasm this prospect raised was so great that it led to a plethora of fairly improbable projects, in which the common factor was the triumph of technology, of the new reality of mechanization, over everything that had been there before: islands and canals were blithely, insouciantly, crisscrossed on the map with bridges and railtracks. A kind of futurism prevailed, highly ordered, but at the same time violently destructive and iconoclastic. Its standard-bearers, naturally, were the architects and the champions of the so-called *cultura degli ingegneri* (engineers' culture), of whom in Venice there were several generations: the first, active in the early decades of the nineteenth century, included Giuseppe Salvadori, Lorenzo Santi, Francesco Lazzari and Alvise Pigazzi, and still had links with the *Accademia* and with Giannantonio Selva; the second generation, active from around 1830, included, among others, the brothers Giambattista and Tommaso Meduna, Giovanni Fuin, Lodovico Cadorin, Giuseppe Calzavara and Federico Berchet, as well as the engineers Luigi Duodo and Giovanni Milani, who, along with Giambattista Meduna, designed the lagoon bridge. The new causeway represented something more than a new means of getting from one place to another: in synergy with the economic, commercial and governmental 'crisis', it shifted the city's centre of

Fig. 6

Lodovico Ughi's plan of the city of Venice, executed
in the early eighteenth century and published in
1729, set a new standard for accuracy and detail in
representation. Around the map are views of St
Marks' and the Piazza, of the Rialto and the gateway
of the Arsenale, and of Palladio's churches of San
Giorgio Maggiore and the Redentore. There is an
allegory of the power of the city at upper right.

The six districts or *sestieri* of the city are named
in largest type, Canaregio to the north-west, Santa
Croce, San Polo and Dorsoduro on the left side of
the Grand Canal, San Marco on the right and
Castello to the east.

The city appears without the excrescences to the
west of the new docks required for larger vessels
and of the railway station; commerce was by water
at the eastern, seaward end (Riva degli Schiavoni).

Museo Correr, Venice, Cl. XLIV, n. 69; photo M44850

Figs. 7,8
These details from Ughi's map (see
opposite page) and from Marco
Perissini's in the fifth edition of 1866 (see
over) show the same area of the Rialto at
the bend of the Grand Canal. In
Perissini's map one finds that buildings of
various kinds that had obstructed the
walkways have been removed, notably to
the north of San Giovanni Crisostomo
(a darkly shaded square in Ughi's map,
marked no. 43 in Perissini's), where a
pedestrian route has been created up to
Campo Santi Apostoli. This route would
later be pushed further as the Strada
Nuova, connecting via filled-in canals
(Rio terà San Leonardo and Lista di
Spagna) to open a pedestrian route from
the Rialto through to the railway station.
On the copy of Perissini's map
reproduced here the new thoroughfare
has been marked in white by Giuseppe
Bianco, who was highly active in the
modernization of the city in the mid
nineteenth century (see over).

See also John Ruskin's remarks on
gaining Campo Santi Apostoli from the
Rialto (p. 127 below).

Though welcomed by many
Venetians, the filling-in of canals was
potentially dangerous, in so far as it
might affect the flow of water through
the city, and perhaps also misconceived.
Among others, the engineer Pietro
Paleocapa criticized the attempt to make
Venice a 'dry-land' city and insisted that,
for Venice, canals were the equivalent of
vehicular roads. It seems an obvious
point, but, when fervour for progress was
reaching its peak, it badly needed stating.

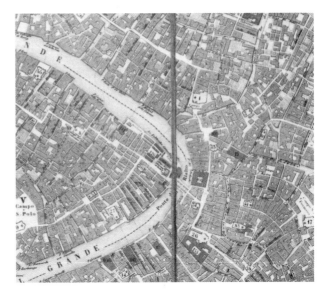

Fig. 9

On his copy of the fifth edition of Marco Perissini's map of Venice, 1866, the chief engineer to the *Comune*, Giuseppe Bianco, has marked in white proposed pedestrian routes across the city. The routes were published by Bianco in his 'Programme for the Enlargement and Shortcutting of Routes and Other Improvements to the Fabric of the City of Venice' of 1866; most of his recommendations were acted on and characterize the city to this day.

Compared to Ughi's map (see previous page), Perissini's shows Venice's changed relations with the world. At top left a miniature train chuffs into the new area of the railway station. At top right, Venice is shown no longer as Queen of the Seas but as a nodal link in the land-based system dominated by the new railways, constituting now an element of the region called 'Lombardo-Veneto'. Of course, Venice at this period was still a major city, not yet a 'museum'; modernization seemed to many not only necessary but desirable. Bianco's new thoroughfares were complemented by many new bridges, including two of aggressively modern iron across the Grand Canal at Santa Lucia and at Accademia (since replaced). Museo Correr, Venice, Cl. XLIV n. 80, photo M16153

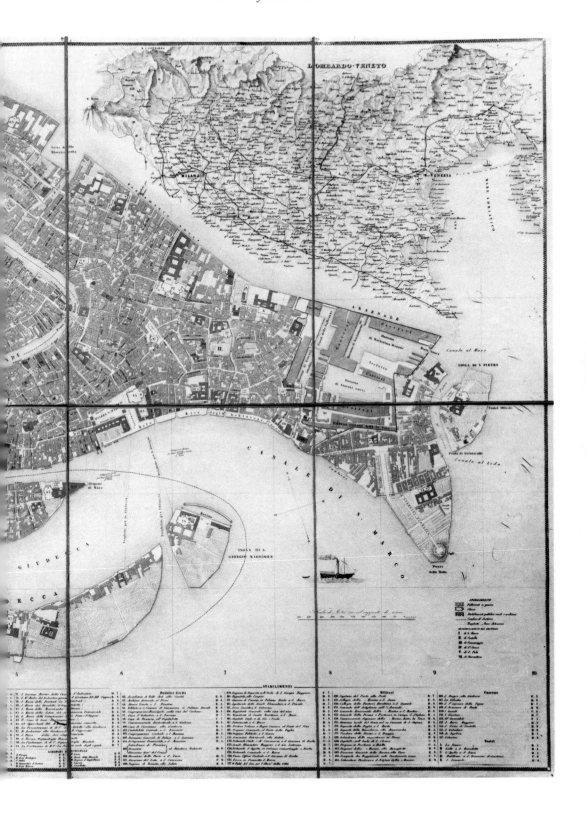

Fig. 10

The construction of the causeway to the mainland changed Venice from an island (or group of islands) into a peninsula, with far-reaching cultural, economic and social effects. It caused the devastation of the western end of the city, not simply through the destruction of churches and palaces it necessitated, but by turning the area into a railway yard and the city's port, for it was soon required that the docks should be moved from the seaward side of the city, from the Riva degli Schiavoni and the island of San Giorgio, to the vicinity of the railway. In 1845 John Ruskin was shocked to find "... where Venice *once* appeared ... the Greenwich railway ... entirely cutting off the sea and half the city, which now looks as nearly as possible like Liverpool at the end of the dockyard wall". Nothing has since improved, indeed the area has become much worse, being now graced with the bus-park of Piazzale Roma and the ghastly car-parks of the Tronchetto. Originally travellers and traders of all kinds had crossed from the mainland or the end of the Brenta Canal at Fusina by boat or barge (the *burchiello*); it is to be regretted that there was never the foresight to stop the automobile at Fusina and re-activate the service.

The causeway has also served as a conduit of fresh water from the mountains to the city, which historically had relied on the cisterns beneath its courtyards and *campi* for drinking water.

gravity to the northwest – the side which in the city's traditional iconography is always represented as a hazy backdrop, as the flank exposed to the 'other' reality of the mainland, in contrast to the opulence and plenitude of the Grand Canal and St Mark's Basin.

The railway bridge upset the already endangered equilibrium of the Venetian environment. Moreover, once it was in place, it gave rise to a new series of designs on the city, in order to exploit the opportunities presented by the new link with the mainland and respond to its consequences. It rapidly became necessary to link the new terminal with the nodal centres of the city by creating new thoroughfares, realised at the cost of filled-in canals and swathes of demolition across the urban fabric. From 1840 onwards, Austrians and Italians, engineers, prefects and administrators, had as their main objective the creation of ready access between the railway station and San Marco, along these routes: Station–Rialto–San Marco and Station–Lista di Spagna–Strada Nuova–Rialto, respectively to the south and north of the Grand Canal, and San Marco–Accademia, an entirely new route, forging a pedestrian link that had not hitherto existed between the *sestieri* (districts) of San Marco and Dorsoduro. The execution of the first of these schemes was virtually painless, involving little more than the construction of a bridge (originally in iron), the Ponte degli Scalzi, between the two banks of the Grand Canal at the station. The second, however, involved the profound alteration and destruction of a considerable proportion of the southern part of the Canaregio district; undertaken gradually, it was not completed until the 1870s (the official inauguration of the Strada Nuova took place on 2 September 1871). The third route required the construction of the Accademia Bridge, erected again in iron by Alfredo Neville in 1853 (replaced in 1932 and again in 1985–86), and the demolition of the houses on Calle Lunga at San Moisè to create the present-day Via XXII Marzo, which became known as the Calle Larga in recognition of its novel and inordinate width – it is indeed a completely inappropriate and out-of-scale segment of the winding route leading from the Accademia Bridge to San Marco. During the 1850s there were numerous further works of pedestrianization: canals were filled in, a considerable number of iron bridges were erected (by the companies Neville and Collalto), and new passageways and *sotoporteghi* (covered passageways, under or alongside a building) were created. In 1858 Campo San Bartolomeo, centrally situated by the Rialto Bridge, was enlarged. All these works were the responsibility of the *Comune*, which generally drew on the services of distinguished individuals such as Giuseppe Salvadori, a disciple of Selva, who was active from 1817 until the middle of the century, and on the recommendations of municipal or external committees, either permanent or *ad hoc*, such as the Napoleonic *Commissione di Ornato*, which remained in being both under Austrian rule and under Italian administration (until the end of the 1860s, when it was dissolved).

As is well known, the old Venice functioned around the system of canals that branched off the Grand Canal and the main waterways in an extending pattern of right angles, while these in turn converged on the Bacino, the Piazza and the Rialto. Areas more distant from the

Fig. 11

One of the routes on Giuseppe Bianco's map (see figs. 8, 9) marked for widening and straightening was that from the Piazza towards Campo Santo Stefano and the newly built Accademia Bridge (before the bridge was built it had hardly been a route at all). From the Piazza the route passed beside and then in front of the church of San Moisé with its late Baroque façade (left), towards Santa Maria del Giglio. This part, though already existing, was widened by demolishing the houses on one side of the narrow *calle*, and so the Calle Larga XXII Marzo was created (named after the first day of Daniele Manin's rebel Republic of 1848). The new *palazzi* flanking its south side were designed in the last two decades of the nineteenth century by Francesco Balduin in an international classical style to provide suitable retail outlets behind the smart hotels that had taken over the Grand Canal frontage to its immediate south – and the street remains tenanted by fashion shops. Out of scale and sympathy with historic Venetian streets or even *rio terà*, it is unique in the city, reflecting a brief period of ambitious attempts to beautify Venice in modern style for modern tourists.

Fig. 12

Though this view down a Venetian canal (the Rio della Toletta in Dorsoduro) evokes the old order of circulation and transport, the central bridge is a comparatively recent one (there were far fewer altogether before 1797) and the railings flanking the bridges throughout the city are all modern. Among the palace façades an example of the use of an over-bright (not lime-based) plaster stands out (see further pp. 161–63).

centre, and outlying islands, were instead used for light-industrial activities such as the storage and repair of boats. The city was organized around the canals rather than the walkways (*calli*) behind them, and it is therefore true that the network of canals was for the city what roads and streets were to other places, its connective tissue. Streets and alleys in Venice fulfilled instead a function mostly of service access; they did not constitute a developed network and did not play a significant role in the city as a whole.

With the new insertions, however, Venice became a city to be traversed on foot, in the least time possible – a 'modern' desideratum which led to ever more visible violence to the city fabric. Today, in order to appreciate how great the impact of nineteenth-century innovations on the city structure was, one has to pursue out-of-the-way itineraries into the innermost parts of the *sestieri* of Canaregio or Castello, where you will almost certainly get lost in a labyrinth of dead-end *calli*, in routes that are incomprehensible from a purely 'land' point of view. The administrators and town planners of the nineteenth century, superimposing on this mixed and polycentric system a series of pedestrian axes, introduced a new element into Venice – a traffic system, an entirely road-related, kilometric phenomenon, measurable in terms of access and distance travelled, and hitherto practically unknown to the city.

After the railway bridge had been constructed the station of Santa Lucia (so called after the church that was demolished to make way for it, together with the convent of Corpus Domini) was completed in 1865, giving rise to new activities and new projects. However, the Venetian economy showed no sign of recovery: in the 1850s economic retaliation against the city for its bloody and futile anti-Austrian rebellion of 1848 succeeded in nullifying the advantage even of the free port that had eventually been conceded after years of indecision: indeed its effect was deleterious to local manufacturing, because it encouraged keen competition from foreign goods imported at low cost. The port authorities vacillated amidst what were by now longstanding problems; nothing was gained by the development of a plan for a canal–railway interchange to be built at the Zattere, extending to the Punta alla Dogana, where a footbridge would have connected the railway terminal with Calle del Ridotto, close to San Marco. The project, presented around 1850 by Giuseppe Jappelli, was not put into operation (although it was taken up again in modified form some twenty years later), but in hindsight it can be seen as a halfway stage in the process which saw the eventual transfer of the port activities of the Bacino and the island of San Giorgio (the location of the free port) to Porto Marghera on the mainland.

In the second half of the nineteenth century – pedestrianized, tertiarized and now also the victim of building speculation – Venice even began to confront, from within, the prospect of relying on tourism to support the economy and fulfil the city's aspirations. As early as 1853 an ill-considered competition organized by the *Comune* gave prominence to a proposal to build a complex 600 metres long and 50 metres deep on the Riva degli Schiavoni, reaching from the Doge's Palace to Castello, consisting of bathing, recreational, refreshment and catering

Fig. 13

Giuseppe Mezzani's Neoclassical lighthouse, erected in 1813, marks a moment of optimism after Napoleon had been petitioned and in 1808 had granted free-trade status to the port of Venice, restricted as such to the harbour of San Giorgio across the Basin of St Mark's. Accompanying the two new lighthouses were new docks and harbour facilities. However, a blockade by the British stifled the initiative. When the Austrians took over the city after the defeat of Napoleon, its port's free-trade status had again to be petitioned for, to be granted only in 1829, and it was lost again following the 1848–49 rebellion. Venice never regained its historic trading prominence. Even under the Kingdom of Italy – and despite the presence of the Italian Navy in the Arsenale – Venice has never been able to wind back its maritime decline. Modern attempts to build up Venice's port – the facilities at Marghera, the welcoming in very recent times of cruise ships (also manufactured in Marghera) – have compromised other aspects and values of the city.

Figs. 14, 15, 16

The Riva degli Schiavoni, the shoreline running east from the Doge's Palace towards the Arsenale, had been the main dockyard area of Venice, and towards its further end it had been dominated particularly by *squeri* or boatyards. One of these occupies the foreground of *The End of the Riva degli Schiavoni* (left) by Myles Birket Foster, an English illustrator turned watercolourist who progressed from rural scenes of England to 'picturesque' representations of the proletariat of Venice (see also fig. 46, p. 83). Some, but by no means the worst, of the squalor in the slums of Venice in the later nineteenth century is depicted in these works, typical of their time in enlivening conventional views of the historic city and its famous monuments with 'genre' elements. A photograph taken of the Riva in 1868 (above right) shows there still to be a 'dock' area, that has been further paved. Today the Riva degli Schiavoni has been paved, cleared and embanked all along its length, and the naval museum stands in for its busy life as a waterfront; it is still used, however, as a moorage for *vaporetti* to the lagoon islands and for visiting ships, now carrying exclusively tourists.

Myles Birket Foster, *The End of the Riva degli Schiavoni*, Sotheby's Picture Library DT7672

facilities, though it housed other activities as well, including a new stock exchange. The project, presented by the builder Giovanni Busetto, known as Fisola, and the architect Lodovico Cadorin, was enthusiastically approved by the *Comune*, but blocked by the *Commissione provinciale* (Provincial committee). Clearly, however, the time was ripe to devote some serious thought to the new face and the new role of Venice. Bravely, the new *podestà* (head of the town council), Pier Luigi Bembo, appointed in 1860, declared that it was not sufficient "for the prosperity of Venice to turn the place into a vast hotel for foreigners attracted by the city's climate, the health-giving properties of its waters, its amusements and diversions, but that there was a need to disinter a few dead industries and inject some life into those still existing".

1.4 The fate of the city's buildings in the first half of the nineteenth century

Before the work of Giambattista Meduna between 1845 and 1847, which provoked the intervention of Ruskin and others and marked a turning-point in the history of the city's fabric, announcing an approach methodologically very different from what had gone before, the most important works of restoration in the city can be divided into three categories. First was the transformation of convents into barracks or other *contenitori* (containers) with a State or municipal function. Secondly there were works intended to combat the critical state of disrepair of many Venetian houses. Thirdly there were restorations of churches and of public or artistically important buildings that had become dilapidated.

In the first category, the conversion of convents was carried out without any particular attention to the artistic and historic value of the buildings concerned, but simply in order to render useable in the least possible time properties expropriated from the Church during the Napoleonic period. There were many such conversions during the 1820s and 1830s, and indeed the Napoleonic requisitions had at a stroke made available an enormous quantity of unbuilt urban land. One can discern two phases in this development: the first, taking place between 1815 and 1830, was aimed primarily at converting huge buildings into barracks or adapting them into premises serving administrative functions. A second phase consisted in the modernization of the buildings already adapted, and especially in a radical re-organization of the barracks. Among the most important sites involved were those of the Frari and the adjacent church of San Nicolò della Lattuga, which, under the direction of Lorenzo Santi, became the *Archivio di Stato* (State archive) in 1815. During those same years, or a little later, the ex-convents of San Sepolcro and of the Celestia were turned into barracks; the ex-convent of San Zaccaria became the seat of the *Ragionateria* (Public accounts department); in another conversion by Lorenzo Santi, the *Tribunale* (Court of justice) was housed in the ex-convent of Santi Filippo e Giacomo and the adjoining cloister of Sant'Apollonia. The ex-convent of Santo Stefano was adapted to house the *Genio militare* (Military engineers or sappers), and the convents of Santa Chiara and Santi Giovanni e Paolo became hospitals, military and civil respec-

tively. Meanwhile Giambattista Meduna, already working on the project for the railway
bridge, was becoming involved in civil construction as well, and between 1835 and 1849 turned
the ex-convent of the Benedictines at San Lorenzo into the headquarters of the *Casa d'Industria*
(Chamber of commerce). None of this had anything to do with restoration as the term is
generally understood: those responsible for these projects and for their end use were not at
all concerned with the repair or re-integration or interpretation of the architectural value and
materials of the buildings concerned. It was a matter rather of adapting their service installations, altering floor and ceiling levels, creating and eliminating doorways and windows, staircases and buttresses so that the building might fulfil its new purpose. In certain cases these
works were so remarkably temporary in nature that a few years later, around 1840, new and
more effective operations were required – a situation that would recur when the reduction of
the military presence in Venice and the re-use of large buildings that had been adapted as barracks in the first half of the century left those reponsible facing considerable difficulties, such
was the poor quality of much of the earlier building work.

By contrast to the conversion of ex-convents, which was a 'one-off' occasion in Venetian
history, the dilapidation of private dwellings was destined to become a constant problem in
the modern city. At its root, in the case of Venice as in others, was demographic decline, in-
ducing reluctance among landlords to invest funds in maintenance and, with the passage of
time, inclining them to consider instead the money that might be made by exploiting the
value of the site. To confront this situation a series of legislative initiatives were taken: in 1805,
for example, property owners were obliged to repair houses declared by the *Comune* to be
"*rovinose*" (ruinous), or else find their property alienated. The regulation had little effect, and so
frequent was the continued recourse to demolition that there was enough rubble to fill in
Sacca Sant'Angelo and Sacca di Santa Chiara. Such infill was an abusive procedure the
Serenissima had always applied sparingly and with an eye to its long-term effects. Its practice
in the modern era (for instance, landfill for the extension of the industrial zone on the edge of
the lagoon) has led to needless ecological destruction and damage to the urban environment.

The activities of the various municipal committees responsible for the urban environment
had little positive effect on the situation, not least because they preferred to address themselves to issues of architectural style and ornamention and to the widening or *rettifilo* (straightening) of streets. The real needs of the city, the population having been reduced by half
following the dreadful famine of 1820, were very different. But no other solution could be
found except to continue with demolition, which in effect the administration endorsed, without attempting to organize or control it. Like the *Commissione di Ornato*, the *Comune* was more
interested in circulation and the easement of pedestrian traffic, and even here it did not always
act wisely: the chief engineer of the *Ufficio tecnico* (Office of works), the aforementioned
Giuseppe Salvadori, even succeeded in getting asphalt adopted as the surfacing for Venetian
calli, in place of the traditional blocks of trachyte.

To complete the picture of an appalling situation, throughout the 1820s projects for work to be undertaken on existing buildings could be signed off (in the fairly rare case that they were actually put in writing) by their owner. A thirteen-point table of building regulations was eventually adopted, but until then authorizations for works were given not on the basis of fixed and institutionalized directives but according to *ad hoc* arrangements made between the workmen and the relevant judicial authorities. The institutions and procedures of the Republic having disappeared, the situation degenerated in a short time into a kind of anarchy.

Despite all this, there was a growing trend towards investment and speculation in property, or rather smart property, for instance celebrated *palazzi* in prestigious locations in the central areas of the city. The most direct consequence was a dizzying rise in prices and rents. Tommaso Locatelli, the proprietor, wrote in the *Gazzetta di Venezia* on 25 November 1843, "… progress is not all pleasurable, as anyone who has to move house realises. Rents now cost a fortune; ideas will move ever forward, but not in all cases will incomes do likewise …" .

As regards monumental buildings, the most significant efforts, as for convents, went into adapting the existing structures to new functions. The most important works undertaken were to the Ca' Valmarana at San Canciano, restructured in 1822, the *Teatro San Moisè*, transformed in 1824 into a carpentry workshop, the Rialto Bridge, of which the main arches were restored in the same year, the church of San Michele in Isola (1827), Ca' Foscari on the Grand Canal (fig. 17) and the ex-monastery of San Giovanni Laterano, which, from 1829, was adapted to house the *Scuole tecniche* (Technical schools) and other educational activities. In the 1830s other ex-convents were also transformed into schools, including the convent of Santa Caterina (which became a boarding school, completed in 1842 by Salvadori) and San Provolo, Santa Maria del Pianto, Santi Rocco e Margherita and the Eremite. The convents of the Terese, San Sebastiano, Angelo Raffaele, the Soccorso and Sant'Alvise were adapted to accommodate welfare facilities for orphans and the poor. From 1836 the *Teatro La Fenice*, designed by Selva, which had been destroyed in a fire, was rebuilt by Giambattista and Tommaso Meduna – the interior decorations, designed by Giambattista, were completed in 1854, and were the subject of considerable controversy. In the same year, the crenellations on the Grand Canal façade of the Fondaco dei Tedeschi (figs. 18, 19), on which work had already been conducted in 1817, were rebuilt. In 1837, continuing until 1848, works were undertaken on the Fabbriche Nuove at Rialto (a project of Lorenzo Santi), and in 1840 Alvise Pigazzi restructured the Magazzini del Sale, the Punta della Salute and a part of the nearby Zattere. During these same years a number of churches were restored, among them San Polo, Santa Maria Formosa, San Luca, San Cassiano, San Geremia, the Gesuati, Santa Maria dei Miracoli, Madonna dell'Orto, the oratory of the Seminario at the Salute and San Giorgio dei Greci; also the Scuola dell'Angelo Custode at Santi Apostoli was converted for the German Evangelists. Last but not least, between 1840 and 1844 Giambattista Meduna converted the church of San Geremia, to the north of Canaregio, into a workshop for the Oexle steam mills.

Fig. 17

The Ca' Foscari on the Grand Canal, reputed in
Venetian guidebooks to have more rooms than any
other palace in the city, was built (or rebuilt) in the
mid fifteenth century by Doge Francesco Foscari.
Following the common fate of grand family houses
in historic cities, it has been converted into
institutional offices, those of the University of
Venice, of which it is the headquarters. Ruskin,
declaring the palace to be "the noblest example in
Venice of fifteenth-century Gothic", added that it
had been "lately restored and spoiled, all but the
stonework of the main windows". An extensive
programme of renovation, begun in 1996, was still
proceeding in 2004.

Fig. 18

The Fondaco dei Tedeschi or 'German warehouse', once the engine of Venetian trade, fell out of use and into disrepair after the Fall of the Republic. In this photograph of 1853, it has already lost the two towers that originally rose at either corner (visible in many paintings by Canaletto and others). In their second edition of 1838 the authors of *Le fabbriche e i monumenti più cospicui di Venezia* (Conspicuous buildings and monuments of Venice) reported with dismay: "When this building was recently restored, the two external *torricelle* were demolished, and for them were substituted *merlature* along the rooftop like those already existing. What may have induced those responsible to do such a thing we have no idea. Obviously the design of the façade has been affected by this alteration. Their action had two other unfortunate consequences: first, that the two historic inscriptions between the windows of the towers ... disappeared; secondly, that the two figures by Giorgione [painted in fresco] were destroyed, and they were perhaps the best preserved among those that survived." Such 'restoration' was evidently widespread in the nineteenth century, though it is very inadequately recorded; this was an episode typical of much more directionless, pointless, careless and uncaring handling of Venice's fabric.

Fig. 19

Today the Fondaco remains an unhappy building. In the 1930s it became the central post office for Venice, and was very radically restored in the 1930s and 1940s. The original structure was transmogrified by the insertion of an iron grid or cage of reinforced concrete, utterly destroying the basis on which the building had been constructed, and irreversible. It is not very much more than a shell, even if its façades appear as they have always appeared (at least in recent times – see opposite). Worse, the insertion of reinforced concrete membering did not and never could solve the problems of the building in the long term, because it did not prevent, indeed it exacerbated, the movement in the remaining parts of the structure (on the drawbacks of the use of reinforced concrete see further below, pp. 128ff., 166ff.). Very recently it was decided to move the sorting office to the mainland, and the building was put up for sale: the only interested buyers were hotel consortia. Determined to prevent such a fate befalling the former foreigners' emporium, the *Comune* successfully negotiated its purchase.

The most significant work of this period was that conducted by Giambattista Meduna from 1842 on the north façade of the Basilica San Marco. It initiated a programme of works that would continue, amid controversy and debate, for more than thirty years, until Meduna was replaced by Pietro Saccardo at the instigation of Alvise Zorzi, an admirer of John Ruskin, and of William Morris's Society for the Protection of Ancient Buildings. Meduna's operations raised the question in very clear terms, for the first time in Venice, of 'restoration' as opposed to 'conservation'. Meduna set to work with the aim first of all of tackling the instability of the Basilica, which permitted him to show complete indifference towards original materials and the documentary value of the architectonic text. In this he had the partisan support of no less an authority than Viollet-le-Duc, who had only praise for his work to stabilize the edifice. Heavy criticism, however, came from Pietro Selvatico Estense, who sought, in 1852, to call in new tenders for the works on the south front. However, Selvatico's comments were mostly concerned with style: it would be twenty-five years before Zorzi produced his lucid and comprehensive assessment of the damage wrought to the building by Meduna in the name of stability, supposed original intention, and *ripristino* (rendering as original, returning to an original, pristine state). Zorzi's list of the errors committed includes complete high-handedness in substituting the original marbles and mosaics with materials that might be similar but were differently worked, or worked in a way that was alien to the fabric of the Basilica; and unconcern for the patina of materials, which had been removed by scraping with abrasive stone-based treatments that caused permanent damage to the marbles and led to their rapid deterioration.

In 1852 it was still too early for general acceptance of the value of the principles of conservation, and, after the proposal to invite tenders to replace him had come to nothing, Meduna was even able to start works (1865) on the south front, which were completed in 1875. The criteria applied were the same as for the northern façade. It was proposed to demolish an altar that had been appended in the sixteenth century to the Zeno Chapel, deemed "crude work"; instead, part of the brickwork was rebuilt. The mosaics of the Zeno Chapel were saved from destruction thanks only to the conscientiousness of a member of the *Fabbriceria* (the Basilica's vestry board), who had them put into storage. The original external marble revetment was replaced and the surfaces that survived were cleaned with acids and abrasives.

Fig. 20

Past the Byzantine 'lily' capitals of the southernmost bay of St Mark's Basilica one can see, lower left, one of the twin antique 'Columns of Acre' commemorating Venice's Levantine victories, the flamboyant late Gothic Porta della Carta marking the ceremonial entrance to the Doge's Palace and the corner of the Doge's Palace itself with *The Judgement of Solomon*. This is historic ground, a millennial and manifold palimpsest of the precious entity that is, or was, Venice. Unfortunately it has not always been treated with the respect or handled with the care that might be expected or demanded; on the other hand, these venerable stones will not look after themselves.

Figs. 21, 22, 23

As seen (above) in an albumen print probably of 1859, St Mark's Basilica had already undergone treatment from Giambattista Meduna, at least on the north side, and the record of what he may have done is very poor. In 1852 or soon after Meduna moved on to the south side (facing out to the Basin of St Mark's), here recorded in a photograph of 1860 (above right). A project survives (below right) for the restoration or rehabilitation of the south façade, involving notably the arbitrary reworking of the pedimented tabernacle-like form on the exterior of the Zeno Chapel (admittedly a recognisably Renaissance intrusion into the Byzantine-Gothic ensemble). Where Meduna was chiefly at fault was in his supposition that what he, the restorer, would put in its place would be more harmonious or suitable than what was there, and would continue to be so with the passing of time (instead of becoming more glaring, as indeed it became to the next century); in his extraordinary lack of archaeological interest in the methods and materials originally used, or in the evidence there available – after all the importance of archival written evidence was perfectly well appreciated by the historians of the day; and in his presumptuous failure to keep records.

While it was the protests of John Ruskin, Alvise Zorzi and the Society for the Protection of Ancient Buildings, whose motivation was not simply scientific but also a little anti-modernist, that eventually put a stop to Meduna's callous work both here and elsewhere – see p. 90 and fig. 51, Ruskin's watercolour of the Ca' d'Oro painted just as Meduna's workmen were "hammering it down before my face" – it was perhaps the disastrous failure of Federico Berchet's restoration of the Fondaco dei Turchi (see chapter 2) that proved still more persuasively the dangers and consequences of a failure to respect the authenticity of a building.

43

Figs. 24, 25
On the south-west corner of
the Basilica, these columns
and capitals and their
surrounding marbles (above
left) are too neat, too clean,
too sharp not to arouse the
suspicion that they may be
nineteenth-century
confections rather than what
was originally put there eight
centuries ago. How the
restorers arrived at their
irreversible new arrangement
is anybody's guess.

Figs. 26, 27

Ruskin had the aim of recording as much and as many as he could of the stones of Venice, which he saw being vandalized before his eyes and which he had ceased to believe would be preserved by the Venetians (or the Austrian authorities). A number of followers assisted him, whether by photography or by such meticulous records as the watercolour on the left above, by an unknown hand in the 1860s or 1870s. The capital depicted is one of the 'lily' capitals on the southwest corner of the Basilica (see also fig. 20, p. 40).

At the same time as he was beginning his invasive and destructive intervention on San Marco, Meduna also carried out a series of restorations on some secular buildings of great prestige – the Ca' d'Oro, 1845–50 (figs. 50–52, pp. 90–91); Casa Meduna in San Fantin, 1846 (fig. 28); Ca' Giovanelli, 1847. In all these cases Meduna took it upon himself to recover the 'original' form. At San Fantin he took his cue from the Gothic structures uncovered during the restoration/demolition to re-cast the entire building in renovated Gothic guise. At Ca' Giovanelli he destroyed the main staircase in order to restore the structure of an older octagonal staircase; at the Ca' d'Oro the staircase in the courtyard was demolished. Here he extensively modified the structural layout and the service installations, and completely relaid the ground floor. In these restorations there was no regard for the conservation of materials, which were freely substituted with similar materials recovered from other buildings in the city, donated by private individuals, or of modern manufacture.

Unfortunately, as is now quite well established, this kind of restoration was typical throughout the nineteenth century, indeed it was distinctively characteristic of countless nineteenth-century restorations. It accompanied the common practice of opening up and filling in doorways and windows, and of 'restoring' architectural elements not merely on the basis of pretty unreliable and arbitrarily treated evidence, but according to an entirely personal aesthetic.

1.5 Early restoration in Venice: remarks on
Giambattista Meduna's interventions

To sum up, Venice was gripped by an economic crisis affecting its port, manufacture and trade, by tertiarization, and by resignation to this condition, while there were also attempts to adapt the city to its new situation, to its pedestrianization and its loss of identity as a seaborne city. These seem to be the *leitmotifs* of the city's evolution in the years between the Congress of Vienna (1815) and the plebiscite which incorporated the city into the Kingdom of Italy (1866). It was during these fifty years that the modern urban structure of Venice was developed and defined. As we have seen, the major transformation of structures and functions led to a corresponding physical transformation of many buildings and of other built parts of the city; there was also some restoration or reconstitution of monuments, but no sense of the modern discipline of conservation. It was not until the 1860s that a practical assessment of the aims, procedures and results of restoration began in Venice.

However, the premises for a serious debate on the issue of conservation were formulated as early as the 1840s. This was the period in which John Ruskin paid several visits to the city, gathering impressions and images of key importance to the development of the ideas and attitudes that were to find expression in *The Seven Lamps of Architecture* and *The Stones of Venice*. Moreover, towards the middle of this decade, for the first time in Venice, procedures, resolutions and intentions towards the restoration of major buildings took on a tenor quite different from that of the past. Giambattista Meduna's interventions on the Ca' d'Oro, Ca' Giovanelli and the Basilica, mentioned above, are examples of this. Something has been said of the character of such works, their tendency to *ripristinare* or clean up, to restore a building to a past it perhaps should have had but never had had, involving the interpolation of extraneous forms, materials, types and images from a notional past. It is also important to emphasize what was distinctively new about them, compared with accepted practice at the time – in a word, their modernity.

This modernity did not reside simply, or so much, in the techniques applied or the practices adopted, as in the application of a new conception of history. The 'founding fathers' of restoration (and of conservation, though it is not the same thing), from Eugène-Emmanuel Viollet-le-Duc to John Ruskin, Camillo Boito and William Morris, self-consciously articulated a new attitude, which they attributed to their own time, the nineteenth century. At its root was an enthusiasm for the past based on a belief in its capacity for regeneration, provided there could be found interpreters culturally equipped to appreciate its genius for renewal. This was the impetus behind these figures' determination to preserve the architecture of the past as "the most precious of inheritances", in the words of John Ruskin.

This movement, as to some extent we have already seen, embraced inconsistent and directly contradictory ideas, in both theoretical and practical terms, which is not surprising given the cultural ferment of the mid nineteenth century. On the one hand, there was faith in what Giacomo Leopardi called 'the magnificent progressive destiny' of the new sciences, which were capable of fathoming the past with professed certainty, of understanding History (and detailed histories) to the extent of establishing a direct relationship with it. Such faith justified reconstructive, corrective and interpretative restoration: it was a legitimate and self-legitimating procedure. Thus the restorer, from time to time, dipped into the past, confident of his accurate translation of his knowledge into concrete form, of his ability to resolve the confusions wrought by time and humanity, of his power to inscribe certainties acquired by sure and verifiable means. An important factor in his thinking was the chance of carrying over suggestions and pointers into contemporary architecture, which, at this time of emerging nationalism in Europe, was striving to find a language in which to express reclaimed traditions, and wanted, as Camillo Boito was to point out on more than one occasion, 'a style of its own'.

Thus nineteenth-century restoration, and modern restoration in general, came into being as a process with an end in view: monuments were interrogated, as it were, in the hope that they would provide new answers to the problems both of creating new architecture and, as a corollary, of establishing criteria for intervention on the monuments themselves. One can apply the following basic model to the genesis of ideas about restoration in the nineteenth century: first the 'lesson' of the historical monuments themselves (achieved by analysis, survey, etc); subsequently the development of 'prescriptions' for a modern architecture,

Fig. 28
The house that Giambattista Meduna built or rebuilt for himself in Campo San Fantin (opposite the Fenice Theatre that he had rebuilt with his brother Tommaso in 1836–37) blends in well enough with its surroundings; one might not notice at first glance that it is nineteenth-century. It has a classical frame adorned with Gothic decoration, such as the windows and the narrow frieze running over the third storey, which has rolling relief 'Catherine wheels' perhaps adapted from the flamboyant Gothic balconies of the Palazzo Contarini Fasan on the Grand Canal. The heavy cornice, a Central Italian import, and the strict horizontal courses insist on structural legibility rather than the colour and movement Ruskin extolled. On the left of Meduna's house is the Ateneo Veneto (see p. 140).

deriving their inspiration from the past in a way that was sometimes 'moral' and sometimes technical. 'Moral' prescriptions might be those identifying regional or national styles, or the spiritualism of Gothic, or the *italianità* of the Romanesque, and so on; as an example of the technical, one thinks of Viollet-le-Duc's comments on the way Gothic buildings were constructed. Then, the 'lessons' themselves can become the object of a deliberate, scientific, application of the new understanding – 'modern' restoration.

Certainly this is the approach that prevailed and was welcomed in most of the cases cited here. It did so not least because it was a long time before a conservation lobby, working from similar premises, presented a united front and articulated a practical approach of its own. It is no coincidence that its earliest and most resolute advocates for Venice were individuals and outsiders in respect of the local technical and political establishment, and, like Ruskin himself, subjective rather than positivistic in their approach. It would indeed be a battle between re-construction, refurbishment and restoration – invasive, destructive, technologically equipped and also highly motivated – and a less directed awareness of the claims of materials, as bearing the marks of time and their own physical history, their own legacy of stratification, their own particular colours and patinas, which would be irreversibly destroyed by such operations, thus impoverishing a heritage felt subjectively but by all humanity. The battle was waged with varying fortunes.

Venice was a city beset by enormous problems of identity in the nineteenth century, and was struggling to tackle problems not only of its 'fall' but of quite a new dimension, such as the effects of industrial revolution, the need for a new infrastructure, a new society, a new economy, not to mention the political upheavals of the Risorgimento. The city could not but turn trustingly to the chance offered by restoration to re-appropriate its past in a manner that was both revitalizing and consoling.

Bearing these considerations in mind, we can better appreciate the modernity of Meduna's restoration of 1845 onwards, compared with earlier such work: his work was carried out while Venice was attempting to confront its 'crisis', its new role in the world, with investments and initiatives that, though very limited, embraced not only the financial and economic spheres but also the cultural. Meduna gave expression to the Venetian awareness of a rupture with the past and of the problems of the present, and he did so in a way typical of the nineteenth century. He presented himself as having a profound (we may add, highly tendentious) understanding of the evidence, and therefore as able to perpetuate its essence and history; but at the same time he consigned the myth of Venice, the continuity of its thousand-year presence on the waters of the lagoon and the routes to the Orient, to history, to the past.

Meduna himself commented on the restoration (or rather demolition) of his own house at San Fantin (1846), which has been recognized as one of the first European renovations in a consciously neo-Gothic style, as follows: "Even though some might now feel the stirrings of warm affection for genuine things, and attempt to conserve the original parts of ancient buildings in renovating them [*ripristinarli*], nonetheless a great many were destroyed, including some of considerable merit, so that hardly any trace remains of that Architecture which might almost be called national, and which was certainly quite widespread. Even in the old house at San Fantin which I demolished there were old windows in the Gothic style, and I have found many more like them. Which is what made me decide to adopt that Architecture in the construction of a façade." Thus Meduna was entirely qualified, and among the first, to enter into the debate on the future of new architecture in Italy and, *pari passu*, on the direction to follow in the restoration of existing buildings – 'restoration', that is, as it was understood at the time.

Meduna's efforts, and those of another leading figure in this field in Venice, Camillo Boito, went into re-creating a national, or rather regional, architecture with great attention to the original form and its reflection of a tradition. It fell to Ruskin and Morris to re-direct attention to the inviolability of materials, so as to ensure the proper protection of the 'messages' that monuments contained and expressed, but this was not to happen until the 1870s and 1880s. By that time the devastation of the Fondaco dei Turchi had been unveiled, and Boito had taken very considerable liberties in his restoration (1879) of Palazzo Cavalli-Gussoni-Franchetti (although here the workmanship was of the highest quality and in the utmost good taste).

Meduna's activities effectively established two methodological norms of restorations for the years that followed: the conception of historical architecture as a lesson for the present, and the conception of restoration as the recovery of the original state of an existing building, or at least of one of its earliest states. These two methodologies would very soon be utterly vitiated by the tendency to interpret the past on the basis of the values of the present – a misguidance that would lead to an ever more extreme distortion and misrepresentation of the former in order to make it compatible with the latter.

NOTES

Essential to the study of building activity in the city in the first half of the nineteenth century is the work of Giandomenico Romanelli, notably his *Venezia Ottocento: materiali per una storia architettonica e urbanistica della città nel secolo XIX*, Rome 1977; with G. Pavanello, *Venezia nell'Ottocento: immagini e mito*, exh. cat., Milan 1983; and *Venezia Ottocento: l'architettura, l'urbanistica*, Venice 1988. A more general introduction to the development of the city, illustrated with a number of maps, is G. Bellavitis and G. Romanelli, *Le città nella storia dell'Italia: Venezia*, Bari 1985.

The suppression of the convents is well detailed in B. Bertoli, *La soppressione dei monasteri e conventi a Venezia dal 1797 al 1810*, Padua and Venice 2002. By the decree of 7 December 1807 about four thousand houses hitherto owned by the monasteries passed to the new authorities; of these some were demolished in pursuance of the projects of Gian Antonio Selva; some were restored to their former owners after 1814; buildings of larger dimensions were for the most part converted to secular use, whether military or civil, by the Austrians on their return.

On the activity of the *Comune* (Municipality) see S. Barzizza, *Il Comune di Venezia 1806–1946. L'istituzione. Il territorio. Guida-inventario dell'archivio municipale*, Venice 1987. The *catasti* or household-tax maps from the period 1801–11 (*catasto napoleonico*) and 1838–42 (*catasto austriaco*) are reproduced in full in I. Pavanello (ed.), *I catasti storici di Venezia 1808–1913*, Rome 1981.

On the *Accademia di Belle Arti* and its professors, beside the fuller E. Bassi, *La Reale Accademia di Belle Arti di Venezia nel suo bicentenario, 1750–1950*, Venice 1950, there is R. Masiero, *L'insegnamento dell'architettura nelle accademie riformate: Venezia*, in G. Ricci (ed.), *L'architettura nelle Accademie riformate. Insegnamento, dibattito culturale, interventi pubblici. Atti del workshop omonimo, Politecnico di Milano, 1989*, Milan 1992, pp. 395–431. However the work that can best demonstrate to the reader with comparatively little familiarity with Italian the intellectual horizons of the leading architects in Venice at the beginning of the nineteenth century is that by L. Cicognara, A. Diedo and G. Selva, *Le fabbriche e i monumenti cospicui di Venezia*, Venice 1815, revised 1838 and 1857, a folio volume of elevations of 'the greatest buildings' of Venice (chiefly Renaissance) in 250 plates of drawings by students at the *Accademia di Belle Arti*, which often 'correct' or 'restore' elements later altered or not corresponding to contemporary ideas of classical style.

On the debate over the proposal and implementation of the railway in Venice, see L. Facchinelli, *Il ponte ferroviario in Laguna*, Venice 1988; P. Redondi (ed.), *Ferdinandea: scritti sulla ferrovia da Venezia a Milano, 1836–1841*, Florence 2001.

The manuscript texts of Pinali, Pyrker and Priuli-Du Bois, from which Romanelli quotes, are in the library of the Museo Correr, Venice. On the careers of Tommaso and Giambattista Meduna there is very little written, though more information has become available in recent studies of the Fenice Theatre and of Palazzo Franchetti.

For the losses during this time to the Venetian fabric and heritage see Alvise Zorzi, *Venezia scomparsa*, Milan 1972, 1984. For Ruskin on Venice, see Sarah Quill, *Ruskin's Venice: The Stones Revisited*, with introductions by Alan Windsor, Aldershot 2000. A compendious general introduction to the culture and history of the post-dogal city is Margaret Plant, *Venice: Fragile City, 1797–1997*, New Haven and London 2002. Two books treating of the cultural aspects of nineteenth-century Venice are John Pemble, *Venice Rediscovered*, Oxford 1995, and Tony Tanner, *Venice Desired*, Oxford 1992.

The quotations from Romanelli in 1.1 and 1.5 are from *Venezia Ottocento*, Rome 1977, pp. 28 and 249 respectively. Ruskin's reference to " the architecture ... of past ages ... as the most precious of inheritances" is from *The Seven Lamps of Architecture*, London 1849, Chapter VI, 'The Lamp of Memory' (Library Edition, 1903–12, *Works* VIII, p. 225).

2 | The Fondaco dei Turchi and Related Issues

In overview and in hindsight, one can see most of the restorations referred to in the previous chapter as attempts to contend with the 'crisis' into which Venice had fallen, its lack of a role and of a self-image consistent with the position it now occupied in the political order and in the economy. Meduna's 'rewritings', the alarming Fisola-Cadorin plan for a bathing establishment on the Riva degli Schiavoni, Jappelli's plans for the free port, and the general approach of the city planners were effectually a series of episodes in a desperate endeavour to give the city back a plausible, lasting, homogeneous appearance that would accommodate new developments and that would define Venice's new identity. This new identity could certainly be attained through new grand projects (the bridge across the lagoon, for instance, and, as we have seen, it did indeed change the face of the city) or also, as in all Europe during this period, through a modern rereading of 'reassuring' images of the past. While Giambattista Meduna led the way in this latter direction, studying Venetian Gothic and carrying out a neo-Gothic restoration at San Fantin, on a theoretical level it was Pietro Selvatico Estense, during the same years, who defined the cultural references for historicist architecture. He proposed instead a return to *lombardesco* (the style of medieval Lombard architecture) or to the style of Bramante, and he soon afterwards won the admiration of the young Camillo Boito, who would succeed him at the *Accademia di Belle Arti* in Venice.

In the critical assessment of this period there is commonly a mistaken assumption that Venetian neo-medievalism was an offshoot of nineteenth-century neo-medievalism in other regions of Italy and in Europe. Such an assumption is methodologically similar to the mistake of failing to distinguish Venice's situation from those of cities on the mainland, and hardly less significant. As a consequence the reconstructions in historical styles, the destructions, the pastiches that took place in Venice are wrongly attributed to the same kind of historicizing revivalism that is found elsewhere. In fact they had a quite different genesis.

The continuity and the homogeneity of Venice's urban fabric made it almost impossible to single out and impose programmatically a particular architectural style that would represent the 'character' of the city. It was not easy to make the kind of categorical distinctions that were being made elsewhere, given the typically Venetian fusion of styles, the organic growth of its fabric and its integration of materials apparently at odds with each other, reflecting a wealth of influences crossing time, and diverse in technique. In view of this continuity, so-called neo-medievalism was (from our point of view) a harmless tendency, or at least could not have been the motivation behind nineteenth-century pastiche in Venice, except in so far as it suggested the use of imported forms as models for a new architecture. In Venice neo-Gothic was primarily a sign of fashion, of novelty, a kind of 'international style' *avant la lettre*, which was employed only occasionally as an inoffensive and rather smart coating to mollify an awkward imposition. It was well received in the city: even the massive neo-Gothic pile of the *Mulino Stucky* (Stucky flour mill; fig. 54, p. 94) at the western end of the Giudecca was inserted without protest into the lagoon skyline. What happened instead in Venice was a faithful revival of the past – though it was a suppositious past shaped by a suppositious fidelity. What was revived, or rather invented, was an *antico volto* (former apperance) of the city, the image of the entity that had been swept away with the fall of the Serenissima. All this had very little to do with the Gothic Revival as such; rather it should be regarded as an overt historical falsification, a fantasy recuperation. Being a fantasy, it not infrequently contrived to produce monsters, or led up to dramatic crises of disillusionment.

Thus one finds that what is called *ripristino*, which means not simply putting things back to the way they were before but also setting to rights, rendering as new, is, regrettably, a particularly Venetian tradition, or is particularly strong in Venice. It is something quite different from revivalism (especially considered as a nineteenth-century phenomenon). Its pernicious influence has been felt at all those moments in the city's history when acute crises have led some to seek comfort in theoretical models, in ideologies and progammatic procedures rather than focus their attention on reality, which, of course, on such occasions has appeared enormously complex and intractable. Unlike stylistic revivalism, *ripristino* is not an historical phenomenon, determinable, datable, and of the past, but a constant.

There are, then, at least two aspects to the 'betrayal' of Venice that has taken place, a betrayal originating in the early decades of the nineteenth-century crisis of the city but continuing with far-reaching and very awkward implications for today. The first consists in the attempt to apply to the lagoon city a kind of urban planning and architecture, as well as an economy, based on the experiences and the example of settlements and functions belonging to the mainland, and therefore 'alien'. The second is a consequence of the recurrent attempt, exemplified in glaring fashion by the restoration of the Fondaco dei Turchi, as we shall shortly see, to force a reading of the evidence without fully understanding it, and to deduce from it rules and principles that are in fact imaginary and distorted. The reality of Venice tends to conflict with tendentious interpretations of the city, whether driven by positivistic certainty or by idealism. Even if these operations start from perfectly lucid premises, the results are at best infelicitous, at worst seriously damaging. What in effect happens is that the building concerned is trimmed, pruned or amputated in order that the forced 'reading' should not be too clearly exposed as such.

This is certainly true of the work by Federico Berchet on the Fondaco dei Turchi ('Turkish warehouse') in the 1860s. The work was carried out with the aim of recovering an image of *Venezia com'era* (Venice as it was), on the basis of long and detailed historical research of the iconographic sources (research, therefore, that was intrinsically poetic, and Romantic) and of the elimination of whatever did not fit with the image thus re-discovered (or invented). In fact, one had only to look at the ruins of the Fondaco, and compare them with its appearance in historic prints, to realise that the Fondaco as a medieval Veneto-Byzantine building was lost and gone for ever and that only by the power of imagination could it be resurrected. That is exactly what happened. Berchet did not hesitate to demolish whatever time had altered and, where necessary, he saw no problem in forcing the material to comply with his requirements (he did not hesitate, for example, to remove the fluting on the columns in order to render them smooth, imitating marble).

What is so striking is that the result was so consistent with the premises as to be grotesque. Berchet, seeking to restore to Venice one of its most prestigious buildings, even re-sorted to Jacopo de' Barbari's view of Venice of 1500 as if it were a plan to be followed. He deduced from it the height of the side towers, though not the slightest physical trace of them remained. He was happy to superimpose his own image on the remains of the building, with absolute disregard for the material reality of what was there. He was therefore able to assert, with total logic, since he was referring to the image supplied by de' Barbari, that "the main principle that prevailed over the project was the scrupulous respect of the original in its every minutest detail". Consistent with this, he believed "the major achievement of the architect [to be] that of not having added anything, not even the smallest moulding profile of his own", and "considering how little survived of the monument, and what was required to make it whole again, then the restoration seems all the more praiseworthy and the time taken to complete it remarkably short ...". The quotations are taken from the article, 'Sui restauri del Fondaco dei Turchi' (On the restorations of Fondaco dei Turchi), which Berchet published in the volume *Venezia nell'ultimo ventennio* (Venice in the last twenty years) in 1887; the volume also includes an article by Annibale Forcellini on the restoration of the Doge's Palace and an article by Pietro Saccardo on the restoration of San Marco. All three are described in the introduction as reports illustrative of "archaeological engineering".

Berchet was thoroughly scrupulous in his reading, and his was by no means an amateurish restoration. On some points of the restoration there were heated discussions, and it was necessary to appoint a committee (made up of Agostino Sagredo, who collaborated with Berchet on the historical research, the two Meduna, Giovanni Battista Cecchini, Andrea Scala and Giuseppe Bianco, head of the municipal *Ufficio tecnico*, or Civil engineering department) to decide whether the *palazzo* should be built on a higher foundation than the original. On 31 May 1864, the committee ruled that the level should remain the same, because "it was thought incumbent on us ... to hand down to posterity every precious monument not only in its original form but also in its first and original position, whatever might have happened to it subsequently, because if a monument is of historical interest, then so too is the level on which it was constructed". Thus the only thing that should have been changed – given that, even then,

Figs. 29, 30, 31

The Fondaco dei Turchi was not built as a *fondaco* like the Fondaco dei Tedeschi (see figs. 18, 19, pp. 38–39) but as a family palace, of the old-fashioned Veneto-Byzantine sort of which few remained in the nineteenth century, and even fewer today. From 1621 onwards it was leased as a base from which they might trade to the Turkish merchant community, hence its name. As shown by Francesco Albotto (1721–1757) it had just been altered, in 1751, but was already in a poor state of repair. In 1838 it was sold to the builder Petich (Antonio Busetto), who made it his office, yard and warehouse. Petich tried several times to obtain permission to demolish it and rebuild on the site. In December 1858 Petich, Federico Berchet and the director of the *Ufficio tecnico* of the *Comune*, Giuseppe Bianco, presented a new project for the building, accompanied by a report on its state of decay quoting from the 1853 edition of Ruskin's *Stones of Venice* ("It is a ghastly ruin ... blanched into dusty decay by the frosts of centuries"). The site was then acquired by the *Comune*, in 1859–60, with the idea of making the building into a museum, accompanying the nearby Veneto Museo (later Museo Correr) which Teodoro Correr had collected in his house. Soon afterwards, in 1860, Berchet and Agostino Sagredo published their research on the history of the Fondaco and their project for its restoration: drawings (right) of its current and proposed future state accompanied the publication.

Francesco Albotto, *The Grand Canale with the Fondaco dei Turchi*, Sotheby's Picture Library JL2812

Figs. 32, 33

Interim work began on the Fondaco dei Turchi, which was tottering on the verge of collapse, in June 1861. The contractor was Sebastian Cadel, who continued the project, approved on 11 March 1862, under Berchet. The work of restoration and reconstruction got under way in 1863 and continued until 1869, when the part of the building intended for the civic museum opened. Work on the façade took place between 1865 and 1869, its gradual progress being reported in logbooks that are now in the Archives of the *Comune*, together with drawings and studies. The reconstruction of the two wings along the flanking canal and *salizzada* was not undertaken until later, from 1880 onwards (on the basis of designs made by Berchet in 1873), and was completed only in 1889, although work continued until 1891 with the construction of a rear wing. In 1887 Berchet described and explained the thinking behind the restoration and reconstruction in a notorious essay, 'On the restorations of the Fondaco dei Turchi'. His efforts were soon fiercely deplored and attacked, notably by Pompeo Molmenti and Giacomo Boni. The Fondaco housed the Museo Correr until 1921, when it became the seat of the *Museo di Storia naturale* (Museum of Natural History). Formerly a "ghastly ruin", ever since a ghastly failure, the Fondaco dei Turchi is probably the most out-of-place building in Venice. It is a joke that it is still described as 'twelfth- or thirteenth-century'.

water was lapping at the entrance of the Fondaco and today, after the effects of subsidence, it flows directly into the building – was preserved.

The restoration proceeded on the basis of some surviving ruins and fragments, and the iconographic sources available: the towers have already been mentioned, and crenellations were also supplied, again in the absence of any reliable evidence. To complete the 'Turkish' look (even though the building had begun its life as a patrician palace, and not as a 'Turkish warehouse' at all), Berchet drew inspiration from the triangular crenellations on the mosque of Ahmad Ibn Tulun in Cairo – which confirms the point that for their style Venetian reconstitutions were not indebted to the *lombardesco* favoured by Boito, to Selvatico's medievalizing eclecticism or to any other extrinsic examples of medievalizing revivalism.

The cladding on the building, though incorporating a few original fragments, was largely provided from the Greek marble left over from the restoration of the north façade of the Basilica, recently undertaken by Meduna. The paterae, the decorative reliefs and the cornices, on the other hand, were retrieved from the attics of half the city. There were lengthy discussions whether or not to polish the marble cladding. In the end Berchet cleaned it severely with a lead-plate polisher.

At any rate the desired end was achieved: Venice had its Fondaco once again, in its 'original', opulent form – an icon, for contemporaries, in both name and form, of the vitality and past glories of the Venetian mercantile class, which many hoped to see flourish once more in the Italian Risorgimento. It is reasonable to assume that Berchet was faithful to the ideas of his uncle Giovanni, a renowned man of letters and advocate of a spirit of national patriotism, who envisaged a leading role in the new State for the emerging middle class, as the motor both for unification and for forward development.

What happened in these years, and especially in the case of the Fondaco, according to Manfredo Tafuri, writing on 'the myth of Venice' in 1985, "was the worst possible betrayal of Venetian 'continuity': in the face of an evident crisis [or rather 'rupture', as we called it] in that continuity, 'hypervenetianism' was invented. There is one name that summarizes all this: Berchet. We know what Berchet did to the Fondaco dei Turchi, but there are other examples of the same kind of thoroughgoing perversity. We have ended up with such fakes that it is necessary to turn to archive sources in order to identify them."

This is the crux. The purpose of this chapter and those that follow is to raise awareness of the extent and impact of operations of this kind, which have in their own terms been remarkably successful, not only in the nineteenth century, but also in the twentieth. There are many other restored 'Fondachi dei Turchi', big and small, in Venice; there are not only frequent such evocations of lost architectures, but many less high-minded ones. The Fondaco dei Turchi is not, as we shall soon see more clearly, a sad monument to a type of restoration that is no longer carried out, but exemplifies the normal prevalent practice of 'restoration' in Venice, conscious or not, yesterday and today.

NOTES

Ruskin had a series of daguerrotypes taken of the Fondaco, one of which, unfortunately illegible, is preserved in the Ruskin Museum in Coniston, Cumbria, and is dated 1851. See further P. Constantini and I. Zannier (ed.), *I dagherrotipi della collezione Ruskin*, Venice 1986, and, on Ruskin as a photographer, M. Hervey, 'Ruskin and Photography', *Oxford Art Journal*, 2, 1982, pp. 23–33.

Federico Berchet and Agostino Sagredo published their research and proposals in the pamphlet *Venezia: studi storici e artistici*, Milan 1860. Berchet contributed his essay 'Sui restauri del Fondaco dei Turchi' to *L'ingegneria a Venezia nell'ultimo ventennio. Pubblicazione degli ingegneri veneziani in omaggio ai colleghi del VI Congresso*, Venice 1887. Pompeo Molmenti attacked him in *Delendae Venetiae*, Venice 1887, and in 'Per Venezia e per l'arte', *Emporium*, 70, 1900, pp. 313ff. Giacomo Boni wrote on the subject in *L'avvenire dei monumenti in Venezia*, Venice 1882, and in *Venezia imbellettata*, Rome 1887. The modern literature on the subject includes R. Codello, 'La ricostruzione del Fondaco dei Turchi in Venezia', in G. Fiengo, A. Bellini, S. Della Torre (ed.), *La parabola del restauro stilistico nella rilettura di sette casi emblematici*, Milan 1994, pp. 313–50; this article depends on the work of S. Boscarino, 'Il cosidetto restauro del Fondaco dei Tedeschi a Venezia', *Restauro & Città*, 3–4, 1986, pp. 58–70. In recent years projects for a restoration of the building have been put forward, following the most up-to-date methodology: see E. Vassallo, 'Progetto di massima per il restauro del Fondaco dei Turchi a Venezia', in G. Carbonara (ed.), *Trattato di restauro architettonico*, vol. IV, Turin 1996, pp. 343–403.

The quotations from Berchet are from his article 'Sui restauri del Fondaco dei Turchi', cited above. For the quotation from Manfredo Tafuri and his idea of *ipervenezianità* see *Rassegna*, 22, 1985, p. 8.

3 | After Annexation to Italy

3.1 New urban projects

The rebuilding of the Fondaco dei Turchi was conducted during the years in which the city passed from Austrian to Italian rule, welcomed in 1866 by a plebiscite in which votes against annexation to the Kingdom of Italy numbered 69 in a franchise of 650,000.

Despite the new government, expectations of improvement were to be largely disappointed. The problems described by the last *podestà* of the Austro-Hungarian administration, the aforementioned Pier Luigi Bembo, persisted unchanged for several years – indeed were aggravated by a virulent epidemic of cholera and an immense *acqua alta* (high tide) in 1866 itself. Equally unchanged were the solutions adopted by the *Ufficio tecnico*, still headed by Giuseppe Bianco. Shortly after the new *sindaco* or mayor of Venice, Giovanni Battista Giustinian Recanati, took over from Bembo, a *Lettera da tredici cittadini* (Letter from thirteen citizens) was delivered, which re-stated, with new hope, what had already been pressing needs during the years of Austro-Hungarian rule – for new streets, for decent housing to replace ancient buildings for the "middle class", and for a *Piano regolatore* (Town-planning scheme) to reform and manage the Venetian urban environment in the best possible way.

The thirteen citizens' requests, as they phrased them, won the support and endorsement not only of the new mayor but also of the highest local representative of the new national government, the *prefetto* or prefect Conte Luigi Torelli, a long-time advocate of the ideas of Giuseppe Mazzini and a fervent patriot who had fought in all the Risorgimento campaigns. Torelli immediately compiled a detailed report to the *Deputazione provinciale* (Provincial delegation) with suggestions for the boosting of the local economy and the improvement of sanitary conditions in the city; particular attention was devoted to the issue of education for the lower classes, with the recommendation that new commercially oriented schools should be established. Also required were regular connections with Alexandria in Egypt and a new Venice–Brenner–Munich rail link, and the construction in the city of new warehouses with rail access, to the benefit in particular of the fishing industry. Also proposed was the widening of the narrow *calli* or alleys of Venice: a rapid survey indicated the existence of 357 *calli* less than 1.5 metres wide, 45 under one metre wide, and 187 coming to a dead end. One of the first results of the new Venetian vigour and of the activism of Torelli (often uncritical and sometimes prevaricatory in his dealings with the *Comune*) was a proliferation of commissions and committees: on 30 November 1866, a *Commissione per lo studio di un piano di riforma delle vie e canali di Venezia* (Commission for the study of a plan to reform the streets and canals of Venice)

Fig. 34
In Campiello Mario Marinoni (Campiello della
Fenice) Venetian independence was celebrated in a
building designed and built by the engineer Carlo
Ruffini in 1869 with a façade decorated with
cannon-balls and shells used by the Austrians to
bombard Venice in 1849; over the door there is a
bust of Daniele Manin, architect of Venetian
resistance, and atop the little building, of course,
there is a Lion of St Mark – a declaration of a
reinstatement. Beside to the left is the modern
Sotoportego della Malvasia, part of another new
pedestrian route through the *sestiere* of San Marco.

Fig. 35
The *Cassa di Risparmio di Venezia* (1964–68) in Campo
Manin is a remarkable and unique intrusion into the
fabric of the city centre; it would never have been built
(by Pier Luigi Nervi and Angelo Scattolin) if it had not
replaced an unloved building designed in 1879, one of
several of the time in this *campo* 'redeveloped' after
Venice became mistress again, to a degree, of her own
affairs. The *campo* was formerly Campo San Paternian,
with the ancient church of San Paternian, known for its
hexagonal *campanile*. In 1871 the church had been
regarded as too far gone to save and was demolished;
nor was the Palazzo del Zane, on the site of the present
Cassa di Risparmio, thought worth saving. In any case
the desire was to transform the area into a celebration
of Venice's liberation, commemorating the
Risorgimento and the hero of the 1848 rebellion against
the Austrians, Daniele Manin. The statue of Manin,
with magnificent lions at the base of the plinth, by
Luigi Borro, was installed in 1875.

was set up to study "the future topography of the city in general and of all its constituent parts"; it had nine members, among them Giambattista Meduna and Giuseppe Bianco. Active at the same time were the *Comune*'s *Commissione permanente edilizia* (Permanent building commission) and the *Società per l'aerazione delle calli* (Society for the ventilation of alleys), set up to address the health concerns in Torelli's report, and the still running *Commissione di Ornato*.

The *Commissione per lo studio* … was dissolved two years later, as was the *Commissione di Ornato*, but not before the former had laid down the guidelines for Venetian planning for the next twenty years. It had projected in detail the axial route Santi Apostoli–Santa Fosca–Strada Nuova on the north side of the Grand Canal, which was immediately put into effect (1867–71), and, following a policy of demolition, proposed the creation of a 'ring' linking the railway station, Santi Apostoli, Santo Stefano and Ca' Foscari, returning to the station through Santa Croce.

The commission then invited all citizens, without distinction, to send in their contributions and ideas for the reform of the city. And the contributions came in: Giambattista Meduna opposed any further filling-in of canals, in favour of maintaining existing routes, with slight modifications to make them broader; Berchet proposed the creation of a 'trans-urban' route from the railway station to Rialto, which was essentially realised. But there were also proposals, some quite mad, involving clearance, demolition and the *interramento* of canals, and a very singular one for the raising of the entire complex of the Procuratie Vecchie in the Piazza in order to protect them from *acqua alta*.

The *Società per l'aerazione delle calli* was particularly active, as long as it was in existence, in encouraging the improvement of sanitary conditions, without losing sight of the advantages of demolitions that would make the city's monuments more prominent. With this objective, for instance, it demolished houses in order to open up space round the apse and south side of the church of Santi Giovanni e Paolo (1889).

Particularly worthy of note in the two-year period 1868–69 are two patriotically inspired initiatives promoted by a private individual, Giorgio Casarini, to celebrate the Risorgimento achievement and the figure of Daniele Manin, leader of the 1848 rebellion against Austrian rule; these were immediately adopted and put into effect by the *Comune*. Calle della Malvasia at San Fantin was widened, to give better access to a courtyard where Casarini constructed an unusual building (fig. 34) in commemoration of the rebellion of 1848; it incorporated remains of Austrian bombs launched against the city on that occasion. Work then proceeded on the expansion and renovation of Campo San Paternian, which was re-named Campo Manin and adorned by the great man's statue, a fine work by Luigi Borro (fig. 35). New buildings designed by Lodovico Cadorin and Giuseppe Bianco were also constructed, and new premises for the *Cassa di Risparmio di Venezia* (Venetian savings bank), designed by Enrico Trevisanato in 1879, involving the demolition of the venerable Palazzo del Zane. (Trevisanato's building was itself replaced, in 1968, with a new building by Pier Luigi Nervi and Angelo Scattolin.)

In addition to the inauguration of the Strada Nuova, the decision was taken in the 1870s to proceed with two further major clearances intended to improve circulation, for the Via 22 Marzo at San Moisè (Francesco Balduin, 1870; see fig. 11, p. 28) and for the Via 2 Aprile at San Salvador (Consiglio Fano and Domenico Colognese, 1875). These would be completed a few years later, and would again involve the construction of new buildings fronting the newly open spaces, designed by the same men.

Extended pedestrianization, with all it entailed, was clearly the overriding objective, and it was welcomed by Venetians. So it is not surprising to discover that there were people who began to think seriously, half a century before it happened, about building a road bridge between Venice and the mainland. Antonio Baffo drew up two projects, in 1875 and 1888, neither of which was acted upon.

There were also plans for a new port, or *Stazione Marittima*. The project advocated by Prefect Torelli was the one realised (1869–80), overcoming opposition from supporters of various different proposals. The issue was decided by a royal commission, chaired and directed by Pietro Paleocapa. In the end the site for the new facilities became the island of Santa Chiara, the strand of Santa Marta (used for the warehouses) and San Basilio (for the free port), following the basic scheme and some features of the first part of Jappelli's project of 1850.

These projects broadly continued a trend already set and even partially implemented during the decades of Austrian rule. Progress was only slightly hindered by the inability of the commission set up in 1866 in order to draw up a *Piano regolatore* to reach agreement – unless, on the contrary, it was helped by the lack of precise directives, which would probably have been more restrictive. Part of the trend were significant industrialization enterprises – the *Cotonificio Veneziano* (Venetian cotton mill) was already active by 1882, and Giovanni Stucky's flour mill started production in 1884 – and the encouragement of tourism, culminating in the 'colonization' of the Lido at the turn of the century.

Meanwhile the restoration programmes on the city's main monuments that had begun under the Austro-Hungarian administration continued, gathering new impetus, new controversies and new precedents and references.

3.2 I grandi lavori *(San Marco, the Doge's*
Palace) and other restorations
Annexation to the Kingdom of Italy encouraged and increased the activity of restoration, which the new government, obviously keen to demonstrate its great interest in the newly 'liberated' city, promoted with incentives. Restoration projects could benefit from tax concessions and financial aid, and it was this that made possible the work both on San Marco, under Giambattista Meduna until 1878 and subsequently, from 1882, under Pietro Saccardo and Federico Berchet (until 1887), and on the Doge's Palace from 1875 to 1888. In addition, surveys and reports were made on churches and *palazzi* that were in disrepair, indeed often on the

verge of collapse, but here the laudable intentions of the authorities and their desire to achieve an extensive restoration of the city were often frustrated. A paradoxical situation arose: the *Comune*, faced with the prospect of having to contribute financially to a restoration, tended to argue the case for demolition rather than repair, while the landlords, the *fabbricerie* (vestry boards), the intellectuals, the architects and, in general, all those who did not want to or did not have to bear the expense of the work argued for their preservation. A corollary was that restorations financed by *fabbricerie* or private individuals without any public contribution enjoyed considerable freedom of action. In 1897, Baron Giorgio Franchetti was congratulated by the *Ufficio Regionale per la conservazione dei monumenti del Veneto* (Regional office for the conservation of monuments of the Veneto) for his restoration of the Ca' d'Oro (see further below), to all intents and purposes without authorization and without the involvement of any municipal or State experts.

The restoration of St Mark's Basilica and the Doge's Palace were the most significant such undertakings of the period, but the contemporary press carries reports on the restoration of several other important *palazzi*, among them Palazzo Cavalli-Ravenna at San Benedetto, Palazzo Farsetti, Palazzo Loredan (both fig. 45, p. 79), Palazzo Tiepolo and Palazzo Franchetti at San Vidal (by Baron Raimondo Franchetti, father of Giorgio; see further below). These works cannot but fuel the sense that there was a general ferment of 'modernization' that certainly affected and changed, who knows in what way, the face and the fabric of the city. The criteria for restoration that prevailed under the Kingdom of Italy were not in fact very different from those observed in the preceding decades, and had the further disadvantage of a pernicious enthusiasm for new materials, for instance Catania marble or *diaspro*, granites and Botticino marble, all of which would deteriorate more rapidly in the lagoon environment than the traditional Istrian stone.

At San Marco, unscathed by the criticism of Pietro Selvatico, Giambattista Meduna continued his works of restoration, moving on from the north façade, where he had been active between 1842 and 1862. In 1860 he consolidated the vaults and the cupolas and their supporting walls, and in 1870 restored the main door of the Basilica, after which he tackled the south façade, work on which was completed by the end of 1875. Meduna several times won the praise of Viollet-le-Duc (who had visited Venice in 1837 and returned in 1871), who credited him with carrying out restorations like those in France and with great professional skill.

Notwithstanding the favourable opinion of the celebrated French architect, the leading authority for much of the nineteenth century on matters of restoration, the day after the scaffolding came down Alvise Piero Zorzi, a Venetian nobleman, painter and later curator at the Museo Correr, compiled (1876) and then published (1877) with the Venetian publisher Ferdinando Ongania his highly critical *Osservazioni intorno ai restauri interni ed esterni della Basilica di San Marco* (Observations on the internal and external restorations of the Basilica of San Marco). The text was published thanks to a financial contribution from John Ruskin, who wrote a long and cordial introduction. Zorzi mercilessly catalogued the damage inflicted on the Basilica by Meduna: the loss of the "precious colour imparted to the columns and other marbles by time", the gratuitous and arbitrary replacement of patterned marble veneers, of capitals and of other stones, the demolition of the rear of the Zeno Chapel, the cleaning of pavings and ancient mosaic surfaces with pumice and abrasives instead of the less invasive techniques traditional in Venice, of which he gave a detailed list, differentiating each for each type of stone.

Taken as a whole, Zorzi's text constitutes a clear and coherent argument in favour of conservation – expressed, even lexically, in Ruskinian terms – rather than restoration. It is dedicated to the defence, in Zorzi's words, not of "an architectural monument, but of a museum of architecture", for which "the idea of Restoration is a very bad thing; even worse is the putting into effect of that idea, and it were better substituted with Conservation. There is a great difference between restoring and conserving. Restoration implies renovation, where the need arises; Conservation completely excludes it …. It appears that, in the restoring, the Basilica has been regarded as some ordinary church in a state of disrepair, not as a museum. The divine patina of the centuries was seen as dirt; wherever possible, the intention was to remove it: who would not have approved? In fact everything that is new, smooth, whitened or scraped meets with the approval of many, who, if they could, would whitewash all the *palazzi*, churches and monuments of Venice …. The modern eye is pleased; *basta*."

This lucid and indignant message was heard by many and initiated a period of sharp controversy. Zorzi had the support of those in Britain with the most progressive views: William Morris asked him to join the newly founded (22 March 1877) Society for the Protection of Ancient Buildings, which on 15 November 1879 held a meeting at the Sheldonian Theatre in Oxford to discuss the state of the Venetian basilica, in the course of which Meduna's work was assessed. The results of the long programme of restoration were denounced, and Restoration itself, which Morris in the Society's manifesto had described in Ruskinian terms as "a strange and most fatal idea", declared pernicious. Among the impassioned speeches made that day was one by the architect George Edmund Street, who had recently visited Venice. He not only described the general replacement of a large proportion of the mosaics, and the loss of freshness and colour in those subjected to restoration, but in a *coup de théâtre* displayed to those present a piece of mosaic from the Basilica, which he had acquired for a few *lire* from the sacristan, who was selling off the debris to tourists. *Basta* indeed: the Society launched an urgent campaign in the international press (with influential contributions from Morris in *The Daily News*, for instance), and at its height sent a petition to the Italian government demanding the suspension of works and the adoption of conservational criteria on their resumption. Although the foreign interference was initially regarded as unwarranted, many Italian newspapers (*La Gazzetta di Venezia, Il Tempo, L'Adriatico, Il Rinnovamento*) soon took up the cry. A commission was appointed to evaluate the charges and to recommend measures to be taken;

its members included the historian Pompeo Molmenti and Federico Berchet, who drafted the final report. The principles advocated by Zorzi were embraced and Meduna's restoration was described as "ill-educated and lacking in taste". Giacomo Boni (on whom see further below) described Meduna in a letter of 1881 to William Douglas Caroë as a "criminal restorer". The contents of the report led the *Ministero della Pubblica Istruzione* (Ministry of public instruction), which at the time was the department responsible for monuments, to take immediate steps for the restoration that he had carried out on the south façade of the Basilica should be reversed. The decision entailed the replacement of Meduna by the engineer Pietro Saccardo, who had been a member of the *Fabbriceria* of the Basilica from 1860.

When Saccardo, continuing the work, began the restoration of the main façade, he was mindful of the conservational advice coming from many quarters, including the Society for the Protection of Ancient Buildings. Symptomatic was his bitter dispute with Meduna about the exact position of the cusps projecting from the façade, which Saccardo did not want to set upright, as he thought they were in the position originally intended (or in any case one that should be preserved), whereas Meduna had intended to straighten them in order to restore them to their putative original state. Saccardo also had an argument with the mosaicists working on the floors and the lunettes, who had altered the names of Sts John the Baptist (Giovanni Battista) and Gherardo into Liborio and Nicolò, their own baptismal names. The episode gives some idea of the casual presumption even the workmen brought to their task, and how intrusive all this dismantling and reassembly of the mosaic surfaces must have been.

The plea for conservation, though well formulated and effective in getting its message across, did not in practice win general support; however, it succeeded, once having been articulated, in limiting falsifications and unnecessary renovations and it became established as a point of reference whenever new restorations of important buildings were undertaken. This was the case with the works on the Doge's Palace (fig. 36), for instance, which, with its fractured capitals and obvious cracks in the walls and columns, was clearly in need of remedial intervention. A first series of works, decreed by a government commission, was directed by Giandomenico Malvezzi from 1872. He reinforced columns with metal hoops and replaced some capitals, but this was not deemed sufficient. In 1876 Annibale Forcellini embarked on new restorations, on the very eve of the heated debate about Meduna's work on San Marco.

Work began on the west façade of the palace, facing the Piazzetta (figs. 37, 38), which was restored by 1884, and had been completed on the corners of the south façade, towards the waterfront, by 1888. Many capitals in the loggias that were cracked were replaced with copies (fig. 40). For Forcellini, this was a case, "in the interests of stability, of sad necessity; sad because, without entering into the exaggerations of conservation extremists, anybody who has a sense of reverence for ancient artefacts cannot but feel sorry to see the original replaced with a copy". The substitution did not pass unobserved, and gave rise to further controversy, which even reached Parliament. Forcellini gave an assurance that there would be "scrupulous conservation" of the originals inside the palace, and the matter was not taken any further. Work was allowed to continue with reconstruction of the transverse arches supporting the north wall of the Sala del Maggior Consiglio and of part of the floors of the loggias at ground level. The reconstruction was carried out using hollow bricks that made it possible to avoid introducing iron rods between the columns, the supports being inserted in the floor. The architrave of the Porta della Carta was also replaced, and a new sculpture was made of Doge Foscari with the Lion of St Mark (the work of Luigi Ferrari, 1885). Forcellini, however, wanted to close three small square windows that opened on the south façade. Camillo Boito, though not of the opinion that they were original, but nonetheless "very old", thought they should be preserved. Forcellini stated that he was aware that "we cannot preserve only the beautiful in monuments, and suppress the ugly, or what seems so to us, but in the conviction that those windows were alien to the original concept of the beautiful façade, and that they were more-over an absurd, superfluous addition serving no purpose, he had proposed removing them: today, however, in the area of conservation any intervention is regarded as dangerous and approval was denied. As a general rule, this is the correct and prudent policy, but one might say that in this particular case prudence erred on the side of excessive caution." He managed in fact to close one of the windows, and also succeeded in demolishing the walls between the columns in the loggias that Antonio da Ponte had put in to support the superstructure after the terrible fire of 1577. For Forcellini, "knocking down the walls that blocked the arches was not destroying history: besides, the main objective of the restoration of a monument is precisely to restore it to the way it was when it was built, unless to do so involves the destruction of works more precious than the monument itself".

These comments of Forcellini begin to pose the question of the conflict between 'historical value' and 'antiquity value' that Alois Riegl would develop a few years later. Forcellini also committed himself to making public the background research and the decisions made during the project: a series of very detailed plans, for instance, indicates, stone by stone, the replacements made and the operations carried out. Every step of the restoration was documented and discussed (see fig. 39), and every decision approved beforehand by a watchdog committee specially appointed to oversee the restorations, demonstrating a more sophisticated level of practice than was usual. That this happened was largely due to the particular climate of those years, to the control exercised by the commissions, and to the awareness of certain of the individuals involved. Prominent among these, though playing a marginal role in the decision-making and executive process, was Giacomo Boni, a man who has not always been appreciated as he should be in Italy. He played an influential part in the field of archaeological studies, and particularly in the early twentieth-century controversy between Italian classical scholars and German palaeographers. Destined for an eminent career as director of the excavations of the Forum and the Palatine in Rome, Boni, still a very young man at the time, served as site assistant on the Doge's Palace project, and in the years immediately following

Fig. 36
"It would be impossible, I believe, to invent a more
magnificent arrangement of all that is in building
most dignified and fair", wrote Ruskin in *The Seven
Lamps of Architecture.*

Figs. 37, 38
An albumen print of 1859, hitherto unpublished, shows the Piazzetta side of the Doge's Palace without the figure of Doge Andrea Gritti kneeling before the Lion of St Mark, removed by Napoleon. Below, railings fend off the public from the two guns that the Austrians kept there at the ready. In 1899 the Venetian authorities could not resist re-installing, *dov'era, com'era*, the Doge and the Lion, newly sculpted by Giuseppe Torres and Urbano Bottasso, and today as much part of the building as if it had never been removed. Similarly, Doge Foscari and the Lion were restored on the Porta della Carta, the public entrance to the palace, in 1885.

Fig. 39
In the course of his restoration, 1876–88, Annibale Forcellini drew the elevation of the south façade of the Doge's Palace (towards the Molo and St Mark's Basin) marking the patches of wall where he had "removed and reapplied" the elements of the surface and where he had "from the need for stability replaced" them. There is no doubt that such scruples and attention to the procedures of restoration, the care to distinguish the fabric as found and the fabric as altered, were the direct result of the fuss made by the Society for the Protection of Ancient Buildings, who thereby encouraged the conservationist faction in Venice itself.

Fig. 40
During the course of his restorations Forcellini found it necessary to replace many of the mid-fourteenth-century carved capitals of the columns of the ground arcade of the Doge's Palace, defusing the criticism this aroused by preserving the originals. One of the most famous of these extraordinary capitals represents (here in the copy *in situ*) human life and love – courtship, marriage, birth and death.

we find him deeply engaged in the conservation of Venetian buildings. He wrote prolifically and polemically on the subject, taking the same line as Zorzi and Molmenti.

It was Boni who in 1889 gave perhaps the most realistic and balanced assessment of Forcellini's work, describing it as "an example of the intermediate type of restoration, between that which replaces anything at all damaged and that which preserves everything possible". His assessment accurately reflects the sometimes contradictory decisions made by Forcellini, which occasionally reveal residual tendencies towards the prevalent nineteenth-century propensity for replacement and casual reconstruction, even if in other cases he took account of the forceful arguments of the new conservationist crusade, which had of course been excited particularly by the major restorations of this period in Venice.

Notwithstanding evidence of a new circumspection on restoration sites, at least at the most important and most closely supervised (also by the press), nevertheless the desire for *ripristino*, for the return to an original (documented or imaginary) *antico*, continued to prevail over respect for the documentary importance of the evidence, taken as a whole, in all its material complexity. Intervening in the dispute that arose over some large windows in the Doge's Palace which Forcellini wanted to *ripristinare* as two-light and three-light Gothic windows, Boito, too, expressed the desire that they should be brought in line with the design of the "first architect", after three centuries of "ghastly mutilation" and "disgraceful disfigurement". That might be tolerated, Boito said, "by those who enjoyed the good fortune of having their own distinctive architecture … whereas we have no architecture of our own but in compensation take a humble pleasure in understanding all kinds of architecture – and is it not our sacred duty at least to correct the artistic mistakes of our fathers?"

Boito made these remarks on the restoration of the Doge's Palace in 1899, but he had already operated in this 'philological' way in Venice as early as 1878–79, when he collaborated on the refurbishment of Palazzo Cavalli-Gussoni for Baron Raimondo Franchetti (figs. 41–44). Together with San Marco and the Doge's Palace, this is one of the best documented restorations of this period, especially considering that it was not a public building but the property of a private individual. Formerly owned by the families Marcello, Cavalli and Gussoni, and subsequently by Conte Pepoli and Archduke Frederick of Austria, the *palazzo* had been inherited in 1848 by Henri, comte de Chambord, who commissioned Giambattista Meduna to turn it into a fitting, albeit austere, official residence. After 1860 Meduna unified the various parts of the building divided in the past between the Cavalli and Gussoni families, homogenized the decoration and created a garden beside the Grand Canal by removing some workshops and the boatyard previously located there. This last was an audacious and almost unique initiative in a city where no waste of space had been allowed and where until the nineteenth century demolitions in the central areas of the city to create open spaces had been unknown. That had applied especially to the Grand Canal, which had long been something of a spectacle, a setting composed by the *palazzi* (or at least *fondachi*) that fronted on to it, not by gardens, which by preference were enclosed within buildings or building complexes or were located on the edge of the city.

In 1878 Baron Franchetti bought the *palazzo* and immediately made arrangements for new works, entrusting the structure to Girolamo Manetti and the decoration to the decorative artist and teacher Carlo Matscheg. In the initial works, concerning the façade overlooking the garden, Meduna may have had some involvement. But the work soon came under the supervision of Camillo Boito, who certainly altered the decorative appearance of this side of the building, by introducing balconies, cladding in Catania marble, and pastiche coats of arms. He, too, conceived the considerable modifications to the Grand Canal façade, and designed a new staircase on the side looking towards Campo Santo Stefano. The façade on the Grand Canal needed most intervention: the central parts of the *piano nobile* were dismantled, the seventeenth-century attic was removed, the small Baroque columns were replaced with Gothic ones. The width of the first-floor balcony was reduced for "reasons of perspective and artistic harmony", and in general all the supposed imperfections of the existing building and its peculiarities were corrected. At the same time new stone panels and coats of arms were inserted. The watergate on the Grand Canal also underwent major alteration, involving reworking Meduna's styling of it and more Catania marble; the new marbles were painted to look like old ones, both their colour and the shape of the chimneys being taken from pictures by Carpaccio. Next, the new staircase was built on the west side of the building, a transparent 'box' with huge windows in late Gothic style, echoing those of the nearby Ca' Foscari on the other side of the canal. In the *Gazzetta di Venezia* of 22–23 December 1880 an anonymous contributor reported that Baron Franchetti "did not restore [the *palazzo*] but rebuilt it, considerably enlarged it and embellished it …. The artistic beauty of Palazzo Cavalli, one of the most commendable examples of Gothic architecture, was not only preserved but completed and enriched in a most extraordinary way …."

Boito's staircase, executed between 1881 and 1884 (the decoration was completed in 1886) was, as has already been said, an extraordinary and inspired piece of bravura. As a compositional exercise in architectural historicism, with references here to the Romanesque, there to Gothic, and the whole thing wrought with great skill, craftsmanship and intelligence, it is undoubtedly a work of taste and refinement. It marks the high point of the search, already mentioned, quoting Boito, for an architectural style for the new Italy. Here it found expression through stylistic elements of the Venetian Middle Ages; later, after Boito moved to Milan, it took on the forms of the *lombardesco*. At the same time this major work of architecture of the second half of the nineteenth century represents a great distortion both of Boito's own principles – during these same years he was engaged in preparing a manifesto, one of the most discerning of the time, on the methodology of intervention on old buildings (the so-called *Carta del restauro* of 1883) – and, obviously, of the building that was there before.

Unfortunately Franchetti's dream, given form by the skills of Boito and Matscheg (more

Figs. 41, 42
The etching (above) and the photograph
(below) show the Palazzo Cavalli-
Gussoni before the restoration – or
transformation – wrought by Boito,
Manetti and Matscheg for Baron
Raimondo Franchetti in 1878–81.
Typically, the attic or *abbaino* would be
removed – these generally 'late' additions
to Venetian palaces were long regarded
unfavourably by restorers, as *superfetazioni*
(accretions), and there are comparatively
few of them left; and much of the
detailing of the decoration would be
freely modified to the restorer's taste.
The building to the left of the palace was
destroyed altogether.

than Manetti), remained unrealised: for various reasons, the works could not proceed beyond the ground floor and the mezzanines. Ironically, the magnificent new staircase was unserviceable for decades. The restoration of Palazzo Cavalli-Gussoni, now Franchetti, therefore remained for some while an empty exercise in the recreation of those fragile vibrations of form, colour and space that Ruskin had detected and passionately pursued in *The Stones of Venice*.

Examples of such casual treatment of the Venetian environment and the Venetian heritage could go on and on. The intentions of the authorities with regard to the Baroque church of San Moisè in 1877, for instance, are well recorded: having no wish to finance a very costly restoration in order to preserve a building that, being Baroque, was deemed of little artistic

Fig. 43
If the Palazzo Franchetti, formerly
Cavalli-Gussoni, is one of the
grandest and most prominent on the
Grand Canal, that is very much due
to its flank being visible; before
Franchetti's restoration it was as
hemmed in as the Palazzo Barbaro
on the right beside it. To its left there
had been a more nondescript palace,
and then an interval in the long
scroll of Grand Canal palaces,
originally occupied by lowly shacks
or workshops; their place was taken
partly by Franchetti's garden and
partly by the Accademia Bridge. (The
workshops were those visible in
Canaletto's *Stonemason's Yard* in the
National Gallery, London, which
looks across to what would be the
Accademia from beside the former
Cavalli-Gussoni.) The exposed flank
was decorated as lavishly as the
Canal façade and further adorned
with Camillo Boito's entirely new,
but perfectly consonant,
grand covered staircase.

value, the *Comune* was considering demolishing it. In the end the *Fabbriceria*, recoiling from such a drastic solution, itself undertook the expense of restoration, and Saccardo was able rapidly to consolidate the façade. This had in any case been transfigured by the continuous removal of its statues from 1820 onwards, occasioning its restoration by Meduna in 1865. In the earlier case the staunchest advocates of preservation had been the municipal authorities, together with many intellectuals, neither of whom were liable for the cost of restoration, whereas the *Fabbriceria*, which would be liable, was proposing demolition. It is worth emphasizing that most Baroque additions to churches and *palazzi* certainly did not enjoy the same happier fate as those of the church of San Moisè, in a period when the overwhelming trend

Fig. 44
A detail of Boito's staircase for
the Palazzo Franchetti, set off by
the foliage of the palace's newly
created garden, shows a
harmonious, confident and
serene handling of the Gothic
idiom of the original fifteenth-
century palace – one indeed
more confident, more serene and
less dense, less cramped than the
original, and in this regard
dependent on the intervening
tradition of classical architecture.

was for a return to a 'pristine state' and a simplicity of line that the Baroque (regarded as 'a scourge of good taste') did not possess.

In addition to the works undertaken on San Marco, the Doge's Palace, Palazzo Franchetti and the church of San Moisè, the restoration by the *Comune* of Palazzo Farsetti, housing its own offices, should not be overlooked. The building was rendered and the *intonaco* painted in imitation of Proconnesian and *cipollino* marble cladding. Its real marble constituents were treated with an oil-based substance, irreversibly. In the face of this kind of falsification and lack of sensitivity towards objects of restoration, one voice of protest at least was raised, that of Giacomo Boni, who gradually took over Zorzi's role in the debate on the restorations of those years. In his article 'Vecchie Mura' (Old walls), published in 1885, Boni, citing Ruskin, de-plored the irresponsible and destructive way in which the surfaces of walls were treated, in programmes of *ripristino* the results of which nearly always left them in a worse state than

Fig. 45

These two venerable Veneto-Byzantine palaces on
the Rialto side of the Grand Canal, the Loredan and
the Farsetti (supposed to have been built by Doge
Enrico Dandolo, who brought back marbles for the
purpose from Constantinople after its sack in 1204),
have inevitably lost much of their earlier character
over the years: additional storeys were added
(though this is the least of it) and their interiors
completely altered. Though the stonework was left
intact, in the late nineteenth century the façade of
the Loredan was arbitrarily recovered. This
extraordinarily casual lack of concern for original
or traditional façade covering continues to plague
Venice today (see figs. 87–91, pp. 161–63). These
palaces cannot be said to have benefited particularly
from passing into municipal possession.

before. Boni also indicted the restorations on the exterior of the apse of San Giovanni Evangelista, which was rendered, then the rendering decorated in imitation of the underlying bricks. Here the works were immediately suspended, but it was only one of many examples of this widespread and rather odd practice. Boni mentions other instances of regrettable restorations, without specifying where they had taken place: we read, for example, of an old *palazzo* where "the ancient coats of arms were removed, plaster was slapped on to the walls by the trowelful, what was left was whitewashed and the Gothic balustrade was removed and replaced with small white columns worked on a lathe ...". At San Polo the *campanile* of the church was repainted "the colour of chocolate". Boni concludes in dismayed perplexity at the works of 'restoration' being carried on, and especially at the unprincipled behaviour of contemporary workmen, illustrated in an amusing little poem by Antonio Guadagnoli that he cites:

> "'E perché dai di bianco alle colonne
> di pietra?" dissi in borgo a un imbianchino.
> "Oh, che vuol. Me l'han detto queste donne
> E accompagno i pilastri del casino:
> Ma per me, se mi dan qualch'altro grosso,
> M'importa assai, le tingo anche di rosso ...".'

> "And why do you whitewash stone
> columns?" I said to a housepainter in town.
> "Oh, well, these women told me to,
> and I make them match the pillars of the house:
> But as far as I'm concerned, if they pay me another grote,
> I don't care, I'll even paint them red ...".

NOTES

Beside the works already cited in the notes to Chapter 1, see the triennial reports drawn up by the *podestà* Pier Luigi Bembo in the 1860s (P.L. Bembo, *Il Comune di Venezia nel triennio 1860, 1861, 1862. Relazione del Podestà*, Venice 1863; *Il Comune di Venezia nel triennio 1863, 1864, 1865. Relazione del conte P.L.B. podestà nel detto triennio*, Venice 1866); A. De Marco, *Progetto per l'assestamento generale delle vie principali di Venezia*, Venice 1866; the various contributions (beside Berchet's, cited in the notes to Chapter 2) to *L'ingegneria a Venezia nell'ultimo ventennio. Pubblicazione degli ingegneri veneziani in omaggio ai colleghi del VI Congresso*, Venice 1887; and the *Estratto delle sedute della Commissione per lo studio d'un piano di riforma delle vie e canali della città di Venezia*, Venice 1867. Several officials in the service of the *Comune* published their projects, including Giuseppe Bianco (*Programma di allargamenti e accorciamenti di vie ed altri miglioramenti nel materiale della città di Venezia*, Venice 1866) and C. Fano (*Sul progetto della nuova strada da SS. Apostoli a S. Fosca*, Venice 1867); and those who saw these modernizing operations as destroying the integrity and character of the city replied, among them C. Boito, 'Venezia che scompare. Sant'Elena e Santa Marta', *Nuova Antologia*, October 1883; G. Boni, *Il cosidetto sventramento di Venezia. Appunti di un veneziano*, Rome 1887; Rullo Bey, *Una voce da Milano sullo sventramento di Venezia*, Milan 1887.

On Camillo Boito see A. Grimoldi (ed.), *Omaggio a Camillo Boito*, Milan 1991; M. Maderna, *Camillo Boito. Pensiero sull'architettura e dibattito coevo*, Milan 1995, with a very complete and useful bibliography.

John Ruskin's *Stones of Venice*, published in London 1851–53, speaks for itself; see also S. Quill, *Ruskin's Venice: The Stones Revisited*, cited in the notes to Chapter 1. On Ruskin's visits to the city and his activity in Venice see further C. Robotti, 'Le idee di Ruskin e i restauri della Basilica di San Marco attraverso le "osservazioni" di A.P. Zorzi', *Bollettino d'Arte*, 1–2, 1976; R. Hewison, *Ruskin in Venice*, London 1978; J. Clegg, *Ruskin in Venice*, London 1981.

For the nineteenth-century restorations of the Basilica see M. Dalla Costa, *La Basilica di San Marco e i restauri dell'Ottocento. Le idee di Viollet-le-Duc, J. Ruskin e le "Osservazioni" di A.P. Zorzi*, Venice 1983, which reprints the entire text of Zorzi's 'Observations' (*Osservazioni intorno ai restauri interni ed esterni della Basilica di San Marco con tavole illustrative ed alcune iscrizioni*, Venice 1877), with notes and commentary. Zorzi also wrote a pamphlet *Sulla demolizione della chiesa di San Moisè*, Venice 1877, and an interesting article, 'Ruskin in Venice', in *Cornhill Magazine*, 122, August 1909. See also M. Dalla Costa, 'Restauro, conservazione e manutenzione: i temi di una polemica ai restauri dell'Ottocento nella Basilica di San Marco', *Restauro & Città*, 3–4, 1986, pp. 40–49, and F. Tomaselli, 'Sui restauri ottocenteschi dei mosaici della Basilica di San Marco a Venezia', *TeMA*, 2, 1996, pp. 59–63. See also, of course, the spectacular publication in several volumes, with contributions by Berchet, Boni, Cattaneo, Molmenti, Saccardo, Zorzi and others, and no less than 650 plates, of *La Basilica di San Marco in Venezia illustrata nella storia e nell'arte da scrittori veneziani sotto la direzione di Camillo Boito*, compiled between 1877 and 1887 and published by Ferdinando Ongania, Venice, 1888.

On the Society for the Protection of Ancient Buildings see first of all the *Manifesto* of March 1877, by William Morris, and the celebrated article, 'Anti-restoration movement', in *The Architect* (the official organ of the Royal Institute of British Architects), 7 April 1877; and otherwise S. Boscarino, *Sul restauro dei monumenti*, Milan 1985, pp. 84–94. A report of the meeting of the SPAB on 15 November 1879 was published in *The Times* of 17 November and in *Il Rinnovamento* on 24 November.

On the restoration of the Doge's Palace see A. Forcellini, 'Sui restauri in corso nel Palazzo Ducale di Venezia', *Giornale del Genio Civile*, Rome 1880, and his contribution, 'Sui restauri delle principali facciate del Palazzo Ducale in Venezia', to *L'ingegneria a Venezia* (cited above); P. Saccardo, *Sulla convenienza di restituire al Palazzo Ducale di Venezia i suoi capitali originali*, Venice 1899; C. Boito, *Il Palazzo Ducale di Venezia. Relazione a S.E. il Ministro della Pubblica Istruzione*, Rome 1899; Trimarchi [Giacomo Boni], 'I restauri del Palazzo Ducale di San Marco', *Archivio Storico dell'Arte*, 10, 1889; P. Molmenti, *Per i monumenti veneziani (dal palazzo Ducale alla Zecca)*, Venice 1903. On the problem of the three windows in the south façade see C. Boito, *Questioni pratiche di belle arti*, Milan 1893, and 'Le trifore di Palazzo Ducale a Venezia', *La Nuova Antologia*, December 1899.

On the restoration of the Palazzo Franchetti see the comprehensive study by G. Romanelli, *Tra gotico e neogotico. Palazzo Cavalli Franchetti a San Vidal*, Venice 1990, amplifying his own previous studies on the subject.

On restoration both in Venice and in other Italian cities in this period see also now C. Di Biase (ed.), *Il restauro dei monumenti. Materiali per la storia del restauro*, Milan 2003.

The quotations from Pinali, Priuli and Du Bois are taken from Romanelli, *Venezia Ottocento*, 1977 (cited in the notes to Chapter 1), which reprints their texts almost complete. The quotations in 3.2 from Forcellini are taken from his 'Sui restauri delle principali facciate ...' (cited above), p. 5. Boito's remarks on the windows of the Doge's Palace in 3.2 are from 'Le trifore di Palazzo Ducale a Venezia' (cited above). The text at the end of the chapter by Giacomo Boni, with the ditty by Guadagnoli, appears in his 'Vecchie Mura', *Ateneo Veneto*, 1885.

4 | Venice after 1890

Between 1885 and 1890, the scheme proposed in Selva's day to develop a network of pedestrian thoroughfares, to be gradually superimposed on that of Venice's waterways, reached completion with the opening of Calle Gallina at Santi Giovanni e Paolo and of Via 2 Aprile at San Bartolomeo. While responsibility for the shift towards the mainland of the city's centre of gravity and the filling-in of many canals can be attributed to the Austrian administration, it was the Italian administration that presided over the rapid opening-up of major new pedestrian routes. By 1889 a total of some 40,000 metres of canal waterways had been filled in (since 1815), kilometres of new *calli* had come into being, and at least forty new bridges. Meanwhile two projects had been submitted to the *Comune* by Antonio Baffo for a road bridge between the city and the mainland.

Poor housing and sanitary conditions in many parts of the city remained both very serious and unsolved: an investigation conducted by the Vatican in 1891 registered the presence of more than 1500 ground-floor dwellings in the six Venetian *sestieri*, countless canals in need of dredging, and a mortality rate as high as three per cent per year. Incentives whereby subsidies were granted to property owners who constructed new housing or refurbished existing accommodation proved to be of little effect. But during the 1880s the first comprehensive attempt was made to resolve this aggravating problem, and a *Piano di risanamento e Piano regolatore* (Sanitary improvement and town-planning scheme) for the city was initiated. Compiled by the municipal *Ufficio tecnico* (Civil engineering department), led by Annibale Forcellini and Girolamo Manetti under the supervision of a ministerial and municipal commission (whose members included, among others, Boito, as chairman, Alfredo d'Andrade, deputy chairman, and Federico Berchet), the plan was approved in 1886, amended in 1889, and then submitted to the *Ministero per la Pubblica Istruzione* (Ministry of public education), which endorsed it in 1891.

The *Relazione della Commissione Ministeriale e Municipale intorno al Piano di risanamento ed al Piano regolatore per la Città di Venezia* (Report of the ministerial and municipal commission on the sanitary improvement plan and town-planning scheme for the city of Venice) explained in specific rather than general terms how the Venetian problem could be tackled – in other words, how to avoid making decisions that would affect the city as a whole (at that time, this seemed an advantage!) and that might undermine "the unique picturesque character of

Fig. 46

Tintoretto was reputed to have had his studio in the
Canale dei Mori in Canaregio, and largely for this
reason the canal featured among the popular sights
of Venice. As remarked above (see fig. 14, p. 32),
Myles Birket Foster liked to spice his watercolour
views of Venice with picturesque genre, giving
some sense of the life in Venice's slums and back
canals that the various programmes of
improvement proposed by the authorities were
intended to make safer and healthier.

Myles Birket Foster, *The Canale dei Mori, Venice – Studio of
Tintoretto*, Sotheby's Picture Library DT7673

Venice". A degree of satisfaction was expressed that the works done had been successfully confined to a series of house demolitions, widening of *calli*, and a few general measures such as the regular dredging of canals, improvements to the drainage network, the cleaning of drinking-water cisterns, the condemning "of low-lying, damp and unhealthy ground-floor apartments", and the granting of subsidies for "building one or two floors on top of the closed-off ground-floor of the dwelling". It should be noted that this final provision was to reappear in article 15 of the Special Law for Venice no. 168 of 3 February 1938, and again in article 14 of the Special Law for Venice no. 294 of 31 March 1956, remaining in force until the turning-point marked by the 1973 Special Law for Venice, which by contrast envisaged subsidies for those who removed extensions and additions. Concluding the Plan was a projection of the demolitions to be carried out and the new buildings to be constructed: relative to demolitions amounting to 276,000 m^3, the aim was for over 400,000 m^3 of new housing to be built, 100,000 of which would be destined for the middle classes and 78,000 for workers.

The provisions of the Plan were therefore in complete accord with the terms of Section VI of Law no. 2359 of 25 June 1865, whereby, under the heading *Piani regolatori*, municipalities with more than 10,000 inhabitants were to institute schemes to regulate interventions on the existing housing stock and "to ensure conditions of salubrity and access" (article 86). The procedure indicated by Law no. 2359 was that of demolition and urban restructuring where it might be necessary in order "to remedy the unsatisfactory position of buildings". Indeed, the twenty-four interventions envisaged under the *Piano di risanamento*, to be carried out within the space of twelve years, were no more than measures for clearing, widening, pulling down and opening up new corridors of access. The schedule for the *Piano regolatore* did not greatly differ from that of the *Piano di risanamento*: consisting of sixteen programmes, to be implemented over a thirty-year period, it used the same terminology and pursued the same ends, with a view more than anything else to the widening of *calli*. In the final analysis, the entire operation amounted to no more than a list of buildings to be demolished, and did nothing about the city's social and economic conditions.

As for the preservation of Venice's artistic heritage, monuments and works of art continued to be entrusted to the goodwill of citizens and of those responsible for work on them, rather than being afforded protection under legislation designed to protect the city, its buildings and its environment. Venice as described and interpreted by the Plan of 1891 is still a two-dimensional, planimetric city, relying on purely geometric or Haussmann-like categories of interpretation and to be read only as a map, with no regard for relief and material. Eyes are raised from the map only to register the picturesque character of the city, leaving to improbable "future arrangements" and "special provisions" the task of dealing with any "infringement on this character". These "special arrangements" were indeed drawn up some time later, but would turn out yet again not to be targeted, effective or clearly defined, but only to display impotence in the face of the need for responsible and specific action in governing and safeguarding the city.

Fig. 47

In Venice, as in every town of Europe in the nineteenth
century, the authorities were intent on both developing
and increasing the standards of hygiene in their food
markets. In Venice, for time immemorial, the main
market for food had been at the Rialto. For the all-
important market in fish an iron covering-structure
was erected in 1884 by Annibale Forcellini; one had
been projected earlier by Federico Berchet. The
completed structure aroused odium and ire; some
twenty years later it was demolished and replaced with
this much more sympathetic and blended Gothic
pastiche by Domenico Rupolo and Cesare Laurenti.
With its outside staircase and graceful arches –
especially in this range along a side-canal – their
Pescheria might pass for a little bit of old Venice, though
it went up in 1907.

4.2 *The activities of the* Ufficio Regionale per
la conservazione dei monumenti del Veneto

The Italian government made attempts during the 1870s and 1880s to establish the necessary conditions and institutions for the preservation of the nation's cultural heritage. However, the project of compiling a catalogue of monuments, such as had been envisaged for all Italian regions since 1875, remained unrealised. So in 1884 the position of *Delegato Regionale* (Regional deputy), directly answerable to the *Ministero per la Pubblica Istruzione*, was created, with the task of initiating new restorations, overseeing restorations already underway, and drafting projects and budgets. In the Veneto the post was filled by Federico Berchet, but it must have had little practical bearing on restoration works at that time, since very rarely is any reference made to it.

In 1891, however, came the setting up of the *Uffici Tecnici Regionali per la conservazione dei monumenti* (Regional offices of works for the conservation of monuments), under the direction of the Regional deputies. The *Ufficio Regionale of the Veneto* was thus entrusted to Berchet, who remained in charge from 1891 until 1902, when, following the collapse of the *campanile* of St Mark's (see below), he was succeeded by Giacomo Boni.

During this period, five *Relazioni sull'azione dell'Ufficio* (Reports on the activities of the Regional Office) were published under Berchet's editorship, at more or less two-yearly intervals. These listed the works carried out or authorized by the *Ministero per la Pubblica Istruzione* and the *Ministero dei Lavori Pubblici* (Ministry of public works), as well as the results of inspections of buildings under restoration, with particular attention to the Doge's Palace and St Mark's Basilica. The philosophy guiding the interventions cited and commented on by Berchet is no different from that we have come to recognize as peculiar to this period, one inspired by a conception of work on existing fabric as a *ripristino* and recovery of a projected completeness. Sometimes, however, this attitude gets ambiguously confused with the profession of conservational priorities: on more than one occasion in the introductions to his Reports the restorer of the Fondaco dei Turchi expresses a conservational intention, respectful of materials and 'accretions' (*superfetazioni*), while at the same time displaying a casual propensity for a complete, artistically motivated and unnecessary renovation of entire sections of the buildings under restoration. His conservational affirmations seem indeed to be made with a certain degree of irony, and at times display a touch of veiled opportunism: in the first Report (1892–93), for instance, it is stated that "monuments, too, have a life of their own, which unfolds over time" and that "the whole of history has claims, and it is not true that a later period must always give precedence to an earlier by reason of its greater antiquity"; but, a few lines on, the restorer reverts to type, reminding us that, "... even though the school of Viollet-le-Duc is now discredited and expert reconstructions, which create illusions and are therefore misleading, confusing old and new, are no longer admired, it is still a matter of restoring to monuments their true physiognomy, in the sense of freeing them of additions and mystifications, which cannot really be described as the colouring of time, of freeing them from super-impositions, from the barbarisms of later centuries".

The "claims of history" defended by Berchet, particularly in relation to the works on the Doge's Palace then proceeding apace, were nevertheless defeated on the very same battlefield of the Doge's Palace in 1899, by Berchet himself. He, together with the *Ufficio Regionale*, carried out an "expert reconstruction" by installing on the balcony overlooking the Piazzetta a new statue to replace the original destroyed in 1797 of Doge Gritti with the Lion of St Mark, executed by the sculptors Bottasso and Torres on the basis of eighteenth-century illustrations (see fig. 38). Berchet proposed following the same procedure for a similar statue to be placed on the south-facing balcony, which would have portrayed Doge Steno with the Lion of St Mark, although it was much less certain that Steno in marble form had ever looked out from the front of the Palace upon the Bacino di San Marco. In point of fact, the group with Steno was never realised, the inscription with his name that appears on the façade being deemed insufficient evidence to justify this particular *ripristino*. However, the temptation was strong.

While Berchet persisted in arguing that it was necessary "to be wary of the danger of recreating instead of repairing" (Report II, 1894), the list of operations carried out on the Basilica of San Marco under the supervision of the *Ufficio Regionale* is truly a catalogue of reconstructions – new bronze doors leading to the loggias, partial *ripristino* of the floor mosaics using old pieces of marble, replacement of the internal cladding of the sacristy with marble facing obtained from "ancient stones", partial rebuilding of the brick vaults and relaying of the mosaics, especially the parts in gold, *ripristino* of the mosaic of *The Apocalypse*, and so forth.

Operations of this kind turned out to be the order of the day in other Venetian monumental buildings too: San Pietro in Castello (fig. 48) regained "its own vaults" (1893), San Giovanni Decollato its original ogival arches, concealed until then by round arches (1895), San Nicolò dei Mendicoli a *bifora* (two-light Gothic window) (1896–98), Santo Stefano seven large windows in the apse (1899–1901), Santi Simeone e Giuda new entrance steps (1899–1901), etc.

Other important work took place on the church of Madonna dell'Orto (figs. 70, 71, pp. 124, 125), where the old plaster was removed and replaced with new, after a greasy substance had been applied to the damp walls (1892–93); at San Giovanni Decollato eight columns of *cipolino* marble that had been "barbarously plastered and coloured" were cleaned (1894); in the church of the Gesuati the *trompe-l'oeil* marbles were cleaned with water and the stone parts drybrushed (1896–98); the plasterwork was removed from the Frari (1899–1901).

During these years there were also two singular and significant events recorded by Berchet, which nicely complete the picture of restoration work in the city. The first was the authorization, regarding the former church of Santa Maria Maggiore, by this time the *Manifattura Tabacchi* (Tobacco factory), for the demolition of walls with frescos painted over stucco: permission was granted on the grounds that the frescos were "of almost no value". The second concerned works carried out without permission by Baron Giorgio Franchetti on

Fig. 48 (left)
San Pietro di Castello, an eighth-century
foundation, was rebuilt in its entirety at the
end of the sixteenth century and the
beginning of the seventeenth (finished 1621);
decoration continued through the
seventeenth century. The church was thus
entirely Baroque, though earlier fragments
remain in or attached to it. In 1807 it ceased
to be the cathedral of Venice (the Patriarch's
seat moving to San Marco, previously the
Doge's Chapel), and its grandeur has ever
since been rather out of place in an outlying
part of the city known chiefly for its poverty
(a 'fisherman's quarter') and peacefulness. In
the late nineteenth century the church was
restored, no doubt removing much
accumulated late Baroque 'excess'; but in the
First World War it was bombarded,
necessitating subsequent repairs especially to
the dome that eliminated traces of the
previous works in their turn; it was restored
again 1970–82.

Fig. 49 (right)
With the justification that it would become a
major exhibition space, the eighteenth-
century Palazzo Grassi at San Samuele on
the Grand Canal (by Giorgio Massari) was
transformed from 1985 by Gae Aulenti and
Antonio Foscari into modern marble palace,
with a gigantic foyer like that of a hotel,
retaining no more than the rusticated
exterior of the grandiose building and its
courtyard, though that was covered in. There
is no doubt that with big money and big
wheels – those of FIAT – behind it, the plans
for an expensive new interior vestment of the
old building seemed attractive enough to
overcome objections of a conservational
kind. The building did indeed become for
several years a venue for major exhibitions,
though its future, following retrenchment by
its owners, is today in doubt.

the Ca' d'Oro, completed in 1895 (figs. 50–52): these were approved by the *Ministero per la Pubblica Istruzione* the following year, while the Baron's initiative earned congratulations from the *Ufficio Regionale*, although, for example, he had an entire floor arbitrarily relaid in order to bring the old flooring closer to its "pristine splendour".

Broadly speaking, the procedures that had been followed in the past at the Fondaco dei Turchi and Palazzo Cavalli-Franchetti, but banned in interventions on public buildings after the bitter controversy over Meduna's restoration of San Marco, returned to Venetian restoration practice by way of private initiatives. These showed the same disregard for what was there before, the same indifference towards materials, the same creative ambitions projected on to the existing fabric, disguised by the belief that thereby the pure, original, true form was being attained. This time the public's satisfaction was united with recognition from the State, which, suffering as usual from lack of funds and in the absence of any clear plans of its own, gave ample scope to anyone who could take the place of the institutions responsible and carry out restorations as they conceived them, so effectively and with such striking results.

This is what happened not only at the end of the nineteenth century but also at the end of the twentieth, and continues to happen. One could mention several recent, highly publicized, privately sponsored works of restoration or rebuilding (fig. 49) which have been greeted with

Figs. 50–52

The sad fact is that the early fifteenth-century Ca' d'Oro, which earned its nickname from the quantity of gold leaf wastefully (since it could not last) expended on its façade, is no more than a shadow of its former state. A comprehensive restoration of the 1970s, concerned above all with the static problems of the building, could achieve little more than cosmetic adjustments to the total refurbishment under Giorgio Franchetti and, before him, by Giambattista Meduna. Meduna's was highly damaging. Ruskin painted his watercolour (above right) in 1845, even "while the workmen were hammering it down before my face" under the direction of Meduna. Ironically, the building is unusually well documented, its original building accounts having survived, so that much of what was heedlessly smashed, dumped or sold off in the early 'restorations' can be itemized.

The photograph (above) shows the building after the mid-nineteenth-century restoration but before that undertaken for Franchetti, which, in most respects, brought about the façade that exists today. However, in the modern restoration the façade lost much of its remaining colour (there is much more in Ruskin's watercolour, and of course he relished the texture wrought by age upon such buildings). Though Franchetti interpreted quite freely, he was rescuing a badly vandalized building; furthermore he deliberately retrieved for it elements such as its *vera da pozzo*, its well-head, that had been sold, and rebuilt an external staircase much on the lines of the one that had been removed by Meduna.

John Ruskin, *Ca' d'Oro*, 1845, watercolour, 33 x 47.6 cm, Ruskin Library, University of Lancaster, by kind permission

a general approval earned primarily by the speed with which the results have been delivered and seldom based on the quality of the work itself. The success achieved by the dynamism of the private sector should, rather, give us cause to reflect on the inertia of the public sector. It is the lack of conservation initiatives or of comprehensive and effective programming on the part of the government that encourages inordinate celebration of isolated operations conducted at the pace of big business, with a time-and-motion approach to restoration, trumpeting a pragmatism that makes every objection that is not of the same practical and concrete kind seem captious and pedantic. The ever increasing influence and credibility of the 'practical solution' is another constant in the modern history of restoration, not only in Venice, and not only in the field of restoration. Consider, for example, the typically Italian legislation granting building amnesties (the latest one in 2004), legislation that seems designed specifically to legitimize *ciò che è* (what's there), licensing its existence in exchange for payment. Furthermore, the pragmatic effectiveness of certain restorations is so persuasive, politically and pyschologically, that it encourages the sector concerned to lobby for deregulation, for the setting aside of the legislative trammels of institutional bureaucracy. This is an attitude to which we shall return (see pp. 175, 203), having paused here to indicate that its roots go back a long way. Unfortunately, the 'practical' approach is invariably piecemeal, nearly always arbitrary, and very often less informed than is supposed. It provides dangerously attractive solutions, which are liable to be distorted and manipulated to serve the most inappropriate ends. It means a do-it-yourself, amateurish kind of restoration, applied in the name of flexibility and efficiency without discrimination. It is, finally, the absence of such 'practicality' – and not either the quality of its results or its cost – that makes the discipline of conservation much less convincing and appealing, and therefore less favoured in general daily practice.

4.3 At the turn of the twentieth century;
an era of optimism

In the 1890s, although many problems remained unresolved, Venice gave signs of a trend towards an overall economic revival: despite the unwelcome presence of the busy port of Trieste, with the opening of the *Stazione Marittima* (Maritime port) Venice seemed to be reliving its past as a major trading centre.

The new *Stazione Marittima* did not, of course, set to rights an economy long deprived of its manufacturing and artisan base, but it did open up opportunities for new entrepreneurial forces that were able to exploit a happy combination of circumstances prevailing throughout northern Italy during these years. As the industrial myth combined with the cultural, the *belle époque* shone more brightly with electric energy; while the various international fairs celebrated the improved standards of living that came with the age of the machine, in Venice the Biennale opened its doors for the first time in 1895, side by side with the factories that the Stucky, the Salviati and the Fortuny were building on the Giudecca and in Dorsoduro.

Alongside their high-profile activity, a variety of lesser enterprises appeared – the *Manifattura Tabacchi* (tobacco), the *Distilleria*, later called the *Birreria Dreher* (beer), the *Cotonificio* (cotton), the restored and expanded Arsenale, the *Istituti per la costruzione di case economiche* (Institutes for the construction of low-cost housing), etc. Only rarely did the establishment of these new activities involve the destruction of existing buildings: in the central areas, where the industrial presence was confined to offices premises only, the clearing of insalubrious hovels and buildings too problematic to restore or too costly to maintain or simply 'in the way', which had been going on for decades, was now complete. The new factories occupied the peripheral areas of the city (especially Giudecca and Castello), away from the railway station and from the recently opened-up pedestrian routes; and these industries confirmed the versatility of the urban fabric, testifying that a distinctively Venetian economic life, supported by and connected with the waterways rather than the pedestrian arteries, was still possible.

With this newly acquired economic prosperity, image became an issue once again. The appearance of the new factory buildings was generally in harmony with the Venetian Gothic tradition, although the *Mulino Stucky* (Stucky flour mill; figs. 54, 55) on the Giudecca paraded Hanseatic origins. The new housing for workers, though occasionally inspired with a touch of eclecticism, was generally flat and dull. Villas on the Lido, though in most cases not progressing beyond the project stage, were almost always pastiches in a Romantic style, nor even were the grand hotels (fig. 56) particularly distinguished. However, the new showcase buildings of the emerging families (Salviati, Fortuny, etc.; fig. 53) spoke the more fluent and dazzling language of early Liberty, a Klimtian Art Nouveau, rich in Byzantine golds and mosaics.

There were also new discussions and controversies on well-worn themes, for instance the question of the compatibility or not of the Venetian tradition and the modern. Thus, Boito, Alfredo Melani and others, while trying to not lose sight of the values and importance of the historic, were caught up in a debate which, owing to the excessive enthusiasm of some and the concealed bad faith of others, became consumed in fine distinctions involving "the nation's ancient tradition", "medieval style", "medievalizing architecture", "the strange naiveties of the new", and so on. Often, as Romanelli rightly declares in his essay of 1985 on the period, "the reasoning and arguments swung fearfully and dangerously between pointless tautologies and obvious contradictions: and all this was dished up in the rhetoric of Venetian one-upmanship and with the critical inaccuracy which were the hallmark of the lagoon city's worst disputes" – and, we might add, so it often is to this day.

During these years of construction activity, entrepreneurial expansion and cultural debate, one cannot but imagine that a radical and extensive refurbishment of private buildings was being conducted: precise data and documentation are lacking, but a very clear idea of the interest in a rapid adaptation of the existing fabric to the new demands of the day can certainly be deduced from the numerous applications for subsidies submitted to the authorities for urgent restoration works to private buildings. In many cases the state of disrepair declared

Fig. 53

Beside the names of Fabergé and Lalique one could rank Fortuny and Salviati, both highly successful propagators of a modern (Art Nouveau) style of revived shining colour and display in materials, fashioned with traditional but also innovative, and highly skilled, craftsmanship. The firm founded by Antonio Salviati in 1859 flourished especially in the 1880s and 1890s, becoming known internationally (above all through trade fairs) for its mosaics and for its glass, and especially its elaborate *tours de force* in glass. Unlike Mario Fortuny, who, though resident in Venice, drew on a variety of models and precedents, Salviati & Co. was rooted in a Venetian tradition and deliberately referred back to the styles and types of old Murano glass. The Casa Salviati on the Grand Canal dates, however, from 1924–26, by G. D'Olivo. The mosaics of the façade advertised its wares to sophisticated clientele staying in nearby hotels or on the Lido.

Figs. 54, 55 (right)

The considerable industrial building that took place in Venice in the late nineteenth-century was generally sited on the outskirts of the city – the *Mulino Stucky* or Stucky flour mill on the Giudecca. It was finished in 1884 by Ernst Wullekopf for Giovanni Stucky. These industrial buildings - including the Dreher brewery on the Giduecca or the Saffa match factory in Canaregio (see figs. 104, 106, pp. 194–95) – have in recent times, after a period of neglect, been converted into residential accommodation (or destroyed to make way for it). In 2004 the Stucky Mill is a wreck, having been ravaged by a fire in the course of its conversion into flats in April 2003; arson, as in the case of the Fenice Theatre, has been suspected.

was not necessarily true, and this was just a way of saving money, exploiting the fact that most restoration costs for monumental buildings were met by the State. The volume of such applications in the last decade of the nineteenth century and the first years of the twentieth was so high that the *Ufficio Regionale* notified proprietors of unsafe buildings that they should apply, in cases of urgency, not to their own department, which was now overwhelmed, but to the *Genio civile* (National civil engineering department). The *Ufficio Regionale* also advised applying to private contractors rather than to the also overstretched municipal and regional offices of works. A vast proportion of building operations on the built fabric, thus officially delegated to the private sector, therefore escaped the administration's control – as it continues to do.

Certainly, the general climate of enthusiasm in the economic upturn at the end of the century, the existence of a *Piano regolatore* (which would remain valid until 1921), and the massive amount of investment and the numerous entrepreneurial initiatives in the city contributed to allowing this dereliction on the part of the central authorities to pass unnoticed. Evidently lacking procedures capable of dealing with the new dimension of the problem, the authorities

Fig. 56
The great bulk of the Hotel Excelsior on the Lido, built between 1898 and 1908 by Giovanni Sardi, is enlivened by domes, turrets and *merlatura* in a pseudo-oriental interpretation of Venetian tradition. In the early twentieth century the Lido became, briefly, a highly fashionable resort – as such, however, having little to do with the historic city of Venice. Hitherto the Lido had hardly been inhabited, and all building on it, even the streets, were new.

It was on the Lido that the doomed figure of von Aschenbach, in Thomas Mann's 1911 novel *Death in Venice*, stayed. The novel reflected in the first place the *haut bourgeois* fashion of tourists on the Lido, but the presence in the novel of cholera, to which Aschenbach eventually succumbs, was also real enough, a consequence of the slum conditions and poverty in which so much of Venice remained, despite the tourists and despite the *piani di risanamento*. And the city itself is portrayed as not so much monumental as a sinister haunt.

Not entirely unrelated were the ideas of the Futurists, led by Filippo Marinetti, who, in Venice in 1910–11, launched a violent attack on the city as pandering to tourists in her putrescence like an old whore. Marinetti sought a forward-looking, manly spirit among Venetians, who could still recall their Republic and the 1848 rebellion and could believe in a future of development.

adopted the tried and tested, easy-going Haussmannian attitude of *quand le bâtiment va, tout va* (if the building's all right, it's all all right). And everything was all right, at least until 14 July 1902, the day the *campanile* of San Marco collapsed.

4.4 *The collapse of the Campanile*
A few years before the fall of the Campanile, in the *IV Relazione (1896–97–98) dell'Ufficio Regionale per la conservazione dei Monumenti del Veneto*, Berchet had written: "... one of those familiar rumours began to circulate that the *campanile* of San Marco was also bound to collapse [along with the Doge's Palace] because, to provide accommodation for a caretaker, some parts of the old wall had been cut away at a point where a crack had started that was worsening all the time". However, when the Campanile did fall to the ground, considerable concern arose for the immediate future of other Venetian buildings, and its collapse lent weight in particular to the prognostications that as early as 1898 had featured in the editorial pages of the *Corriere della Sera*, envisaging the imminent collapse of the Doge's Palace. After 14 July, as Massimiliano

Ongaro, appointed to the position occupied by Berchet from 1 April 1905, relates in his *Cronaca dei restauri, dei progetti e dell'azione tutta dell'Ufficio Regionale ora Soprintendenza dei Monumenti di Venezia (in seguito alla V Relazione dell'Ufficio Regionale)* (Chronicle of the restorations, projects and action of the Regional Office, now Soprintendency of the monuments of Venice (annexed to the fifth report of the Regional office)), Venice fell silent, the bells no longer rang and even the traditional midday gun-shot was abolished, though it resumed shortly afterwards, on the Lido. According to Ongaro, the *Ufficio* compiled a worrying list of "bell-towers and churches at risk": twenty-seven sacred buildings and twenty-seven *campanili* turned out to be seriously damaged and on the verge of collapse, and among these were some of the most important monuments in Venice, from St Mark's to the Frari and Santi Giovanni e Paolo.

Over the next few years the city was obliged to undertake a lengthy series of operations for the consolidation of public and private buildings. The psychosis of the collapse outweighed legislation in putting a stop to improper works, and it took only a rumour, in 1910, of serious new cracks in the Doge's Palace to create a wave of panic, slow to abate even after a reassuring report issued by the *Soprintendenza* (as the *Ufficio Regionale* had now become) after an on-site inspection. It seemed that the city would have to resign itself to abandoning a considerable proportion of its historic buildings to their sad fate, and in many cases building interest and investments moved to the Lido, where there were plans for the development of a garden city and where villas and new leisure and sports facilities were becoming ever more numerous.

However, the rebuilding of the *campanile* of San Marco, *com'era e dov'era* (as it was, where it was), was immediately projected, amid bitter disputes that pitted the so-called 'traditionalists' against the advocates of a different solution. It was clear straightaway that the Venetians wanted their emblematic bell-tower back, "in the same form and in the same position", as Pompeo Molmenti emphatically declared to Parliament. The contributions to the debate that came from the world of architecture during that period nearly all tended in the same direction: "I understand that there are some who think that, since the Campanile has fallen down, it would be better to forget about it; but, if it does have to be rebuilt, it should be constructed in the same place, in exactly the same form" (Camillo Boito); "There is a wish to rebuild the Campanile, and when we have a reliable and accurate plan for it, it will be possible. But were it to happen, and out of respect for history, it must be erected on the same site" (Corrado Ricci); "... identical to the one that fell down, and in the same place" (Guglielmo Calderini, of the ministerial commission set up to establish the causes of the collapse).

Dissenting voices feared the enormous costs of reconstruction, and suggested levelling the ground, or rebuilding only Sansovino's Loggetta, but there were also those who, while accepting the argument for rebuilding, wanted a different building, either being inclined to get rid of obvious later additions, for example "... rebuild with what is left, but without replacing the top part, which is a sixteenth-century addition" (Giacomo Boni), or favouring something new in a modern style (Otto Wagner). The *Accademia di Brera* of Milan devoted one of its annual competitions to the subject, without, surprisingly, setting any "restrictions on dimensions, forms, decorative features". Other leading theorists of the discipline of restoration spoke out on several occasions against this interpretative freedom – Gustavo Giovannoni, for instance, in 1912 ("If the innovators had prevailed, we would now have a building in the effete Liberty [Art Nouveau] style, which is now so old-fashioned it's scarcely remembered"), and above all Luca Beltrami, who in 1903, when the foundation stone of the new construction was symbolically laid (25 April), was called upon to investigate the causes and the dynamic of the collapse.

Beltrami identified the causes of the collapse not in the sinking of the foundations, or in the consequences of ill-advised works carried out by the *Ufficio Regionale* shortly before the tower came down, but in the collapse of the Campanile's internal shaft, which had previously been damaged. Some sections of it were insufficiently robust to support the weight of the upper parts, a situation aggravated in the sixteenth century by the addition of the heavy bell chamber. Beltrami proposed building a structure similar to that of the collapsed Campanile, with two brick-built shafts, but erected on a larger foundation platform, modifying the dimensions and redistributing the load, and making the upper parts lighter. At the same time, he controversially renounced any position of responsibility for managing the project and overseeing the works, in a famous letter sent to the *sindaco* or mayor of Venice, Filippo Grimani, on 11 February 1903: "... you tell me that I would find people there eager to assist me and I do not doubt it; but I would nevertheless have to be in constant contact with the Ministry, with which it has been my sad experience to be acquainted for almost twenty years, and therefore I have a clear vision of the fate that would await me and the situation in which I would shortly and inevitably find myself. I should have to come to you, as you rightly observe, invested with full powers, and after the disaster of 14 July I had hoped that there would be a real appreciation in Rome of the needs to which the present situation gave rise: but my hopes were dashed. In Venice I would soon become both the instrument and the butt of the mistakes and incompetence that rule the Ministry."

The task of implementing the project was entrusted to a commission headed by Gaetano Moretti, subsequently replaced by Daniele Donghi, who in fact drafted the new project. Donghi brought more than a few variations to the project outlined by Beltrami: in particular he introduced the use of reinforced concrete for the flights of steps inserted between the two brick-built shafts, which, most importantly for the belfry and pinnacle, served to lighten the building by about 2000 tons compared with the previous Campanile.

The works were, however, suspended a few months after they began, in response to a series of objections, especially regarding the decision to build the Campanile with all five original steps of the base, instead of the three that were visible at the time of the collapse (the other two had been buried in the process of raising the level of the Piazza). The supporters of

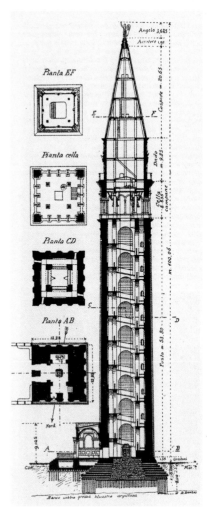

Figs. 57, 58, 59

The new *campanile* at St Mark's (left) differs from its collapsed predecessor (above left) chiefly in its interior structure (above right), in which the stairway running the height of the building is of reinforced concrete.

The old tower had given ample warning of its impending collapse, showing cracks, letting fall fragments of masonry; on 12 July the *biffe*, glass tubes measuring the progress of the cracks, had split altogether, and on Sunday 13 July the police had cleared the Piazza of protesting Venetians who had come to hear a concert. On Monday 14 July an inspection of the tower by the *Genio civile* at 9.30 am had hastily to be abandoned; the tower crumpled in a heap at 9.47 am. Fortunately, the Basilica was untouched, though the Loggetta beneath the Campanile was totally destroyed and also a corner of St Mark's Library (both were reconstructed).

The collapse of the Campanile, which, despite the warning signs, few had anticipated, sparked a campaign of restoration in Venice that has been equalled only in the aftermath of the flood of 1966.

com'era, dov'era protested, and a commission was appointed, but on 2 May 1907 the commission allowed the works to proceed, and they were completed in 1910.

There then arose the problem of the reconstruction of Sansovino's Loggetta, the sides of which were totally destroyed. The solution adopted was to re-use as much as could be recovered from the rubble, while for the sides a new design was drawn up by Gaetano Moretti in 'Sansovinian style', which was executed after the population had been given the opportunity to judge its merits from a full-scale cardboard model. On 25 April 1912, Venice inaugurated the simulacrum of its beloved Campanile.

At this point, one cannot avoid reflecting briefly on the fate of the slogan, which is by no means exclusively Italian, *com'era, dov'era*. What has been the reaction and the consequences for monuments that have fallen down or been destroyed in the hundred years since the collapse of the *campanile* of San Marco? With rare exceptions, the pressure to build a replica has prevailed, and all the more so where the impact of the reported event on public opinion has been greater and the circumstances sadder. The most recent example, in Venice itself, has been that of the *Teatro La Fenice*, destroyed by arson on 29 January 1996. True to its name, it has risen from its own ashes, in a project of reconstruction in which the first step was to get rid of almost everything the fire had spared, although that was very little.

NOTES

See the notes for Chapter 1. The drafting of the *Piano di risanamento e Piano regolatore* of 1891 was preceded and accompanied by proposals and debates of which one finds echoes in A. De Marco, *Progetto per l'assestamento generale delle vie principali di Venezia*, Venice 1886; A. Cadel, *Case sane*, Venice 1887; P. Molmenti, *Delendae Venetiae*, Venice 1887; L. Ongaro, *L'ingegneria sanitaria a Venezia*, Venice 1893. The *Relazione della Commissione Ministeriale e Municipale intorno al Piano di risanamento ed al Piano regolatore per la città di Venezia*, Venice 1891, has recently been reprinted, edited by the Istituto Universitario di Architettura di Venezia. The state of Venice at the beginning of the twentieth century is recorded in a rare document, the mosaic aerial photograph or *fotopiano* of the city of Venice at 1:2500 undertaken on the initative of Cesare Tardivo, head of a special department of the *Genio civile*, which was completed in 1911 after five years of photography from a balloon; see further F. Guerra and M. Scarsò (ed.), *Atlante di Venezia 1911–1982. Due fotopiani a confronto*, Padua and Venice 1999.

The *Uffici Tecnici Regionali per la conservazione dei Monumenti* were created in 1891. Federico Berchet was the first director for the Region of the Veneto, remaining in office until the arrival of Giacomo Boni in 1902. Also in 1902 legislation was passed which led in a few years to the substitution of these *Uffici* by *Soprintendenze*, each divided, as today, into three, one for buildings (*Monumenti*), one for antiquities (*Scavi, musei e oggetti di antichità*), one for art (*Gallerie e oggetti d'arte*). A survey of the restorations carried by the Venice *Ufficio* is to be found in the *Relazioni annuali dell'Ufficio Regionale*, published under Berchet in 1894, 1895, 1896, 1899 and 1901, covering the entire period 1892–1901.

On the story of the collapse and reconstruction of the Campanile there is plenty of information, notably *Vedute, disegni e calcoli di stabilità dell'antico campanile di S. Marco e del progetto per la sua ricostruzione, presentati dalla Commissione ricostruttiva all'on. Giunta comunale di Venezia il 31 dicembre 1905*, Venice 1905; A. Fradeletto, *Il campanile di S. Marco riedificato*, 1912, and *Il campanile di San Marco. Il crollo e la restituzione, 14 luglio 1902–25 aprile 1912*, exh. cat., Cinisello Balsamo, 1992. My summary of views on whether and how to reconstruct the Campanile is indebted to the useful synthesis by B. Colombo, 'Venezia: Il campanile di San Marco (1902–1912)', *ANANKE. Cultura, storia e tecniche della conservazione*, 4, 1993, p. 42. For subsequent developments see G. Mariacher, *Il Campanile di San Marco 1912–1962*, Venice 1962.

Issue no. 4 of *ANANKE*, 1993, is devoted to the tradition of restoration embodied in the tag *com'era, dov'era*.

The quotations from Berchet in 4.2 are taken from the *I Relazione (1892–1893)*, 1894, pp. 13, 15, and the *II Relazione (1894)*, 1895, p. 39. The comments of Giandomenico Romanelli quoted in 4.3 are drawn from his 'Nuova edilizia veneziana all'inizio del XX secolo', *Rassegna*, 22, 1985, p. 11. Beltrami's rejection, quoted in 4.4, of the invitation from the mayor of Venice, Filippo Grimani, to direct the reconstruction of the Campanile is the main feature of the memorandum *Venezia e Luca Beltrami (a proposito della questione del campanile di S. Marco): Relazione documentata della Giunta al Consiglio comunale*, Venice 1903.

5 | Restorations from the Collapse of the Campanile to the First World War

In the early years of the century, until the First World War, *Soprintendente* Massimiliano Ongaro played a key role in restoration in Venice. Under Ongaro's influence, a generation of restorers came into being destined to dominate the Venetian scene in the decades to follow, most notable among them Ferdinando Forlati, himself a future *Soprintendente* and responsible for many of the most important operations of the years to come. Besides Forlati, Federico Rosso, Domenico Rupolo, Clotaldo Piucco and the by now aging Alvise Piero Zorzi worked as inspectors. Their main concern was, as already noted, the consolidation of unsafe buildings, while the interminable works on the Doge's Palace and St Mark's Basilica continued.

Ongaro's attitude towards buildings in need of restoration was certainly more progressive than that of Berchet or Meduna. In particular, Ongaro openly declared himself against *ripristino* and reconstruction: Viollet-le-Duc's operations at Pierrefonds he described as "not so much restorations as total falsifications [in which] one can admire the patient research, the ingenious contrivance, without any sense of enthusiasm". At the same time, however, his attitude to the past was still romantic – almost a contemplative position, which led him to "enthusiasm" during the restoration, with Aldo Scolari, in 1911, of the abbey of San Gregorio, where, thanks "to the detailed study of remains revealed by initial minor works, one was left in no doubt as to the existence of a corner loggia, since traces of abutment were discovered on the wall, and a piece of architrave. It remained to be discovered what form it had, and this was supplied by some eighteenth-century prints". Thus 'historical' restoration, recalling the approach of Luca Beltrami, who had already been active for some years in Milan, accompanied the 'philological' and conservational tendencies that were part of Ongaro's complex professional training. On other occasions, however, Ongaro's response, echoing Ruskin in *The Seven Lamps of Architecture*, was: "No! Monuments should be preserved, and not imitated or recreated, because imitations and recreations, like waxworks, which neither colouring nor form can make lifelike, have no power of expression". Ongaro continued: "The restorer of monuments should show the greatest self-abnegation, he should be able to efface himself in the presence of the monument, being content to do whatever he can to enable the work of art, the record of past glories, to continue to defy the ravages of time". Thanks to his appreciation of the colour and 'picturesque' appearance of monuments, in their originality and totality (though it did not extend to all colours and all totalities), and to his desire to establish a 'pristine' status not as suggested by tradition, imagination or civic pride but as documented with certainty by the evidence of the site, Ongaro ran the institution of which he was director with considerable judgement. He was little inclined to concede to a desire to introduce Byzantinizing 'retouches' or to allow the privileging of particular aesthetic or formal preferences in the restoration of buildings.

Fears of the imminent collapse of the city in the wake of the collapse of the Campanile would have scarcely have been allayed by Ongaro's already mentioned *Cronaca* of 1912. It is a terse, precise and alarming document:

"... bits of cornice fall off the façade of the Scuola Grande di San Marco and from Santi Giovanni e Paolo (1903); a floor gives way at the Palazzo dei Camerlenghi under the weight of numerous levels of *terrazzo* paving, laid one on top of another over the centuries, following long-established Venetian practice (1907); the *biffe* [crack-monitoring devices] break under pressure from developing cracks and *biette* [locking bars] fall out in the Cappella del Cristo at the Frari (12–13 October , 1902); the *biffe* in the church of Santa Maria Mater Domini break and bricks fall from the *campanile*; a piece of cornice (1903) and bits of marble (1906) fall from the façade of San Stae; a cornice falls off the church of San Simeone Picolo; bits of rendering fall off the façade of San Giorgio (1910); a capital from the Vivarini window at Santi Giovanni e Paolo falls to the ground; cracks appear in the Fondaco dei Tedeschi (1906)." An inspection of the Procuratie Vecchie, after the proprietors were asked to grant free access to inspectors (order of the day, 24 July 1902) produced "a shocking report: the building's foundations were so inadequate that extremely serious cracks had resulted ... each of the numerous proprietors had altered his own premises without taking into consideration anyone else's, creating apertures, reducing the thickness of walls. In the rear part of the building, walls were found suspended in the air, almost not resting on the foundations ...."

Drastic steps were taken, however. 'Accretions' (*superfetazioni*) and all those parts deemed of scant artistic value weighing on structures on the verge of collapse were demolished. Among other such operations, there was a plan to demolish the two upper floors that had been added to the cloister of Sant'Apollonia (fig. 102, p. 171), but in the end, in order to counteract the shifting of the east wall, two arches were filled in and large buttresses were constructed in the middle space of the cloister, as an interim measure (which remained there until Forlati's restoration of the 1960s). Authorizations were given for the demolition of Palazzo Fondi in Salizzada San Luca; of one floor in a house adjacent to the church of San Bartolomeo; of the church of San Leonardo (though this was not implemented); of the ex-convent of San Girolamo; of houses adjoining the south apses and the sacristy of the Frari; of the *campanile* of the church of Santo Spirito; and of numerous other buildings.

The *campanile* of the church of Santo Stefano, having been condemned by a government commission to lose most of its upper parts, instead was successfully consolidated with funds raised somehow or other by the *fabbriceria* responsible. This is a case like that in the nineteenth century of the façade of San Moisè, and demonstrates once again that the propensity to preserve rather than to demolish is often directly related to the financial contribution the interested parties have to make to any restoration. Another similar case was that of the church of San Salvador, a building weakened by the several shops that had been built up against it, the owners of which, in order to gain space, had cut into the wall of the church, carving out alcoves and cupboards. In response to the *Soprintendenza*'s request that they should rebuild the wall, the proprietors refused to take any action, maintaining that the church did not qualify as a monument of artistic value. A few months later, however, there were infiltrations of water into the shops through the walls of the church; since the responsibility and costs of the restoration now fell to the State, the proprietors did not hesitate to invest the building with dignity as a monument and to make repeated calls for the intervention of the *Soprintendenza*.

As an example of a kind of insensitivity that has little improved today, it transpires from Ongaro's report that the inspectors of the *Soprintendenza* registered a total of ninety-six telephone lines attached to the *campanile* of San Bartolomeo, lamenting their very displeasing aesthetic effect.

Apart from conducting inspections and negotiating permissions to proceed with demolitions, the *Soprintendenza* itself intervened in many buildings, consolidating them usually by introducing iron stays or metal reinforcement rings to the parts in danger. Particularly exacting, however, were the restorations of the Doge's Palace and of the churches of San Francesco della Vigna, Santo Stefano, the Frari and Santi Giovanni e Paolo, where the works went on for a number of years and were of major structural and decorative importance.

Works at the Doge's Palace included rebuilding the wall between the Sala Bessarione and the Quarantia Civil Vecchia, which had been cut away some years earlier, and inserting two iron girders in order to create a small lift. In the Sala del Maggior Consiglio, in view of the poor condition of the east wall, it was decided without hesitation to slice in two a fresco of the fourteenth century, by Guariento, in order to facilitate its transferral to another room. Then some joists in the floors were found to be partially carbonized from the fire of 1577, though miraculously still supporting the weight above them; the most badly damaged were replaced or reinforced with iron girders.

In the church of Santo Stefano, windows in the wall of the apse were opened up again, two lunettes either side of the façade were replaced with two-light ogee windows. A vault was demolished, at the suggestion of the Prefect, so that light should reach its venerable wooden ceiling.

In the church of San Francesco della Vigna the subsidence of a pier had caused a general disjointedness in the vaults and arches, as well as the bulging of the perimeter walls, and the truss rods carrying the saddle of the roof had come out of their sockets. So the foundations were rebuilt or strengthened with reinforced concrete, the vaults and chapels of the south transept were completely demolished, then rebuilt; the organ wall was rebuilt and the ceiling was completely reconstructed using softwood battens covered over with plaster.

Figs. 60, 61

Among the many buildings restored between 1902 and 1912, in the great campaign of restoration that followed the shock of the collapse of the Campanile, was the Ca' da Mosto on the Grand Canal. Its original two storeys are Veneto-Byzantine of the thirteenth or even twelfth century. It was later extended with two further storeys and during the seventeenth century it became a celebrated inn, the 'White Lion' (*Leon Bianco*). In the early twentieth-century restoration, as one might expect, the arches of its waterfront entrance were opened up again (the photograph above shows its prior state). Since those times the building has decayed, having passed in recent times to a buyer who had intended to refurbish it but has not obtained the necessary funds.

Although this venerable and historic palace surely requires conservation, it may be asked how desirable it is that it should be pristine? Is there not something rightly appealing about its faded and makeshift state? Has it not undergone eight hundred years of history? Has it not been "blanched into dusty decay by the frost of centuries"? Should it be presented in such a way that its history is denied, rendered like a corpse in a funeral parlour to a decent state for viewing, to a state of some kind of perfection, as if it were what it once was, though it is not? Surely a sensitive restoration, or rather a minimally interventionist conservation, should do no more than is necessary to ensure the statics, the continued life, of the building, the whole building?

Figs. 62, 63
The lowly shacks (left) interloping along the flank of the right transept of the Frari (Santa Maria dei Frari, the Franciscan church in Venice) were not likely to survive the zeal of authorities keen not only to preserve but to reinstate and re-affirm the lost dignity and grandeur of Venetian monuments; they were removed as *superfetazioni* (unwanted accretions) in the city-wide campaign of restoration following the collapse of the Campanile in 1902. It is not immediately clear that they posed any great threat to the structure of the church.

At Santi Giovanni e Paolo, too, the instability was fairly severe, mostly, according to the diagnosis made at the time, because of inadequate foundations and the lack of bonds between the various parts of the large building. In the Cappella dell'Addolorata there was a bulge of 25 cm in a wall 15 m high, while a wall of the Cappella del Rosario was 51 cm out of line at 16.5 m above ground. The remedial measures undertaken consisted of the insertion of dozens of metal braces into the brickwork, so as to connect the walls of the chapels with those of the nave; the extension of the foundations, with new subfoundations of reinforced concrete and linking *chiavi* (keys), also of reinforced concrete; the replacement of cracked columns and of part of the masonry, and finally the filling-in, with 43 m^3 of new brickwork, of the altar niches in the area surrounding the Vivarini window.

Venice's second most important church, Santa Maria Gloriosa dei Frari (figs. 62, 63), was in no better condition: the *campanile* had subsided 30 cm on the side of the Cappella di San Pietro, tilting 76 cm at a height of 42 m, dragging down with it part of the church walls. Cracks in the vaults and the load-bearing parts, inadequate braces, and advanced deterioration of the floor joists required reinforcement measures and the levelling of the foundations, while the roof beams were connected together "to prevent lateral thrust". This consolidation made it possible to re-open a series of windows in the outside walls, at the cost, however, of closing up

the large lunettes above them. The external paintwork, applied in the seventeenth century, was described as "unpleasant", and was also removed. The restorations also involved the adjacent sacristy, where an external buttress and a drainage pit under the foundations had occasioned subsidence and the leaning of the walls, causing cracks throughout the vault; there was surprise when it was discovered that the space between extrados of the vaults and the joists of the floor above was filled with debris. Many of the wooden beams were rotten, and the connecting rods between the corner piers of the Sala Margherita, in rusting, and therefore increasing in weight, had actually weakened the walls and piers. In the end the outer walls were largely rebuilt, to the same dimensions as the original ones; vaults, ties, beams and stained-glass pieces were replaced. The drainage pit was filled in with common lime, hydraulic lime and sand. Finally, three windows in the end wall of the Sala, of which vestiges had been found, were reinstated in place of the semi-circular lunette.

It seems clear, in all these cases, that the interventions undertaken were comprehensive and major, in the hope that they would prove definitive remedies to situations of extremely serious structural degradation. In such situations, there was little concern for the conservation of the original materials; the preference was to replace the ailing, disintegrating or 'stressed' material. Questionably, this remains the approach today.

Fig. 64
The statue of the *condottiero* or general Bartolomeo Colleoni, by Andrea del Verrocchio, an unprecedented and unrepeated glorification of an individual during the Republic (although some rather vainglorious and lavish tombs were set up in churches) has had to endure weather and the other vicissitudes of a public placement for over five hundred years. What one cannot expect is that a restoration, no matter how thoroughgoing or how technologically advanced (always a comparative) will be definitive; sooner or later there will need to be another one. It goes without saying that a little often serves better than a lot infrequently.

Undoubtedly the seriousness of these problems of instability, the intrusive and ominous presence of the rubble of the Campanile in St Mark's square, and the pressure of public opinion spurred the institutional officers to work speedily, with results that were often rather crude and scarcely conservationist. Their task was generally one of repair, and as such was, in fact, very effective and on a scale completely new compared with previous years, and indeed unmatched in later ones, at least as far as State action is concerned.

Again, there was no lack of criticism, polemics and accusations, especially with regard to the materials used in the restorations and the methods used in cleaning stones and surfaces. The marble façade of the Scuola Grande di San Marco may have been washed with "pure water", but in the process of consolidating Verrocchio's nearby monument to Bartolomeo Colleoni (fig. 64) a paste made of oil, white lead, powdered marble and a greasy substance was applied, and it completely lost its lustre. Meanwhile a statue cleaned during works at the Scuola di San Rocco became, in Ongaro's words, "white, too white", so much so that it was put in storage, where "it lay waiting for the colour to return to it in due course".

Not very creditable results of this kind prompted official reaction: in 1905, for instance, the *Commissione centrale delle antichità e belle arti* (Central commission of antiquities and fine arts), including among its distinguished members Camillo Boito and Corrado Ricci, published a

Relazione intorno ai lavori di ristauro di Santa Maria Gloriosa dei Frari in Venezia. Sui lavori compiuti nelle chiese di San Giacomo dell'Orio, San Francesco della Vigna, e San Niccolò dei Mendicoli in Venezia (Report on the restoration work on Santa Maria Gloriosa dei Frari in Venice. On the works conducted in the churches of ...). Reference was made and a response given to a memorandum of the *Collegio della Accademia di Belle Arti* of Venice, in which the *Ufficio Regionale* was criticized "for having embarked on many works at the same time and for not having finished any of them, whereas it would have been commendable if each undertaking had been started and finished in accordance with those artistic criteria that a distinguished monument demands". This protest from the *Accademia*, which saw itself increasingly sidelined with regard to restoration in the city, may lead us to suppose that the officers of the *Soprintendenza* were actually being, according to present standards, rather restrained, concentrating on rescuing buildings rather than on going in search of images and suppositions in order to re-make them.

But if the *Soprintendenza* under Ongaro to a large extent resisted the pressure and emotion of the aftermath of the collapse of the Campanile, it is also clear that at the first opportunity even its very capable and dedicated restorers might be prompted once again to take an artistic approach – re–creative, improving, romantic. Ongaro himself, in his *Cronaca ...*, admitted, surprisingly – though he was perhaps being ironic – that, during a period in which "everyone dreamt every night of finding something, a pleasure anyone can easily obtain, for instance by scraping the wall of an old church and uncovering the underlying fresco, it would have been a disgrace if the Doge's Palace had not yielded any find". He was referring to the discovery of a small archive in a hidden space that came to light when a wall was knocked down.

Such activity on the part of the *Soprintendenza*, supported by suitable funding from the various ministries and by public interest, were, however destined to be short-lived, as much more serious and more fundamental problems arose. Preparations were being made for the First World War, which was to be fought only a few dozen kilometres from Venice. Futurist iconoclasts targeted Venice, demanding that the city should be modernized and its canals filled with asphalt and cars. As a result both interest and interventions rapidly dwindled. Identifying the months around 1910 as the last of "the brief golden age of the Venetian building industry, when numerous consolidations and improvements were carried out", in 1935, Angelo Fano would write, "We have returned to the old state of neglect".

NOTES

A survey of the restorations carried out by the authorities in the period 1902–12 is to be found in the *Cronaca dei restauri dei progetti e dell'azione tutta dell'Ufficio Regionale ora Soprintendenza dei monumenti di Venezia (in seguito alla V Relazione dell'Ufficio Regionale)*, ed. M. Ongaro, Venice 1912. Ongaro's judgement of Viollet-le-Duc and other remarks are taken from M. Ongaro, *I monumenti e il restauro*, Venice 1906 pp. 13, 39 and 40; other quotations are from M. Ongaro, *Cronaca*, as cited, *s.v.*, and from A. Fano, 'Danni e pericolo negli edifici veneziani', *Ateneo Veneto*, 1935, p. 147.

6 | The Interwar Years

6.1 'Greater Venice': Expansion on the mainland, the first Special Law (1938), another Piano di risanamento

The First World War did not cause very great damage to Venice, although it hindered many activities not linked to the war industry. The Italian Navy had its headquarters in the city, and the Arsenale, which since 1870 had been stocked and made ready constantly, became the base from which naval operations directed against Austrian forces departed. During the war Venice suffered aerial bombing, which caused many deaths and some damage to buildings close to military targets: the church of the Scalzi, next to the railway station, was hit, and lost its roof; the Sala di San Marco at the Ospedale Civile (Scuola Grande di San Marco) was destroyed; the vaults of San Pietro in Castello, close to the Arsenale, were damaged. But much more significant for the city were the industrial developments involving the mainland port of Marghera, which had been initiated before the war and continued during it, but which made their impact felt only after it.

A proposal to transfer the port of Venice from the city itself to the shores of the mainland, in order to facilitate that large-scale expansion for which hopes had already been entertained during the nineteenth century, was formulated by Luciano Petit as early as 1902. Petit at first envisaged building the new port near Mestre, on the saltmarshes of the San Giuliano area, but in 1904 he amended his proposal, locating it to the south of the railway bridge, in the area of the Bottenighi, close to the fort of Marghera. What followed, and led to the creation of the blight of Porto Marghera, is emblematic – a typical example of the close connections betwen 'big business' and politics, both Venetian and Italian, and of the interests that these bring into play. It enabled huge riches to be generated, though shared among very few, and at the expense of an unhappy future both for the lagoon environment and for the health of its inhabitants.

The main 'players' included one of the leading representatives of Venetian capitalism, Piero Foscari, who was closely connected with the higher echelons of the *Banca Commerciale Italiana* (Italian merchant bank), founded in 1894. This bank was involved in the financing and therefore control of the most promising sectors of the expanding Italian economy of the early

Fig. 65
Venice and its lagoon as photographed from a satellite in March 1997
Courtesy Consorzio Venezia Nuova/Magistrato alle Acque - Servizi Informativi

twentieth century: navigation (*Società Generale di Navigazione Italiana, Lloyd Italiano, Italia Veloce,* etc); the chemical industry (*Montecatini,* owned by the Donegani brothers); the iron and steel industry (ILVA, *Savona, Piaggio*); energy. With the involvement of the *Banca Commerciale,* the *Società Adriatica di Elettricità* (SADE) was founded in Venice in 1905, and subsequently took over the major companies owning Alpine plants for the production of electric energy. The company would become notorious after the tragedy of the burst hydro-electric dam at Vajont on 9 October 1963, which killed more than 1900 people.

In 1912 Giuseppe Volpi took over as head of SADE, and he ran it until 1943, earning the title of Conte di Misurata from the Fascist government. Foscari, Volpi and the *Banca Commerciale* initiated and oversaw the construction of the Montenegrin port of Antivari (1909), where they started a tobacco trade and obtained a monopoly for it. Antivari was a foreshadowing of the Porto Marghera scheme, where works began that same year, after the Petit project of 1904 had been developed by the Venetian section of the *Genio civile* (National civil engineering department), and then sent to the *Commissione per il piano regolatore dei principali porti del regno* (Commission for the development plan for the main ports of the kingdom), instituted by ministerial decree that same year. The development plan for the new port was approved by the *Commissione* in 1907 and immediately underwritten by the Italian State. Works were, however, suspended in 1913, on the eve of the First World War, by which all the above-mentioned industries profited immensely. In 1917 there were founded, at Volpi's instigation, the *Cantieri navali ed acciaierie di Venezia* (Shipyards and steelworks of Venice), in which SADE had an interest; the *Società veneta di beni immobili per la compravendita di aree fabbricabili* (Venetian property company for the acquisition of factory development areas), and the *Società italiana costruzioni* (Italian construction company), which would build the first workers' housing estate in Marghera. Also set up – secretly – was the *Sindacato di studi per imprese elettro-metallurgiche e navali* (Research association for electro-metallurgical and shipbuilding companies), which brought together the leading figures in Venetian finance and industry (Volpi, who was president, Stucky, Nicolò Papadopoli and others).

The *Sindacato* commissioned detailed plans of the new port from Enrico Coen Cagli, who had also been responsible for planning the port of Antivari. He envisaged four different sectors operating over a vast area: a commercial port, a petroleum port, several industrial zones and residential quarters for 30,000 people, as well as a new canal, seven metres deep, connecting the port with the Giudecca, St Mark's Basin and the Lido. The plan was dated 10 May 1917; within just five days, and in time of war, it was approved by the highest ministerial body, the *Consiglio superiore dei Lavori Pubblici* (Higher council for public works). One month later, the *Porto Industriale di Venezia* (Industrial port of Venice) was set up as a company, with, needless to say, Giuseppe Volpi as its president. It was only on 15 June, after the event, that these manoeuvres were made public, prompting a profoundly hostile reaction from, among others, the Venetian Chamber of Commerce. A contract between the Italian State and the *Porto Industriale,*

Fig. 66

Seen between Santa Maria della Salute on the right and the Molino Stucky on the left, Porto Marghera seems an extraordinary, unbelievable intrusion on the Venetian skyline, one that, surely, no one can ever have wanted. Ultimately, however, the creation of Porto Marghera was driven by the needs and perhaps pretensions that Venice still had, in the early twentieth century, as a capital city, as the leading centre of its region: it needed to find employment and prosperity for a large, urban population that its vicissitudes had impoverished and diminished but not removed. At the beginning of the twentieth century, when Marghera was initiated, Venice was still seeking a future in the modern world – as something other than the prostitute of tourism (though that also). It is in fact to Marghera, to Mestre, to the new-build sprawl of its former marshy hinterland that Venice has successfully 'lost' its population, a population that now, of course, no longer exactly is Venice's. If Venice itself has no economic future except as a centre for tourism – though some of it will be highly developed tourism (so one might describe its very successful university) – so be it. But the destructive abomination that is Porto Marghera must, sooner or later, be removed, or at the least disarmed, and the damage that it has done and continues to do to the environment and the city must be repaired, or allowed to repair itself; the mainland will have to make its own way, economically and otherwise, and Venice must become again, in Francesco Da Mosto's words, "virtually separate".

Fig. 67

The lowering smokestacks of Porto Marghera emit
in particular sulphur dioxide, which tends to create
a ceiling of polluted air over the city which prevents
other pollutants (from central heating and the like)
from being released; ultimately the dioxide finds its
way down to the stonework of the city, which it
corrodes. It is disputed how much harm the
channels cut through the lagoon bed to permit
ships to reach Marghera really do, but they cannot
contribute positively to the preservation of the
lagoon, and certainly cause the washing away of silt
that is vital to it. Largely thanks to Marghera, there
is an imminent danger that the lagoon will evolve
into a marine bay, with all sorts of consequences
both for its wildlife and habitat and for the human
traditions of the lagoon.

granting permission to build the port, was signed immediately and implemented by special decree on 26 July 1917, although it was not ratified until 1924, when Mussolini in one fell swoop approved more than 2500 decrees issued since 1907. In 1925 Volpi became Mussolini's minister of finance. By the terms of the agreement, the *Porto Industriale di Venezia* was responsible for the costs of building the industrial installations and the railway, while title to the hitherto publically owned area of Marghera was granted to it by the State with no financial strings attached. If this was a colossal gift, it was not the only one, because the dredging of the canals, too, was carried out at the expense of the State, the roads, sewers and water supply were financed entirely by the *Comune*, and the *Comune* was also responsible for the cost of building the residential quarter, though this remained the property of the *Porto Industriale*. The areas that were in this way developed might then be sold back or leased by Volpi's company, which had sole rights, and thereby generated enormous profits, which, moreover, under the terms of the decree, were exempt from tax.

The works at Porto Marghera were therefore able to proceed rapidly, despite a feeble attempt by Breda, an Italian metallurgical giant, to steer the production centre to Sacca Fisola. In fact the Breda works were among the first to be established at Marghera; other factories soon followed, some already recognized to be emitting extremely high levels of pollution: the thermo-electric power station (SADE, obviously), *Società Italiana Coke, Vetri e Cristalli* (Italian coke and glass company), two plants for processing pyrite cinders, the *Società Italo-Americana del Petrolio*, AGIP, the *Società Italiana Allumina* (Italian aluminium company), ILVA, *Leghe Leggere, Elettrometallurgica Veneta San Marco* (another steelworks). The *Banca Commerciale Italiana* and the various bodies headed by Volpi were involved in many of these companies. The industrial complex was completed in 1932. It would grow further in the years to follow, and its plants would gradually be converted to newer technologies, leading up to the development of a petrochemical complex of enormous impact on the environment and on the health of the workers and other citizens drawn to the housing estates built round the factories.

The time was now ripe for the construction of a new bridge from the mainland to Venice for road and pedestrian traffic, the Ponte Littorio. After the early projects submitted by Antonio Baffo, new solutions were put forward with a certain regularity: in 1899 Giuseppe Torres and Luigi Vendrasco presented a scheme for widening the railway bridge on the north side; in 1906 Daniele Donghi proposed a similar project. In 1916, in the midst of war, Fulgenzio Setti advanced plans for two possible road links, the first of which would have connected Mestre with the Sacca della Misericordia, in Canaregio, while the second would have run out from Mestre to the southern tip of the Giudecca and extended to the Lido, where a 'garden city' would grow up. Typically, the fate of Venice continued to be planned more in relation to the mainland than to the water, a tendency firmly endorsed by the *Comune*, which, in 1919, opened a competition for the new bridge, though nothing came of it until the beginning of the 1930s, when a scheme designed by Vittorio Umberto Fantucci was constructed under the supervision of Eugenio Miozzi.

Meanwhile, Marghera expanded, "on the initiative of Conte Volpi di Misurata and thanks to the Fascist government", as the town-planner Gustavo Giovannoni later justly commented. Marghera soon took over and choked the area bordering on the lagoon and to the south-west of the port. The opening of the Canal Nuovo to the north of Venice, in 1929, and the building of the road bridge alongside the railway bridge, between 1931 and 1933, signalled the definitive exclusion of the island city of Venice from any significant productive activity. Mestre, too, was affected by the presence of the new industrial area, its population having become by 1935 five times greater than in 1871, and having spread like oil slick as a consequence of the indiscriminate parcelling out of land for building development and absence of any concern for urban and environmental values.

Before long Porto Marghera, which had been intended to provide employment and support for the Venetian economy from the outside, began instead – of necessity, and in line with social policy – to take on the role of a relief valve, allowing the evacuation from the city of the proletarian and working classes that had settled there in great numbers between 1915 and 1921 in order to escape from the war zones, building shacks or occupying insanitary and dilapidated dwellings. In 1925 some 4000 people were living in deprived conditions, requiring aid from philanthropic societies and charitable institutions. The mayor had more than once pleaded for a "total exodus" and for the removal of the shacks. With the advent of the Fascist regime efforts were made to tackle more effectively these problems of overcrowding and poor hygiene, by building semi-rural overspill communities on the mainland. Here the influx of population could be accommodated, and it would be possible to obviate the "distressing sight of the beggars that throng the streets of the city centre and the environs of the main monuments", and to demolish "the slums and hovels that infest Venice and extract the wretched families that would be left without a roof over their heads". The *Quartiere Urbano* (Urban district) of Porto Marghera, established between the main road to Padua and the Bottenighi wharfs (in terms of the prevailing winds, downwind of the industrial zone), seemed more than ever suitable, a place where "the worker or employee who will be constrained to seek this latest source of employment, got away if possible from cramped Venice, should find an environment that compensates him for city life and attracts him to the healthier life of the countryside".

However, Marghera and Mestre grew and grew without the exertion of any control, despite the plans drawn up in 1925 by the *Comune* of Mestre (merged with that of Venice in 1926) and subsequently by the *Comune* of Venice in 1927, 1933 and 1934. In 1934 the public announcement of a "competition for a *Piano regolatore* [General town plan] for the zone of Mestre and Marghera" stated as its objective "to establish a network providing easy access between the main arteries of the hinterland and the bridgehead, and to link closely the island part of the city with the neighbourhoods that already exist or will come into being on the mainland, so

that the Ponte Littorio can become a linking thoroughfare within Greater Venice, the administrative centre of the Veneto Region". From the proposals submitted, in 1937 Antonio Rosso
compiled a comprehensive Plan for further residential expansion in a broad curve from
Mestre to the San Giuliano marshflats, along six hundred metres of lagoon shoreline, ignoring
altogether the by now 'saturated' Marghera district.

That there were problems inherent in these measures seemed evident to the *Consiglio
nazionale dell'educazione, delle scienze e delle arti* (National council for education, sciences and the
arts), which produced a revised Plan, moderating the crudity of the development scheme but
extending the zone available for urbanization by another 1200 metres of shoreline. Even with
these modifications the Plan came to nothing, chiefly because it was in fact incompatible with
the terms of the law governing town-planning no. 1150 of 1942. No further solution to the
problem of Mestre's expansion was or has since been found, despite the much publicized
competition that would be organized in 1959.

In the period during which this *Piano per la terraferma veneziana* (Plan for the Venetian mainland) was being drafted, public health conditions in the island historic centre became critical.
It was a problem that evidently could no longer be deferred. In 1935 Raffaele Vivante, medical
officer to the *Comune*, compiled a register of uninhabitable houses and buildings for clearance
numbering several hundred units. The provisions adopted were, however, contradictory:
while on the one hand it was the policy of the Fascist regime to reduce the population in the
city centre, on the other hand the royal decree of 21 August 1937, no. 1901, which was converted into a Special Law for Venice on 3 February 1938 as *Provvedimenti per la salvaguardia del
carattere lagunare e monumentale di Venezia* (Provisions for the preservation of the lagoon and
monumental character of Venice), devolved responsibility for the soundness of buildings to
anyone with the power or interest to assume it, giving no indication of any required method
or means. Article 15 of the Decree affirms that "... completely new buildings, superstructures
and added storeys, as well as buildings that are radically transformed and in major part reconstructed, with complete or partial rebuilding of the outside walls, or with complete gutting in
order to create a number of dwellings with appropriate dividing walls, floors and ceilings, will
enjoy a twenty-five-year exemption from the tax and surtax on buildings, on condition that
the exemption is applied for in order to further the works provided for in the decree and in the
slum clearance plan, and within the time envisaged for the carrying out of the latter". The
Special Law made provision for the slum clearance plan to which it refers to be drawn up
within ten years.

What this was in essence and effect was an appeal and incentive to private initiative and
independent construction in the city centre. The State, and the Special Law, made no attempt
to formulate the means and manner in which the renovation of the city should be carried out,
implicitly delegating that to a new slum clearance plan, the *Piano di risanamento*, which itself
did not provide the answers, either. The same formula would, significantly, be followed

twenty years later, in Article 14 of the Special Law, no. 294, of 31 March 1956, from which one may deduce that not only was the failure to set criteria not reversed in 1956, but that there was still no ability or willingness to tackle the issue, except by handing it on to the private sector and individual initiative.

The new *Piano di risanamento*, drafted by Eugenio Miozzi, chief engineer of the *Ufficio tecnico* of the *Comune*, was dated 9 March 1939. It is very similar in its lack of substance to the Plan of 1891 (see Chapter 4.1), of which it is actually a continuation. It was perhaps, however, closer to the intentions of the regime – and to real events – than were the provisions of Article 15 of the decree of 1937. That is due not so much to the nature of the improvements proposed, of which there were some thirty, involving (once more) the widening and rationalization of streets and improvements to the circulation of traffic, as to the desire expressed in the *Relazione al Piano* (Preamble to the plan) to respect the 'Venetianness' (*venezianità*) of the city, to restore to some extent the water network that had previously been dismantled, and to build "outlying neighbourhoods".

The Plan was submitted, that same year, to the *Consiglio Superiore delle Scienze e delle Arti* (Higher council for sciences and the arts). Here one of its members, Gustavo Giovannoni, proposed modifications and made suggestions in what he defined as a *Carta del rinnovamento di Venezia* (Charter for the renewal of Venice). Giovannoni advocated the idea of 'thinning out' (*diradamento*), as opposed to the practice of wholesale clearance (*sventramento*) and "beneficial demolition" then in vogue, and claimed for Venice, as he had for other Italian cities, the simultaneous need to "redevelop the old quarters, especially where there was a high density of population and the living conditions were unsanitary, and not to alter the character of this wonderful city which is in its entirety a beautiful monument, not only in the great works of art with which it is studded, but also in the picturesque value of the ordinary urban fabric". This was a global vision of the city that also took account of its 'minor' buildings, though still in terms of the picturesque, of the superficial image. Giovannoni saw Venice above all as a city requiring reclamation, and the Plan as "a felicitous solution ... for saving the lagoon city, the city of Rialto, from every contamination".

Thus Giovannoni makes three main points in the *Carta*. The first is a call for the complete preservation of the "topographical character of the island city". The second is a hope that "in the redevelopment of the old quarters there should be strict adherence to the principle of thinning out buildings, making improvements to blocks from within, by opening up spacious courtyards without altering the external aspect; if necessary, demolishing houses in a state of total dilapidation; removing habitation from the ground floor and transferring the families crowded into them to the new outlying neighbourhoods; and above all ruling out the clearance of large areas that would inevitably lead to the construction of the large tenements favoured by building speculation ...". The third point is a challenge "to emulate, in new building, even in a modern form, Venice's vibrant and ebullient urban style, consisting of the free grouping of small details, bright colour, harmonies or contrasts to which any geometric rigidity of line is foreign".

Giovannoni confronted Venetian problems in a judicious and flexible manner, but he did not overcome the failure, also inherent in the 1937–38 Laws, to take any interest whatsoever in the possibility of a solution developed from the inside, one which might envisage salvaging the city's own structural and social dynamic instead of depending on external finance or action. These large-scale State-sponsored projects descended without any real sensitivity for its reality on what was regarded essentially as a passive body. When Giovannoni states that the Plan is "in the nature of a preliminary programme, devised to grant private individuals who wish to pursue their own initiatives the concessions provided for by the legislation", the suspicion arises that in order to tackle the question of redevelopment it was considered sufficient to talk of financial concessions and tax relief.

Historically, perhaps ever since the Fall of the Republic, the lack of direction and directives, the lack of a programme or of clear objectives, has been a constant of the Venetian situation. In particular the city would be condemned, in the years after the Second World War, to an extraordinary paralysis, to an irresolution that inevitably encouraged the growth of bureaucracy, a bureaucracy that at one and the same time allowed free scope to operations it could not control and created huge obstacles to progress for those within its grasp.

Apart from the guiding principles adopted and developed by Giovannoni, the most interesting part of the Plan was undoubtedly the proposal to restore the viability of the waterways, including some that had been filled in over the preceding decades: had it happened (but it did not), the re-opening of canals would have given districts lying out from the historic centre more flexible and rapid communication with the heart of the city, from which the inhabitants of 35,000 new homes would not have been estranged. But Venice would enter the Second World War subject to a major contradiction, the coexistence of an enormously ambitious Plan for new construction and a law that favoured, and subsidized, widespread restoration of the existing fabric, both to be implemented by the self-same municipal authority.

6.2 Interwar restorations: the quest for Venice's
antico volto; *new technologies*

During Mussolini's regime, in the 1920s and 1930s, no more than a limited number of restorations were carried out in Venice: these involved mostly the renovation of decorative elements and architectural details and the consolidation of public buildings, but also the meretricious salvaging of fragments of Venice's *antico volto* (former appearance). The absence of any vestige of Roman antiquity meant that the Fascist regime had little interest in encouraging or financing any major operations, which may well have been a good thing.

Generally, the restorers' aim became that of ridding Venetian buildings of neo-Gothic accretions, especially those of the nineteenth century, which were considered oppressive and clumsy, and alien to the lagoon tradition. Nineteenth-century Gothic was now cast as the antithesis of Renaissance colour and light, of the free Venetian Republic, Italian mistress of the Mediterranean, and began to attract the kind of hostility that had earlier focused on the Baroque. Certainly the work of Giambattista Meduna did not escape this surge of purism, and was regarded with suspicion – not so much, however, for the arbitrary character of his restorations (as one might have hoped), but for his "tasteless Gothic reconstructions".

The 'new era' of restoration began in the 1920s, with works undertaken on the Rialto Bridge, the Ateneo Veneto, the church of San Fantin and the Osteria del Selvadego; but the most important and significant operations were carried out in the 1930s, coinciding with the professional debut of Ferdinando Forlati, who would also play a key role in Venetian restoration after the Second World War.

In 1931, for instance, the church of Madonna dell'Orto (fig. 70) was again restored, being "rescued from the ghastly decoration, in the rudest transalpine Gothic style, that had camouflaged it in German guise and decked it out as if for a village fete" – a reference to Meduna's restoration, carried out about 1869. At the suggestion of the *Soprintendente*, Gino Fogolari, Vittorio Invernizzi, who was in charge of the project, endeavoured "to find out if any of the old decoration remained, not with the intention of taking it further, and thereby falsifying it, but, even if only fragments of it were to re-surface, in order to conserve them so that they might again be enjoyed". Inside the church, the paint with which they had been covered was removed from the columns, bringing to light decorations painted in 1399; "encouraged by this wonderful discovery", Invernizzi had "all the other walls stripped, but no further trace of ornamentation was found". The objective was "to remove the most tasteless Gothicisms so that everything should once more become correct and seemly, just as it should be in a Venetian church, regaining all of the picturesque and quintessentially Venetian overlay it had accumulated over time".

Such statements convey a clear desire to find a 'pure' architectural language, free from contamination and accretion (*superfetazione*). In preparing to carry out their cleansing intentions, the Venetian restorers, instead of washing their dirty linen in the Arno, as the expression goes, washed them in the Grand Canal, at Campo San Marcuola, right opposite the Fondaco dei Turchi. The concept of *restauro* was becoming dangerously indistinguishable from that of *restaurazione*: restoration in the sense of returning to a good state what was actually there was being elided with restoration in the sense of putting back what was no longer there.

The operations on the Madonna dell'Orto also reveal a 'de-restoration' purpose in the mentality of those working in the field at that time. They readily took issue, whether for ideological or for common-sense reasons, with many nineteenth-century interpolations, although the suspicion arises that this was hardly different from the usual intolerance of *superfetazioni*, now confronting the no longer recent works of the nineteenth century.

Figs. 68, 69

On one side of the church of the Carmine (Santa Maria del Carmelo), the Carmelite church in Venice, there is a fourteenth-century porch (or *protiro*) decorated with Veneto-Byzantine roundels and also, as the photograph of 1870 (above) shows, with crumbling plasterwork or *intonaco*. In the late twentieth century, under the direction of the *Soprintendenza*, following 'philological' or archaeological principles, the plaster was removed and the bare brickwork revealed in order to set off the roundels. This is a classic example of *ripristino*, of returning to an original, pristine state which cannot, however, be known to be authentic and too often in fact involves the imposition of a contemporary, rather than an original, ideal or standard. What gets lost is the evolved, 'lived-in', organically historic patina of the building or element of the building; the tidy version that we have today is an archaeologist's specimen, redolent of gallery displays, and emphasizes the roundels at the expense of the Gothic porch as a whole. The demand for bare brick is really a twentieth-century taste. Notably the stripped down churches of Santa Fosca and Santa Maria Assunta on Torcello have been restored in a very similar vein. In the same programme of restoration the Baroque 'oculus' visible in the background of the 1870 photograph was also removed. Such *superfetazioni* or accretions are typical targets of *ripristino*.

Figs. 70, 71

The Madonna dell'Orto is one of the most restored churches in Venice; that means inevitably that much of the later restoration has involved disentanglement from previous restoration. Restorations of the church are recorded in 1837–48, about 1869 (by Giambattista Meduna), in 1892–93, in 1930–37 (by Vittorio Invernizzi for the *Soprintendenza*), in 1964, in 1968–70 (for the Venice in Peril Fund and the *Soprintendenza*) and in 1993 (in the photograph on the right).

Invernizzi's stated intention in 1931, "to remove the most tasteless Gothicisms so that everything should once more become correct and seemly, just as it should be in a Venetian church, regaining all of the picturesque and quintessentially Venetian overlay it had accumulated over time", would itself seem excessive and unseemly today, above all because the idea of a 'pristine', truly 'Venetian' state is a pernicious one – and essentially the same one that led Meduna to implant his "Gothicisms" in the first place. Invernizzi, intemperately, went on to strip the walls of the church of their remaining *intonaco*, permanently depriving the church of an essential element of its patina; against these bare walls the detached paintings by Tintoretto appear like artefacts on display and the whole church as frigid as a Victorian museum.

Figs. 72, 73

The Ca' Falier at Santi Apostoli belonged, by repute, once upon a time to the infamous Doge Marin Falier, executed for treason against the State in 1355. The palace has indeed ancient windows, giving "a very distinct idea of the second order in its perfect form", according to Ruskin. As Ruskin also noticed, and as one sees in the photograph above of 1920, "The balcony is, of course, modern, and the series of windows has been of greater extent, once terminated by a pilaster on the left hand, as well as the right; but the terminal arches have been walled up". Restorers in the 1930s, as one sees today (right), first of all destroyed the *intonaco*, though there was nothing dissonant and undesirable about it, and then made the outlines of the missing light on the left and its immured capital pedantically visible; at the same time they saw fit to remodel the flanking windows, presumably to make them more consonant with the prized 'second order'.

Beneath Ca' Falier runs a portico (or *sotoportego*) resting on ancient columns, though which nowadays snakes the pedestrian traffic from the east side of the Rialto Bridge along the north side of the Grand Canal ultimately to the station – and in the opposite direction. Despite other such operations in this area during the nineteenth century (see pp. 23ff., 63ff.) this element of the pedestrian throughfare could hardly be widened. Ruskin, in whose time, of course, it was still normal to move about the city by gondola, remarked on the uniquely Venetian "extraordinary involution of the alleys leading to it from the Rialto". "In Venice the straight road is usually by water, and the long road by land; but the difference of distance appears, in this case, altogether inexplicable. Twenty or thirty strokes of the oar will bring a gondola from the foot of the Rialto to that of Ponte SS Apostoli [shown in the foreground]."

It is worth drawing attention to one other aspect of the restoration of the Madonna dell'Orto – financial considerations, which came to the fore when, in the eastern part of the church, "the walls and apse were stripped of the pretentious nineteenth-century painting and the bricks were left bare, even where they were in need of repair, because as a whole, in its quiet luminosity, it was serene and ... there were no funds for anything".

The same kind of objectives and practices as those of the restoration of the Madonna dell'Orto recur in a whole series of other restorations carried out in the early 1930s, though they were less extensive: some windows, including a four-light Gothic window, were opened up in the church of Santa Maria Mater Domini; so were a three-light window in a house in Campo Santi Filippo e Giacomo, ogee windows in Ca' Venier, and a two-light window in the church of San Polo. The Fenice Theatre, however, was extensively restored, ridding it of the effects of the operations that the Meduna brothers had carried out some one hundred years earlier. It was a small war that was being conducted against accretions, occlusions and additions, forgetting many of Boito's teachings, certainly, but respecting those, for instance, of Article 2 of the *Carta italiana del restauro* (Charter for restoration in Italy) of 1931, which expressed the hope "that the problem of a *ripristino* prompted by reasons of art and architectural unity, in conjunction with historical judgement, should be addressed solely on the basis of absolutely reliable data supplied by the monument destined to undergo the *ripristino*, and not of hypotheses; of elements mostly already existing rather than mostly new". It was not until 1938 that this outdated guideline was to be superseded by Article 3 of the *Istruzione per il restauro dei monumenti* (Instructions for the restoration of monuments): "In the restoration of monuments and works of art, any completion or *ripristino* or any addition of elements not strictly necessary for the stability, conservation and consolidation of the work is to be ruled out absolutely".

Apart from the removal of "very unfortunate additions" carried out to restore the *antico volto* and get back to "the way the work was originally made", Venetian restorers had to confront major problems of consolidation in famous monumental buildings, and in their operations they often made use of a material that was now sanctioned even by restoration charters – reinforced concrete. Reinforced concrete, though so widely used, is a material intrinsically alien to, indeed directly in conflict with, Venetian traditions of construction (figs. 74, 75).

During this period consolidation works were carried out on Ca' Corner (housing the *Provincia*), the Ateneo Veneto, the church and *campanile* of San Vidal, the Ca' d'Oro (figs. 50–52, pp. 90–91) once again, the Palazzo dei Camerlenghi and the Fondaco dei Tedeschi (figs. 18, 19, pp. 38–39). In all these cases reinforced concrete and iron were used. All were somewhat complicated operations, those on the Ca' d'Oro and the Fondaco dei Tedeschi being of particular note, because of the fame and the size of these buildings. In 1935 Ferdinando Forlati anchored the facade of the Ca' d'Oro to the building structure behind, and reinforced capitals and column bases with internal supports of stainless steel. In the same year, the Fondaco dei

Figs. 74, 75

Although the use of steel and concrete
has enabled the comparatively economic
and effective repair of statically unsound
buildings, it brings with it still more far-
reaching problems for the future,
because its rigid structure is so
diametrically antithetical to the 'softer'
principles of Venetian building tradition.
Unlike Venetian walls of brick and joists
of wood and floors of polished *terrazzo*,
iron and concrete do not give or move,
and are therefore unable to absorb the
shifting forces of the essentially unstable
Venetian subsoil.

The technique shown is the insertion
of steel armatures *in rottura di muro*, that is
'breaking' them into the ancient
structure while it remains suspended by
centering. It necessitates a considerable
wastage of the original material of the
building, which is not desirable in itself,
and it is not the 'once and for all'
operation that major restoration works
so often are supposed to be. It creates
problems for the remaining, original
parts of the building at the same time as
solving them.

Tedeschi, owned by the *Ministero delle Poste* (Ministry of postal communications), which had always been liable to serious problems from the degradation and degeneration of its materials, was closed. Already by 1908 the stability of the building had worsened considerably, but the most effective consolidation works were carried out later, in three successive phases, from 1929 to 1933, from 1934 to 1938, and from 1938 to 1939. The building received the attentions, successively, of Ferdinando Forlati, Giuseppe Pession and Gino Vittorio Ravà. They were able to avail themselves of the results of laboratory tests, of the kind that in the years to come would prove of invaluable support to conservation. At that time the tests were of course still of a 'destructive' nature, involving the removal of samples of building materials. In the case of the Fondaco dei Tedeschi, these made it possible to identify as causes of the very serious decay "the inferior quality of the bricks used (insufficiently baked bricks made of inferior clay) and the poor quality of the sand used to mix the mortar (unwashed marble sand)".

Following the scientific investigations, the aim of the static restoration, carried out by the *Genio civile* (National civil engineering department), was to pin the various parts of the building together, after removing occlusions and walls added in the past to counteract its imbalances. The pinning was carried out by inserting reinforced concrete girders *in rottura di muro* (by breaching the wall), to form a frame of superimposed grids, one to each floor. The girders were put in place by cutting through all the outside walls and horizontally sectioning the building. The procedure consisted of removing part of the wall, while jacks held up the unsupported masonry above, in order to create continuous beams of reinforced concrete.

The structure of the Fondaco was thereby completely inverted: from a system of load-bearing brick walls, without toothing, which allowed the entire building to react in a non-rigid fashion in response to differentiations in subsidence due to the particular characteristics of the Venetian substratum, it became an extremely rigid vertical sequence of rectangles. As a result, perversely, the walls became the 'weak points' of the system: they would be the first to crack and to give way, at the least stress, and this would no longer have a merely local impact, but would affect practically the whole building.

Similar operations, involving the insertion of reinforced concrete girders *in rottura di muro*, were conducted on the Palazzo Corner and the Palazzo dei Camerlenghi, also by the *Genio civile*, and the practice was to become common in restorations of the 1950s and 1960s, despite the fact that the rigidity introduced into the building's stable equilibrium often wrecked the walls and floors. These, if they had not already been substituted with new structures in reinforced concrete, would be damaged or fissured shortly afterwards by the failure of the new structural parts to accommodate their movement.

NOTES

The founding and development of Porto Marghera have been widely recounted and discussed: see notably C. Chinello, *Porto Marghera 1902–1926. Alle origini del 'problema di Venezia'*, Venice 1979, and *Forze politiche e sviluppo capitalistico: Porto Marghera e Venezia 1951–1973*, Rome 1975. On the industrialization of Venice see *Venezia città industriale. Gli insediamenti produttivi nel XIX secolo*, exh. cat., Venice 1980.

The history of SADE and of the industrial zone of Porto Marghera is closely intertwined with some of the most unfortunate catastrophes that have struck modern Italy. The construction of the hydro-electric dam at Vajont (near Longarone, in the province of Belluno) was pushed through even though the geology of the valley was clearly unfavourable. The artificial lake was allowed to rise to a greater height than safety permitted and, on the evening of 9 October 1963, a colossal landslip (of which there had been numerous warnings) fell into the basin, creating an enormous wave that engulfed the little town of Longarone, killing more than 1900 people. As Tina Merlin, a journalist who had drawn attention to the grave threat the dam posed several years beforehand (and had been prosecuted, and acquitted, in 1959, for spreading "false and misleading rumours"), wrote at the time, "It was a massacre ... one, however, that had long been foreseeable, ever since, when the works on the huge hydro-electric dam began, the experts recognised that they were building on a kind of clay liable to slide down a hill, which, therefore, might very well precipitate a catastrophe". There was a judicial inquiry. It lasted four years (1968–71) and reached the verdict that most of the staff working at the plant were indeed guilty of criminal manslaughter.

In the aftermath of World War I much was published about the damage to the Venetian heritage caused by the conflict, some of it clearly propagandistic and anti-Austrian: see A. Moschetti, *I danni ai monumenti e alle opere d'arte delle Venezie nella guerra mondiale 1915–1918*, Venice 1932. The restorations undertaken in Venice between the two world wars are documented for the most part by reports in newspapers and journals and by monographic publications on individual buildings, for example Tridenti , 'L'antico volto di Venezia: il restauro dell'Osteria del Selvadego', *Il Giornale d'Italia*, 14 May 1926; V. Invernizzi, 'Lavori alla Madonna dell'Orto', *Bollettino d'Arte*, 1931, pp. 232–37; Provincia di Venezia, *Il restauro di Palazzo Corner*, Venice 1935; anon., 'Opere di restauro e consolidamento del palazzo dei Camerlenghi a Venezia', *Annali dei lavori pubblici*, 11, 1936. During this period the first publications of Ferdinando Forlati appeared: 'Restauri a Venezia', *Le Vie d'Italia*, 1937; 'Il restauro del Fondaco dei Tedeschi', *Palladio*, 7, Rome 1943. On the subject of the sanitary conditions in the lagoon islands the contributions of Gustavo Giovannoni should be mentioned: G. Giovannoni, 'Venezia, il risanamento urbanistico', *Palladio*, 6, 1939, pp. 273–74; also Comune di Venezia (Direzione generale dei servizi tecnici), *Progetto di massima per il piano di risanamento di Venezia insulare: relazione*, Venice 1939; and, more strictly on the hygienic and social aspects, the numerous publications of Raffaele Vivante.

On the use of the new technologies in older buildings see Gino Vittorio Ravà, *Nuovi metodi impiegati nel restauro di alcuni palazzi veneziani*, Rome 1936.

The complete texts of the Italian charters for restoration are to be found in A. Bellini, *Tecniche della conservazione*, Milan 1986. The quotation on Marghera in 6.1 is taken from P. Somma, 'L'edilizia residenziale pubblica dall'inizio del secolo alla seconda guerra mondiale', *Edilizia Popolare*, 175, 1983, p. 28. The observations on the brief for the competition of 1934 are drawn from R. Chirivi, 'Eventi urbanistici dal 1846 al 1962', *Urbanistica*, 52, 1968, *passim*. The remarks by Giovannoni in favour of *diradamento* (thinning) instead of *sventramento* (demolition) appear in G. Giovannoni, 'Venezia: il risanamento urbanistico', cited above. Quotations regarding the restoration of the Madonna dell'Orto are taken from V. Invernizzi, 'Lavori alla Madonna dell'Orto', as cited above.

7 | Venice and Marghera before 1966

7.1 Awaiting the Piano regolatore: *the 1950s*

Venice emerged from the Second World War practically unscathed physically, or at least the island city did – the industrial plants of Porto Marghera suffered serious damage. The war had interrupted the attention being given to the problem of expansion on the mainland, but this, by the end of the 1940s, had taken on such proportions that it became the most pressing issue of all confronting Venice. Owing to out-of-date building regulations, dating back to 1929, and to the lack of a *Piano regolatore*, the 1942 version not having been approved, Marghera and Mestre surged ahead side by side with their uncontrolled urban sprawl, organized solely on the basis of the division of the land into some one hundred allotments. The *Piano di ricostruzione* (Reconstruction plan) approved in 1951 was of no more use in this respect, since it was concerned primarily with the zones that had been affected by bombing.

The influx of population from the Venetian hinterland meanwhile continued, increasingly taking on the characteristics of a real and proper migration. It more than fulfilled the labour requirements of Marghera, and was pushed on to the other industrial areas of northern Italy. By 1961, as Vittorio Emiliani was able to declare, "Volpi di Misurata's projects have had a reverse effect" – referring to the fact that Marghera was no longer a part of Greater Venice but had developed as an independent entity, while the Venetian population, still on the increase despite the fact that only ten per cent of the active labour force was employed at Marghera, continued to suffer from overcrowding, unemployment and unhygienic conditions of the kind that had been endemic for decades.

Even in these pressing circumstances, however doubtful it might seem that the development of Marghera had contributed or would eventually contribute to a resolution of Venetian problems, a solution was not sought in Venice, for Venice, but the usual path was taken of looking outside the city, by seeking to extend the industrial zone of Mestre ever more in the direction of Padua, Treviso and San Donà. This had terrible results, as we all know, both for Marghera and for Venice. The growth of the industrial monster was indiscriminate, in the wrong place and out of all proportion. "Marghera is neither a city, nor a community, but a jumble of factories, pipes and chimneys, facing Venice, which looks on appalled at the monster it has pupped .... Venice is dying: hence the grief throughout the world. But let it be clearly understood, Venice is dying by its own hand, and too many of its citizens deserve the fate of Marin Faliero .... Rather than pity, this city inspires rage." Thus wrote Cesare Brandi, founder of the *Istituto Centrale del restauro* (Central institute for restoration), and a learned scholar and

Fig. 76
What is quite clearly a modern office building occupies, tactfully enough, a site on the Rio Nuovo, itself created in the early 1930s (under the direction of Eugenio Miozzi) to improve a route from the Tronchetto and railway station to the Accademia Bridge avoiding the bend of the Grand Canal (it has since been closed to *vaporetti* because of the excessive wash they create). This postwar but still rather fascist building for SADE (*Società Adriatica di Elettricità*; Adriatic electricity company), by Angelo Scattolin and Luigi Vietti, was begun in 1954 as part of a wider development of this rather 'dead' area south of the of station, bordering on the port. Tactful though it is in its elevations, and though other modern buildings in Venice lacking its integrity are undoubtedly uglier or more discordant, Scattolin and Vietti's office is also brutal in its forward-marching modernism and its contempt for the picturesque, and as such is redolent of the environmental neglect and political manipulation of Venice's real needs not only before but no less after the Second World War.

theoretician of the discipline, in 1970, contemplating with indignation and dismay the results of the ill-conceived planning and industrial policies for Venice in the early post-war period.

Marghera and the lagoon skyline as we know it today grew up during those years. As early as 1953, at the first signs of recovery after the slump of the Second World War, the *Genio civile* prepared a provisional *Piano regolatore* for the exploitation of the saltmarsh between Fusina and the Brenta Canal, which was immediately approved by the *Consiglio Superiore dei Lavori Pubblici* (Higher council for public works). At the same time another draft project was prepared, for a new canal from Malamocco to Fusina. A plan took shape for Marghera's second industrial zone, a continuation of the first zone along the western shore of the lagoon. This governed the terms of the important public competition for the *Piano regolatore di Venezia*, published in 1956, notably its *Norme tecniche di attuazione* (Technical regulations for implementation), where we read (article 15, paragraph 3) this ominous and in some respects incredible provision: "To be located in the industrial zone are mainly those plants that discharge smoke, dust or emissions harmful to human life into the atmosphere, that discharge poisonous substances into the water, and that produce vibrations and noise". Eugenio Miozzi immediately completed, in 1957, a preliminary project for a new oil depôt on the edge of the lagoon, near Sant'Ilario, with direct access across the lagoon from the Bocca di Malamocco. His was a revival of the plan drawn up by the *Genio civile* in 1953: it marked the first stage of planning for what became the notorious 'tanker canal', and intimated the future use of the second industrial zone as a petrochemical complex. In the competition for the new *Piano regolatore* it was expressly required that part of the area should be allocated to small and medium-sized enterprises, but before long almost the entire area (80 per cent) had been acquired by *Montecatini* (which within a few years took over SADE) and *Edison*; then in 1964–65 these two companies would merge to form the Italian chemical giant *Montedison*, effectively the only beneficiary of the new industrial area. A new *Consorzio per l'ampliamento e lo sviluppo di Porto Marghera* (Consortium for the expansion and development of Porto Marghera), which was swiftly established, approved the construction of the industrial zone, in a situation where there was effectively no control exercised by the local authorities and no obligation to give priority to works in the public interest.

At the same time plans were being drawn up for a third industrial zone, adjacent to the second. This was established by Law no. 397 of 2 March 1963, under the terms of which the *Comune* of Mira formed part of a new consortium, the objective of which was the construction of a steel-making complex and an oil pipeline for central Europe. The *Piano regolatore* for the third zone was approved and ratified in 1965. Nothing was done to check the indiscriminate expansion of the factories until, *in extremis*, the prospect of the utter destruction of the lagoon's ecosystem became real.

7.2 *The Soprintendency of Ferdinando Forlati*

In the 1950s the issue of the reconstruction of monuments damaged or destroyed in the war was the main focus of restoration debate. All over Italy – and Europe – restorers were grappling with the same dilemma that the Venetians had faced in 1902, the day after the collapse of the Campanile.

Debate in the cities affected took the form of 'how to reconstruct' and 'how not to reconstruct' – the historic centres of Florence, Milan, Verona, Padua, Treviso and Genoa had suffered such extensive damage that it would have been impossible to stick to conservational principles without ending up with a landscape of ruins. It came down in the end to the creation of an image of the past: the bridges of Santa Trinita in Florence and of the Castelvecchio in Verona, for example, were reconstructed *com'erano, dov'erano* (as they were, where they were); the Palazzo dei Trecento in Treviso was to all intents and purposes rebuilt. In other cases, however, the few remains still standing were patiently consolidated; cloisters, façades and similar architecture were reconstructed by piecing together and building round the surviving fragments; masonry and decorations were re-created on the basis of photographs, surveys and documents predating the conflict. In these various procedures, however, there was, unfortunately, no shortage of questionable or misguided decisions.

The *soprintendenti* of the various cities carried out the reconstruction of damaged monuments with some rigour, but not with sufficient rigour to prevent the entire discipline of restoration from contamination by anomalous and irregular activity. The relaxation of the hardline conservationist approach, necessitated by the new but temporary exigencies, favoured the development and defence of a tendency still not eradicated among workers and technicians – the tendency to interpret the monument, to restore it according to an image of its original form, to a completeness it never had, to modify or perfect it "with the aim of increasing the value of the monument itself", in the words of a great theoretician of restoration, Renato Bonelli, in 1972.

Thus, what should have been a last resort, to be adopted once and for all in exceptional circumstances, became, for some, a profound human need, and the task of the restorer became, in Bonelli's words, "that of identifying the value of the monument, in other words, to recognize in it the presence or otherwise of artistic quality. But this recognition is a critical act ... and upon it is based ... the task of recovering, restoring and releasing the work of art, that is to say, the entire complex of figurative elements that constitute the image and through which that image realises and expresses its own individuality and spirituality".

It was during these years that the principles of so-called 'critical' restoration were codified, embodying demands of the kind we have seen expressed, in different form, in earlier periods. In its less sophisticated versions it gave respectability to interpretative freedom and wide scope for interference with materials and forms that might not conform to the "individuality" and "spirituality" of the monument. In the event that recovery of the image might be "interrupted by destruction or visual impediments, the critical process would be obliged to draw on the imagination to re-create the missing parts or to reproduce those concealed and so finally to regain the complete unity of the monument". Widely accepted at a time when re-construction and, ultimately, falsification of material were "necessary", 'critical' restoration had much deeper implications because, again in its less sophisticated versions, it sanctioned arbitrary, substitutive and destructive approaches to the built fabric.

In Venice, during this period, restoration in the sense of reconstruction was not wide-spread, because of the absence of any great war damage; it manifested itself mostly in that ex-cessively 'philological' approach which had guided certain restorations of 1920s and 1930s, which was in fact an expression of the desire to purge and cleanse buildings of accretions con-sidered to be alien. It would have pernicious consequences when, in due course, there was an attempt to return to more objective parameters, in so far as it made building typology an obligatory consideration in determining project decisions (see pp. 182ff. and 212–13). But it was another decade before this development occurred, and the most important works in Venice during the 1950s were still conducted on moderately conservationist premises, and in sym-pathy with the philosophy that had governed the restorations of twenty years earlier (at the church of Madonna dell'Orto, for example). However, considerable destructive intervention was made necessary by the objective requirement to disencumber certain buildings of truly inappropriate nineteenth-century distortions dangerous for the conservation of the structure, as in some of the works that Ferdinando Forlati conducted on the ex-convent complex on the island of San Giorgio Maggiore between 1951 and 1956 (figs. 77–81).

Here Forlati found himself confronted with sixteenth-, seventeenth- and eighteenth-century convent structures that had been turned into barracks in the nineteenth century and now appeared in a serious state of degradation, especially as a consequence of humidity. His operations focused first on the dormitories and the Renaissance buildings by Giovanni Buora, on the western side of the island: some of the deteriorated brickwork was replaced with new by the traditional method of *scuci-cuci* (unstitch, stitch); horizontal cuts were made into the walls to insert a barrier against the rising damp; gravel beds were laid under the ground-floor pavements, while the *terrazzo* floorings of the upper storeys were patched or repaired; the roofs of the dormitories were given new wooden struts and centering, and, once the brick-work had been brushed, the walls were re-plastered with a mixture of hot tar, lime, sand and ground shards of old terracotta roof-tiles, applied in several coats, and dusted with talcum.

It was then decided to raise the floor of the Sala Capitolare (Chapter house) to the same level as the rest of the complex, while the foundations and columns of the cloister *degli Allori* (of the Laurels) were reinforced, and the occlusions between the columns removed. The restoration required for the refectory, built by Palladio, amounted to a total *ripristino*, which did not fail to give rise to argument: the space had been turned into a theatre for the soldiers, destroying the original floors and considerably raising the floor level. Forlati removed the

Fig. 77

After suppression in 1806, the monastic buildings lying south of the church of the Benedictine foundation of San Giorgio became redundant; they had little relevance for the port (see p. 31) that was built on the north side of the island in the first half of the nineteenth century. From 1851 they became barracks, and continued to decay until 1951, when they were ceded by the State to the Giorgio Cini Foundation, set up by Count Vittorio Cini in memory of his son. For the *Soprintendenza* Ferdinando Forlati carried out a large-scale restoration and renovation intended also to serve the purposes of the Foundation, on the one hand a scholarly institution requiring a library (for which it took over Longhena's monastic library), exhibition space, conference room, lecture theatre and appropriate offices, on the other (more to the south of the cloisters proper) a naval training school. The monastic gardens were also refurbished, by Luigi Vietti, though he did not attempt a reconstruction. The monastic buildings contained monumental buildings by architects such as Palladio and Longhena, among them the refectory (see over), built by Palladio about 1560, in which once hung Veronese's *Marriage at Cana*, removed by Napoleon to the Louvre and never returned (a painting by Tintoretto and assistants takes its place today). Though some criticisms can be and were made of Forlati's restoration, the rescue of the complex for the *Fondazione Giorgio Cini* has been from almost all points of view a success – the buildings were rescued, are maintained, and are appropriately used.

Figs. 78–81

Above on this page, the refectory of the monastery of San Giorgio, built by Palladio about 1560, as it was in 1950; below, the refectory immediately after Forlati's restoration, in 1953. Forlati seems to have been influenced by the fashion which saw Palladio as a precursor of modernism, introducing light and clarity and sweeping out clutter; but the resulting space corresponds to no known or possible phase of the building's history and is incoherent in itself. The theatre (below on the opposite page) was less equivocally a modern structure inserted into a badly damaged shell (above on the opposite page), altered to suit its function.

nineteenth-century structures and 'put back' the sixteenth-century arrangement, provoking criticism from Roberto Pane, among others, who maintained that, for the sake of consistency, the semi-circular 'thermal' windows that had been inserted in the eighteenth century but closed up for the theatre should be re-opened.

'Disencumbrance' did not stop there, but also extended to the nineteenth-century additions to the cloister, which were removed – recalling the similar fate in the same period of the cloisters of the Ospedale Maggiore in Milan, which Liliana Grassi was repairing after the serious damage caused by bombing in 1943. Baldassare Longhena's library on San Giorgio regained its staircase, and work also began on Palladio's church itself and on its *campanile*, both of which were in a critical condition. Forlati took action to remedy the subsidence of the supports of the dome and of the belfry, which was very serious. The dome was reinforced externally, supporting it while reinforced concrete girders were inserted and liquid cement injected; and the work on the *campanile*, extremely difficult because of its terrible condition, involved the insertion of a large reinforced-concrete strut and the securing of precarious parts with rust-proof metal stanchions.

A few years later, in 1959, Egle Trincanato used similar methods in the restoration of the Procuratie Nuove, destined to become part of the Museo Correr, in Piazza San Marco. The entire building had previously been converted from offices to apartments for habitation, inserting intermediate floors and partitions, "wrecking the walls with chimney flues and holes for floor joists and stair treads", re-laying the floors with poor-quality *terrazzo*, replacing the plaster and washing it with lime and glue, and rebuilding or refitting the ceilings. The restoration involved general re-plastering and re-surfacing and the replacement of many floors and of some fixtures, others being kept, "although of quite late construction". The brickwork was consolidated with the insertion of reinforced-concrete girders, the surviving floors were strengthened with iron beams and finally the old beam heads were reinforced with iron and concrete sections.

Both Trincanato's intervention on the Correr and Forlati's on San Giorgio had as their first objective the preservation of large structures in a serious state of disrepair. In making them safe they repeated what had been done in the 1930s, continuing the practice of inserting rigid structures into these old buildings. Forlati was responsible for one of the first ever restorations involving the complete replacement of the original structure of a monumental building with another in reinforced concrete, in operations conducted on the Scuola di Santa Maria e San Girolamo in Campo San Fantin, better known as the Ateneo Veneto (see fig. 28, p. 48), between 1956 and 1958.

The building had already been restored several times, in 1826, 1849, 1896 and 1912 (by Gino Fogolari), but was still in terrible condition: in particular, the roof, the attic and the reading room were completely unsound as a result of water infiltration and lack of maintenance. Forlati inserted two parallel reinforced-concrete girders, running from one end of the building to the other, at eave height, connected by pillars to two beams lower down, at the level of the floor below (the reading-room floor), which was suspended by the structure thus formed. The roof supports, which were entirely ruined, were completely rebuilt; the floor just below (the reading-room ceiling), that had rotted away almost completely as a consequence of the leaking roof, was relaid as a tile-lintel floor. Forlati also restored the building's façade, which was cleaned, repaired and consolidated. His attempt, however, to preserve the internal walls from humidity with "several layers of insulating treatments, of gesso" remains puzzling.

To conclude this survey two more significant restorations, of 1958 and 1959 respectively, at the church of San Lorenzo and at Ca' Pesaro, should be mentioned. The first involved the use of pre-stressed reinforced-concrete girders of great length (two pairs 21 m long and two pairs 17 m long), and the second, the immediate precursor of the better known restoration of the building by Salvatore Boscarino in the 1980s, involved the rebuilding of the brick walls, their stripping and re-plastering, and the use of *cappotto* (capping) insulation.

This brief examination is sufficient to illustrate all the salient characteristics of restoration practice in the 1940s and 1950s – moderate effort to return to original forms, frequent resort to reinforced concrete, indifference towards the historical and documentary value of original materials. Even if these characteristics do not, in themselves, show any significant development compared with previous years, it is nevertheless possible to identify three trends that would grow in importance over the next twenty years – the emergence of a technology capable of replacing rapidly, at reasonable cost, one material with another (this latter mostly reinforced concrete); the end of comprehensive, large-scale restoration projects – San Giorgio was the last major operation of its kind; and the decisive contribution of external funding to the costs of restoration (in the case of San Giorgio the *Fondazione Giorgio Cini*).

In addition there is the very unusual case of the 1954 restoration of St Mark's Basilica. As early as the 1820s, the then Patriarch of Venice, Ladislao Pyrker, had sought to remove the church's imposing iconostasis, executed in the late fourteenth century by Pierpaolo and Jacobello dalle Masegne, on the grounds that it blocked the view of the altar from the nave and transepts and had been erected to create an exclusive space to which only the Doge and his entourage had access and from which only they could enjoy the spectacle of the religious ceremony. Fortunately, the project had come to nothing. In 1954, the Patriarch of Venice Angelo Roncalli (who was to become the much-loved Pope John XXIII, 1958–63), acting on the same completely erroneous assumption, authorized a partial modification. The plutei or marble panels were sawn off at the base and put back on metal hinges that allowed them to be folded down, thereby making the whole presbytery visible from the centre of the nave.

Figs. 82, 83

Restorations during the early 1960s falsely and arbitrarily transformed the Palazzo Tiepoletto on the Grand Canal south of the Rialto Bridge (on the right in the photographs, beside a nameless 'infill' palace in between and the Palazzo Persico or Giustiniani-Persico on the left). The broad and spacious sixteenth-century Palazzo Persico has long been prominent on the Grand Canal thanks to the deep red hue of its *intonaco*. The comparatively minor Tiepoletto (so-called to distinguish it from the larger Palazzo Tiepolo on its other side) is currently described in guidebooks as 'Gothic, late fifteenth-century', and so it may once upon a time have been, but its ogival windows are modern reconstructions: before the restoration the palace had been given standard post-Renaissance square-cut Istrian-stone windows. The lower floors and their fenestration were also drastically altered in the 1960s restorations, re-imposing a 'normal' pattern of water-level floor and *mesà* or middle floor of smaller rooms beneath the *piano nobile* with its series of large windows.

7.3 The Piano regolatore and
the third Special Law (1956)

The Marghera 'solution' had failed, the *Piano di risanamento* of 1939 was obviously out of date, and the resident population had started to fall alarmingly (the rate of abandonment of the historic centre reached a peak in the period 1956–62). Meanwhile the city was finally obliged in the second half of the 1950s to set about the drafting of the measures envisaged by the *Legge urbanistica* (Town-planning law) no. 1150 of 17 August 1942, namely a *Piano regolatore generale* (General town plan) and accompanying *Piani particolareggiati* (Detailed plans), or, in their respective acronyms, PRG and PP (we will call them 'General Plan' and 'Detailed Plans').

The interministerial decree no. 391 of 11 May 1954 called on the *Comune* of Venice to honour its obligations under the law of 1942, but to no avail. One may date to this moment a typically Venetian situation that prevails to this day – non-fulfilment of obligations, the failure to programme or plan and, consequently, to act. This inertia, this *immobilismo*, however inadequate it may be, might be read as a kind of resistance to external intervention; this evasion of the laws of central government could be seen as a romantic and irresponsible nostalgia for the prerogatives of a city that was once mistress of its own destiny, but had now been forced to submit, especially in the nineteenth century and the 1920s and 1930s, to pointless, inefficient and painful measures. On the other hand this history of negative experiences of 'outside' measures, and the resultant mistrust and failure to act, whether 'native' or in reaction, have reduced Venice over these last fifty years to a sort of no-go area, where the weakness or absence of any kind of effective government has allowed scandalous exploitation, speculation, destruction and decay; the city has undergone an economic, cultural and social debasement that has transformed it into a boutique for tourism and betrayed any vestige of the traditions of its past.

The above-mentioned decree 391 of 1954 having produced no results, Parliament approved Special Law no. 294 of 31 March 1956 (*Provvedimenti per la salvaguardia del carattere lagunare e monumentale di Venezia attraverso opere di risanamento civico ed interesse turistico*: Provisions for the preservation of the lagunal and monumental character of Venice through works of civic improvement and of touristic value), the third special law in Venice's history, after that of 1938 and the financial measure no. 945 of 17 April 1948. The new Special Law imposed a deadline of 28 April 1958 for the adoption of a General Plan and corresponding Detailed Plans, clearly specifying that approval of the General Plan was dependent on the Detailed Plans being drafted at the same time. Thanks to the interest of the newly elected centre-left *giunta* or coalition, a *Comitato redazionale del Piano regolatore* (Supervisory committee) was quickly nominated.

Soon afterwards, on 9 June 1956, a competition was declared – a *Concorso nazionale di idee per l'impostazione del Piano regolatore generale del Comune di Venezia* (National competition for the implementation of the General town plan), for which the entries were to be delivered by 15 November 1957. There were thirteen projects submitted, among which five were awarded prizes: in first place the Amati-Pastor-Pastorini-Salvarani group; in second the Astengo-Coppa-Trincanato group; in third the Calabi-Gaffarini-Caiani-Paccagnella group; in fourth the Quaroni-Benvenuti-De Carlo (Adolfo) group; in fifth the Bellemo *et al.* group. All of them sought to provide Venice with new communications with the Lido and Marghera, or to improve the existing communications; also envisaged were an increase in port activities, the development of the urbanized area of the San Giuliano saltmarsh, and an in-depth study of the physical characteristics of the historic centre as a prelude to a more detailed restoration strategy (the Astengo-Coppa-Trincanato project makes references also to an unlikely "conservational restoration" on the basis of a map to a still quite inadequate scale of 1:200).

Suggestions forthcoming from these submissions were to be used for the subsequent drafting of the General Plan, which was drawn up in broad outline in 1958 by the *Comitato*, in collaboration with the *Centro Studi Economici* (Institute for economic research) of the University of Venice at Ca' Foscari and the *Unione delle camere di commercio delle Venezie* (Union of the chambers of commerce of the Veneto), and approved on 16 April 1958.

On the eve of the presentation of the General Plan to the *Comune*, there was a budget debate in which the ruling coalition fell apart. A government commissioner was appointed to run the council, and it was to him that the task fell of adopting the General Plan, on 20 March 1959, despite the fact that the Detailed Plans were missing and new building regulations did not yet exist. The *Provincia* or provincial administration, on examining the Plan, imposed a fifty per cent increase on the building targets, so that the additional 85,000 habitation units that had been anticipated became 152,000, considerably inflating the previsions for the San Giuliano area. The General Plan was then reviewed by the *Comitato*, which was unanimously opposed to the adjustments of the *Provincia*, but was forced nevertheless "to resign itself to not resisting, in general terms, acceptance of the provincial administration's ultimatum, simply in order to deflect from the outset the clear intention, in what others had proposed, of scuppering the result of long months of careful and dedicated study carried out by a qualified commission, that was legally constituted and legally operating; and above all in order not to impede later the expected return to normality and full development in the field of private housing in the municipality".

Thus the General Plan was able to progress: on 9 July 1958 it was approved by the provincial administration, and on 16 March 1961 by the *Consiglio Superiore dei Lavori Pubblici*, with a few reservations, overcome, after some alterations to the project, on 31 October 1961. A decree of 17 December 1962 ultimately ratified it. The final contents of the Plan embraced the idea of a new administration district between Piazzale Roma and San Basilio – an idea which was immediately scrapped – a series of new development areas and a general commitment to "strict conservation of the appearance of the city and to keeping the city alive in its traditional forms". To achieve this, Detailed Plans were required, for without them virtually no work was possible: and so there began a lengthy process, destined to come to an end only after the promulgation, in 1973, of a fifth Special Law, with the approval of the Detailed Plans the following year. In 1965 a *Commissione Tecnica per i Piani particolareggiati* (Technical commission for the Detailed Plans) was set up, and approved by the *Provincia* in June 1966. Shortly afterwards, the commission having produced no results, a fourth Special Law (no. 526 of 5 July 1966) laid down as a deadline for the approval of the new Detailed Plans the end of July 1968, and also made the General Plan effective, even in the absence of the accompanying detailed apparatus. In July 1968 the Detailed Plans had still not been drawn up, and Law no. 161 of 8 April 1969 granted a further year in which the Detailed Plans might be drafted, putting forward in their stead the *Piano di ricostruzione* (Reconstruction plan) of Law no. 1402 of 1951. Other extensions of time continued to defer the matter, prompting government intervention with the promulgation of the Special Law of 1973 (which will be considered in a later chapter), but by this time the problem of programming restoration projects had reached such proportions that it could not be dealt with solely by means of the Detailed Plans – or at least this was to be the argument put forward by the administrators. It would lead in the end on the one hand to the formal adoption of Detailed Plans that were practically useless, and on the other to the creation of what would later be called the Venetian 'legislative arsenal', an expression coined by the *assessore* or councillor for town planning for the period 1975–85, Edoardo Salzano.

While the affair of the Plans dragged on from 1956 to 1974 (or, from another point of view, to 1979, as it was not until then that the *Norme tecniche di attuazione* or technical guide to implementation were adopted), Venice gave over to degradation and speculation two whole decades of 'post-vacant' institutional anarchy. The results will be examined in later chapters, but it can be stated in advance that when at last the General and Detailed Plans were approved they were already obsolete and unusable, because they related to provisions, conditions and dynamics that were decades old. Of this the consequence was a call for more plans, more wrangling, more waste.

NOTES

Between 1998 and 2001 there was an important court case over the damage to the environment and to the health of the workers in the petrochemical complex at Marghera, one of the flagships of the Italian economy in the 1970s and 1980s. The executives of Enichem and Montedison (companies evolved from the earlier AGIP and Montecatini originally established in Marghera) were accused of criminal manslaughter and mass murder (in hundreds of cases of cancer caused by chloride of vinyl and PVC) and of environmental damage, the environmental defence group Greenpeace having brought a civil action during the course of the manslaughter trial. As early as 1971–72 a survey by the *Istituto di medicina del lavoro di Padova* (Paduan institute for health at work) of the health of children at a primary school in Mestre had produced shocking results: only fourteen out of 116 pupils had no disease or pathology, and 70% had pulmonary problems. In 1973 the *Ispettorato del Lavoro di Venezia* (Health and safety inspectorate of Venice) occasioned a great scandal by making it compulsory for all workers at Mestre to wear protective masks, given that there were scores – scores! – of escapes of toxic gas every year, and that cases of death by cancer induced by chloride of vinyl were already appearing. In 2001 all those accused were acquitted, on the grounds that Montedison and Enichem could not have known at the time of the toxic effects of their production and that they had responded in good time to new regulations. On the second count, of environmental damage such as poisoning the marine fauna and the acquifers, the court accepted that the industrial canals were polluted but, following the guidelines of the World Health Organization, held that they did not constitute a real danger to health; it was declared that the pollution had originated in an earlier period when there were no regulations governing environmental hazards, for these had not come into being until the 1970s and 1980s. To this trial and the tragedy at Vajont (see Notes to chapter 6) the Venetian actor and writer Marco Paolini has devoted two *orazioni civili* or public lectures, *Il racconto del Vajont* (1993) and *Parlamento chimico. Storie di plastica* (2002). See further most recently the exposé of S. Bettin and M. Dianese, *Petrolkiller*, Milan 2002. On 28 November 2002 an explosion, followed by a fire and the escape of a cloud of toxic gas, created panic amongst those living and working in Marghera. The plant concerned was that of Dow Chemical, owners of Union Carbide, the company responsible for the disaster at Bhopal in 1984.

Returning to restoration, the career of Ferdinando Forlati can be traced through the notes that appeared regularly in the annual periodical *Arte Veneta*, especially his work at St Mark's, and in several specific accounts, such as 'The work of restoration in San Marco', in O. Demus, *The Church of San Marco in Venice*, Washington, D.C., 1960; or *S. Giorgio Maggiore. Il complesso monumentale e i suoi restauri (1951–1956)*, Padua 1977. He also published more strictly technical reports, such as 'Problemi di restauro monumentale e la restituzione dell'Abbazia di San Giorgio Maggiore', in *Actes du XVII.me Congrès international d'histoire d'art*, The Hague 1955; or 'Metodi di restauro monumentale nuovi e nuovissimi', in *Atti del II Congresso internazionale del restauro*, Venice 1964–69.

Contributions that have opened up new ideas and horizons include Egle Renata Trincanato's text of 1948 dedicated to the less well-known, vernacular buildings of Venice, with the resonant title *Venezia minore*. At the same date the question of sanitary conditions was taken up again by experts in various institutions, among them R. Vivante, *I pianterreni inabitabili di Venezia. L'abitato di Mestre. Nuove indagini sulle condizioni igieniche delle abitazioni del Comune*, Venice 1948, and by architects: E.R. Trincanato, 'Salvaguardia e risanamento di Venezia', *Urbanistica*, 32, 1960. New directions for restoration were outlined in a series of conferences and studies leading to the drafting, in 1964, at the Second Congress of Architects and Technicians of Historic Monuments (Venice 25–31 May), of the Venice Charter, while the fashion for new technologies became ever more prevalent (see, for example, R. Ravà, 'Nuovi sistemi per la conservazione degli antichi edifici veneziani', *Rassegna dei Lavori Pubblici*, 11, 1959), and also new techniques of investigation in the project stage of operations: here the important text is that of S. Muratori, *Studi per un'operante storia urbana di Venezia*, Rome 1959, which indeed greeted the new dawn of 'typological' research and *ripristino tipologico*.

The tireless but widely ignored voice of Piero Gazzola, whose *Venise sombre lentement*, Paris 1965, appeared before the disaster of 1966, deserves greater recognition.

On the events and debate surrounding the General Plan (*Piano regolatore*) for Venice in the 1960s and 1970s see F. Benvenuti, 'La legislazione per i centri storici: l'esperienza veneziana', and E. Salzano, 'Produzione di piani a mezzo di piani', both in *Casabella*, 436, 1978, pp. 14–15 and 18–22.

For the context for the planning and management of *centri storici* in Italy there is E. Vassallo, *Centri antichi 1961–1974, note sull'evoluzione del dibattito*, constituting a special issue of the journal *Restauro*, 19, 1975.

The quotation in 7.1 is from C. Brandi, 'Marghera', in *A passo d'uomo*, Milan 1970. The citations in 7.2 are drawn respectively from R. Bonelli, 'Il restauro architettonico', in C. Brandi (ed.), *Enciclopedia universale dell'arte*, Milan 1972, *s.v.* 'restauro', and from E.R. Trincanato, 'Il restauro architettonico all'edificio' (on the Procuratie Nuove) and G. Perocco, 'Restauri e prospettive per Ca' Pesaro', both in *Bollettino dei Musei civici veneziani*, 2, 1960.

8 | 4 November 1966

8.1 Before and after the flood of 1966

From the general outlines accompanying the projects for the *Piano regolatore* (General Plan) submitted in the competition of 1956–57, and in particular from the one that accompanied the project that won second place (Astengo-Coppa-Trincancato), one gains the impression that strenuous efforts were being made to gain acceptance for a new approach to the cultural heritage from those active in the field. Some of these ideas had already become current in wider debate.

In the first place the growing need was felt for continuous and programmed action for the upkeep of monuments. Italian laws relating to the issue, nos. 1089 and 1497, formulated in 1939, guaranteed effective protection only to buildings of recognized artistic or historic value, even though Law no. 1089 theoretically allowed the extension of legal protection to any building. Although the object of protection was not specifically defined, Law no. 1497 marked a great step forward in stipulating that *Piani regolatori* could not be approved without the consent of the *Ministero dell'Educazione* (Ministery of education), and had to be drawn up under the supervision of the *Soprintendenza*: protection thereby officially became part of planning, even if it was not absolutely clear what should be and could be protected, or how it was to be done.

Secondly, the need was felt for the safeguarding of the artistic and environmental heritage on a completely new scale. At the end of the 1950s, the destruction of the built heritage that had been carried out and was still being carried out led to the birth of various associations (*Italia Nostra*, for example) described, rather pejoratively, as 'protectionist', to denunciation of the 'new vandals' by such notable figures as Roberto Pane and Antonio Cederna, and to the organization of conferences addressing the issues of the city and of urban planning, and particularly the problem of preserving historic centres.

It was only natural that during the period of reconstruction after the war the concerns of those active in the field and of their critics should have focused primarily on the problems inherent in single buildings to be restored. The discussion developed, from around 1950 onwards, into a heated debate on the co-existence or otherwise of new-built and old architecture in historic nuclei. The problem was presented at first mainly in formal terms, but in turn gradually stimulated a search for definitions and guidelines on the modern role of historic centres and in that light the problem of their preservation and re-use. This move towards a new approach to the pre-existing fabric, even though it did not succeed in preventing the the 'tertiary colonization' of the 'heart of the city' (as the historic centre was defined at the

Fig. 84

The *acqua alta* above differs from those of the
present day because it could still take the city by
surprise: these tourists cut off beneath the
Campanile in the Piazza were unable to make their
way to a drier place using *passerelle* or raised
footways that the city nowadays has ready for such
all too frequent occurrences.

The *acqua alta* of 4 November 1966, at 1.94 m
above mean sea-level, surpassed all previous known
(the first was recorded in 782) and has not (yet) been
repeated, although the number and magnitude of
acque alte has been increasing regularly. In the 1920s
there were 385 *acque alte* at least 60 cm above mean
sea-level, and in the 1990s there were 2464. In 2002
the city suffered 108 *acque alte* over 80 cm, but not
quite so many in 2003 and 2004.

International Congress of Modern Architecture held in 1951 at Hoddesdon), did lead neverthe-less to a significant step forward in the consideration of these problems, with the formation in 1960 of ANCSA or *Associazione nazionale per i centri storici e artistici* (National association for his-toric and artistic centres) and the creation of the *Carta di Gubbio* (Gubbio Charter).

One might have hoped that in Venice, where the issue of the geographical definition of the historic centre obviously did not arise, the newly developed theoretical ideas about ancient nuclei might have found instant application: at the time of the Gubbio conference (1960), the *Piano regolatore* was still work in progress, and through it there might have been promoted direct and far-reaching action in urban improvement and restoration, financed by the State and the local institutions under the guiding hand of the *Soprintendenze*. Yet, as we know, this qualitative leap did not take place: the General Plan ignored the new proposals, and its lack of substance, together with the deplorable absence of any other institutional initiatives, meant that Venice never did become the workshop of regeneration and conservation that it should have been and might have been.

Restoration nonetheless was continuing, even though a gulf had opened up between the technological and financial means available (there were many State subsidies for structural restoration and consolidation) and resources for the monitoring of the ends to which they were applied. It is evident from the record of building permissions that the number of works undertaken was multiplying dramatically, but they were carried out on the basis of outdated building regulations and the new and insubstantial General Plan. The usual purpose, which was almost always achieved, was to exploit the site value or to let prestigious premises to tertiary-sector companies and the wealthy. In any case, there was a notable increase in invest-ment in property in the city and – thanks also to the now steady decline of the population – an expanding stock of unlet housing, which, once prices had risen again, re-emerged on to the market in the 1990s.

In this situation, while laborious efforts, as we have seen, were being made to put together the Detailed Plans to accompany the General Plan, and to formulate a body of provisions and procedures that would permit management and restoration of its historic centre, Venice suf-fered enormous damage following the flood or *acqua alta* of 4 November 1966.

Acqua alta has always been an inevitable hazard in Venice, repeated at more or less regular intervals several times a year, especially during the winter months. The *acqua alta* of 4 November 1966 was disastrous not so much for the level the water reached, though this was exceptionally high, as for the length of time the high water lasted. For a whole day the city was submerged, without electric power or heating. The most serious consequence, however, was the leak of inflammable liquids from the tanks of central heating systems. Fuel oil, being lighter than water, was flushed out of tanks by the rising waters and then settled everywhere, marking with iridescent black trails the various stages in the waters' retreat.

In a city inured to walls permeated with water and salt, and to *intonaco* plaster detached from façades, the high water did not cause enormous structural destruction, except to edifices already seriously damaged and to external claddings already in a bad state of repair. The flood did, however, once more bring to notice problems that should have been tackled earlier, in particular the failure to maintain the city's buildings in a good state of repair as constantly as possible, and the failure to finance and to make preparations for operations at a high technical level at short notice. What first made itself felt was the lack of funds available for restoration, and indeed funds were the first thing the Venetians asked for. Hitherto, works undertaken by the private sector with State subventions (awarded after much effort and delay) or by the various ministries (whose activities were confined to monumental buildings) had been fairly limited in scope. After 4 November, in effect, every single building in the city was in need of immediate cleaning and repair, before the water, salt and fuel oil ruined walls and surfaces. Private residents were practically abandoned to their own devices, apart from contributions set aside by the *Comune* and the assistance provided by the staff of an office of works that was clearly unprepared and impotent faced with a catastrophe of this magnitude. As a consequence, there was a much higher tolerance of works undertaken by the private sector – for only the private sector was in a position to take significant action – than there should have been, and some things done were really questionable.

Nor was there in the years that followed any acceleration in planning action, or any significant technical or administrative development. On the other hand, monumental Venice increasingly became the recipient of quite lavish funding from all over the world, provided by specially constituted committees and fund-raising organizations, since the city was regarded no longer as the patrimony solely of Venetians, but as part of the cultural heritage of all. By an ironic twist of fate, this response exactly answered the hopes expressed thirty-five years earlier in the Athens Charter and reiterated in the manifesto declared by the Second International Congress of Architects and Technicians of Historic Monuments (25–31 May 1964), which, since it took place in Venice, is known as the Venice Charter (*Carta di Venezia*).

8.2 UNESCO and the Committees for Venice

It was only a few days after 4 November 1966, once the damage began to be tackled, that the gravity of the catastrophe in Venice was fully appreciated, for at first it had taken second place to the dismay aroused in Italy and the rest of the world by the terrible damage wrought on the same day by a devastating flood in Florence.

A debate then began that was destined to continue for many years and continues to the present day, on the relation between the problem of *acque alte* and the effect on the ecosystem of the lagoon of the works of man. It was realised that the dredging of new canals, the reclamation of saltmarshes, the creation of lagoon fishing grounds (*valli da pesca*) and the failure to maintain the former Republic's elaborate waterworks had undermined the regular functioning of the tides in the lagoon.

The reactions were in some cases incoherent: for example, blame for the catastrophe was ascribed to the Malamocco–Marghera canal (the 'tanker canal'), on which work had actually only just begun, and to its transfer of the excavated mud into the reclamation areas. Environmental organizations such as, for example, *Italia Nostra* that had in previous years endorsed the go-ahead for a second and a third industrial zone at Marghera, and for the 'tanker canal' (even criticizing the delays in the work on it), now for the first time looked at the lagoon from an ecological point of view, and began claiming that its ecosystem should be inviolable and was incompatible with industrial installations and twentieth-century policies for their development. Dredging for the 'tanker canal' was indeed suspended, and plans to expand the third industrial zone, and for a fourth and a fifth zone extending as far as Chioggia, were frozen soon afterwards, amid widespread controversy, by the Special Law of 1973. The regulation of the flow of the tides through the channels linking the lagoon to the open sea became a new engineering challenge, with various proposals being made for creating barriers capable of arresting major tidal surges.

However, the most pressing problem was the need to start work straightaway on repairing the entire city. The Italian Government, aware of the imbalance between the resources available and the huge task at hand, launched a worldwide appeal, which was formalized at the fourteenth session of the General Conference of UNESCO. UNESCO then launched an International Campaign for the Safeguarding of Venice, instigated and participated in the formation of an International Advisory Committee for Safeguarding Venice, and drafted a dramatic and unflinching *Report on Venice*, which was published in 1969. In 1967 UNESCO convened an International Meeting for the Protection of the Cultural Property of Florence and Venice, chaired by Sir Ashley Clarke. It funded the compilation of a list of buildings in danger and, after pressure from its director-general, René Maheu, opened an office in the city, made available by the Italian Government and run by Joseph Martin.

In 1973 UNESCO published the first edition of *Venice Restored*, in which were described all the works carried out since 1967 by the Italian and foreign committees. In the same year it became directly involved in commissions appointed by Italian government bodies, though without exercising any real power. At the same time, the Italian government requested the world's major financial bodies to cover without security a forecast expenditure of £200 million sterling in the value of the time. It had been an official of the *Banca Commerciale*, Raffaele Mattioli, who had first proposed, in 1971, a huge international loan, underwritten by banks and private companies, with UNESCO's guarantee, to finance works in Venice. The funds were indeed found and were put at the disposal of the Italian government, but they never arrived in Venice. They were used instead to cover the State's expenditure and the Italian budget deficit, as were also many billions of *lire* intended for Venice in the years that followed, as indignantly pointed out in foreign publications such as *The Sunday Times*.

In 1974, the support of the Council of Europe was added to that of UNESCO, and the

European foundation *Pro Venetia Viva* was instituted, which in turn founded the European Centre for the Training of Craftsmen in the Conservation of the Architectural Heritage, based in the Scuola di San Pasquale Baylon in the *sestiere* of Castello. In the same year, frustrated by the difficulty of taking action with any speed, by the inertia of the Italian Government and by the paucity of funds reaching Venice, UNESCO, in the course of the meeting of the International Advisory Committee, raised the possibility, later retracted, of closing its office in Venice. On the same occasion, the chairman, Sir Ashley Clarke, revealed that the Italian Government was quietly intending to include VAT at 12% on the bills for works met by funds collected abroad for restoration – from which invoices handled through UNESCO were exempted only from 1977. The International Advisory Committee met again in 1978, but did not do so again. The Italian government was responsible for calling these meetings. Why it did not do so again is not recorded.

UNESCO also laid down directives for restoration, which, however, were dangerously favourable towards the *ripristino* of dilapidated buildings, excepting their decoration. In the 1969 *Report on Venice*, the very brief chapter devoted to 'Restoration: Technical Aspects' states: "From the technical point of view, the restoration of buildings of historic and architectural value in a state of great deterioration is a prodigious undertaking. To guarantee structural stability, the simplest method would be to demolish and rebuild, but then the decorative elements would be at risk (not all sculpted friezes and surface claddings lend themselves to dismantlement and reconstitution). In any case, it has been possible hitherto to avoid such traumas, at least for *palazzi*, and even to adopt the best architectural interpretations and formal solutions." The language used here and the thinking behind it are very far removed from the much more cautious and judicious tone of the Venice Charter, and the International Advisory Committee's last session condoned some highly questionable examples of *ripristino*. However, UNESCO also organized a series of meetings for the definition of its recommended methodologies, with the cooperation of both the *Comune* and the University of Venice (which for some years had been carrying out detailed research in Venice's urban morphology and building typology), and to them invited as expert consultants the Italian Pier Luigi Cervellati, head of the vast project for the restoration of the centre of Bologna, the French Bernard Huet and the West German Wolfgang Wolters.

The international assistance organized for Venice certainly benefited from its co-ordination under the aegis of UNESCO, with all its prestige and influence, but the moving agents were primarily the dozens of committees and associations that were specially formed to gather funds for the restoration of the monumental buildings of Venice. Some initiatives were quite novel: for example, the International Fund for Monuments, founded by James A. Gray in 1965 to save the sculptures on Easter Island, formed a Committee for Venice which had begun work by 1969 (it restored the paintings of Tintoretto in the Scuola di San Rocco) and was able to raise significant funds in the following years, notably by arranging a discount card with which contributors could obtain reductions in hotels and restaurants in the United States. The International Fund for Monuments also launched a crusade against pigeons, whose droppings were erroneously held to be the primary source of damage to the stones of monuments: some 25,000 of them were caught, but this made little difference, and associations for the defence of the pigeons objected. So then a massive amount of food treated with contraceptives was distributed, again without appreciable results, because the pigeons inexplicably continued to reproduce. The British Venice in Peril Fund financed the restoration of the Porta della Carta of the Doge's Palace with funds largely raised by its chairman, Lord Norwich, from the Sainsbury Foundation (in other words, from supermarket profits) and by means of programmes on London Weekend Television. An anonymous German donor financed the restoration of the synagogues of the Ghetto. In another initiative of the Venice in Peril Fund, thanks to the enormous enthusiasm of its vice-chairman, Sir Ashley Clarke, urgent operations were undertaken on the endangered church of San Nicolò dei Mendicoli (opposite what is now the *Istituto Universitario di Architettura di Venezia*, the Venice University institute of architecture [IUAV], occupying the former cotton mill at Santa Marta). When the works were completed, a central heating system was installed. Its exhaust pipe was concealed, so as not to affect the external appearance of the church, but provoked such furious complaints from the inhabitants of the neighbouring houses that in the end it had to be allowed to emerge from the roof. The parish priest then changed the height of the altar without authorization, and for this was tried and condemned to pay a heavy fine, later suspended.

In less or more bizarre circumstances more than fifty different associations succeeded in financing at least one restoration operation in Venice. They brought to Venice not only money, but also an attitude of pragmatism, which meant that action was taken, but not infrequently precipitate action, taken without proper regard for the principles of conservation. One thinks, for example, of the initial operations for the static consolidation of the church of the Gesuiti (or Santa Maria Assunta), described by UNESCO in 1973 as the most unstable church in Venice, which were undertaken with funds from John McAndrew's Save Venice Inc. The works had hastily to be revised while in progress, thanks to an elderly American naval engineer, Robert Maccoun, who realised that serious mistakes were being made and drew attention to the inadequacies of the project. If problems of this kind were not infrequent in the first years of the emergency, that was also due to the relative autonomy of the international committees, who tended to employ on the work their own trusted technicians, non-Italians who sometimes had little familiarity with Venetian conditions. In some cases, this was a good thing, in as much as the particular skills and experience of outside professionals stimulated very useful discussions. One example is the research on the causes of the decay of stone and on the methodologies of cleaning, consolidation and protection of Venetian stone carried out by Kenneth Hempel, a restorer from the Victoria and Albert Museum in London, Giorgio Torraca and other researchers before the operations of the 1970s, in particular before the first restoration of the Porta della Carta of the Doge's Palace. A counter-example might be the cleaning of the stone revetments of many monuments with avant-garde techniques: many were sealed with irreversible heat-cured resins (the Loggetta of the Campanile, in 1972–74; the spiral staircase of Ca' Contarini del Bovolo, 1980–86; fig. 85), or with products that darkened their colours; in some cases concrete and reinforced concrete was even used (the chapel of San Saba in the church of Sant'Antonin, in 1968; the cloister of Santissima Trinità in the Convento dei Frari, in 1971–73; the Rialto Bridge, in 1973–74).

In many cases the restoration was supposed to produce a final resolution of the monument's problems, which justified resort to technologies of major impact. For example, the problem of the infiltration of water into the interior of a building was solved by creating impermeable underground cisterns (*vasche*), which necessitated entirely removing floors and their foundations and constructing platforms of reinforced concrete anchored to the ground with steel rods and sheathed in a coating resistant to sea-water; but the prior removal of floor and foundations was not always followed by their replacement (Scuola di San Giorgio degli Schiavoni, 1971–72; San Nicolò dei Mendicoli, 1972–73; Santa Maria del Giglio, 1970–73; Scuola Grande di Santa Maria del Carmine, 1972–76, 1979; Oratorio dei Crociferi, 1982–84). In order to protect buildings from the water walls were in some cases rebuilt to a height of two or three metres above their footing (Palazzo Fortuny, formerly Ca' Pesaro degli Orfei, 1971–74; San Nicolò dei Mendicoli, 1972–73; Oratorio dei Crociferi, 1982–84). Roofs, too, were replaced, sometimes preserving only the terracotta tiles (Italian Synagogue, 1974; Scuola Grande Germanica, or German Synagogue, 1975–79; San Stae, 1977–79), or their elements were even substituted with reinforced concrete (Scuola di San Pasquale Baylon, 1967–68). Partial substitution (San Zaccaria, 1967–82; Santa Maria dei Miracoli, 1969–77; San Martino, 1971–84; Scuola Grande di Santa Maria del Carmine, 1972–76, 1979; Levantine Synagogue, 1974–81) was more the exception than the rule.

Almost invariably, the attempt to eliminate the causes of deterioration led to the removal and replacement of fragile and decayed materials. At many sites the inside walls were totally replastered and the floors totally relaid (San Sebastiano, 1967; Santi Giovanni e Paolo, 1967–79; San Zaccaria, 1967–82; Madonna dell'Orto, 1968–70; Scuola Grande di San Giovanni Evangelista, 1969–81; Palazzo Barbarigo della Terrazza, 1970–71; the flooring of San Giovanni Crisostomo, 1973–74, relaid on asphalt; of the Levantine Synagogue, 1974–81; of the Squero, or boatyard, of San Trovaso, 1978–83; fig. 86). External *intonaco* rendering suffered the same fate (San Moisè, 1967–68; Santi Giovanni e Paolo, 1967–69; the Pietà, or Santa Maria della Visitazione, 1971–78; the Levantine Synagogue, 1974–81; San Stae, 1977–79). Only where significant quantities of original *intonaco marmorino* (a stronger plaster, mixed with marble dust) had survived was the resurfacing of façades only partial (Santa Maria della Salute, 1965–75; San Pietro di Castello, 1970–82; the Gesuati, or Santa Maria del Rosario, 1971–72, 1981; Santo Stefano, 1971–73; Scuola Grande di San Giovanni Evangelista, 1969–81).

Fig. 85 (left)
One of the more famous secrets of Venice, the Scala del Bovolo (literally, 'of the snail'), the outside staircase of the Palazzo Contarini del Bovolo, huge in its rather small courtyard, was restored in 1986 using heat-cured resins to seal the Istrian stone that flanks and lines the brickwork, a technique also used on the Loggetta beneath the Campanile in the Piazza. This technique, new at the time, is no longer favoured because it is not reversible.

Fig. 86
The *squero* or boatyard at San Trovaso in Dorsoduro is about the only one in the city or its surrounding islands that retains an old-fashioned aspect. Once there were hundreds of such yards, which, with their makeshift wooden sheds, were far from prepossessing to look upon even if they were pre-industrial and were not yet littered with rusting boilers, throughout the city and especially along the Riva degli Schiavoni. This one, dedicated to the making and repair of gondolas and other special Venetian oared craft, is now deliberately preserved, and indeed was restored from 1978 to 1983.

Likewise, frames and casements were substituted just about universally (Scuola di San Pasquale Baylon, 1967–68, 1970, 1976–77; Santa Maria dei Miracoli, 1969–77; Santa Maria del Giglio, 1970–73; San Pietro di Castello, 1970–82; San Pantalon, 1971; San Martino, 1971–84), and in some cases entire wooden partition walls (Scuola di San Giorgio degli Schiavoni, 1971–72; Arsenale, Portale di Terra or Land Gate, 1973–76, 1984).

Similarly, without compunction, other ancillary or insignificant decorative elements were removed, or buildings were 'cleaned up' (*rimessi in pristino*), or their parts dismantled and re-assembled (Redentore, 1971–73; San Martino, 1971–84; Arsenale, Portale di Terra or Land Gate, 1973–76, 1984; Torre dell'Orologio di Piazza San Marco, or Clocktower, 1975). A building restored with the funds of the world had to justify the world's expenditure in the eyes of the world, and had therefore to appear as new, splendidly new, better than it was before, and, implicitly, rescued once and for all from the passage of time.

In fact, as time went by, the international committees modified and nuanced their attitudes, especially as the *Soprintendenza* and the *Istituto Centrale del restauro* (Central institute for restoration) in Rome became more closely involved, usually managing, especially towards the end of the 1980s, to impose more cautious practices. Indeed more than a few of the international associations still active, it should be emphasized, have adopted conservationist methodologies in line with the current direction of the discipline, and in particular Venice in Peril has, from the 1990s, included minor architecture within its scope.

8.3 The role of the Soprintendenza
in the 'emergency' years

The restorations carried out by the *Soprintendenza* from 1959 until the promulgation of the Special Law of 1973 numbered around seventy. As already mentioned, for the most part they concerned churches and *campanili*, and only in a few cases were there works on secular buildings, and only on parts of these. Among the most important restorations were those completed on the Portale di Terra or Land Gate of the Arsenale, on the façade of the Scuola Grande di San Marco, on the Salone delle Cerimonie of the Palazzo Patriarcale and on the surroundings of Palazzo Pisani and of the *Istituto Manin* (formerly the Spanish Embassy). Operations most frequently encountered in *Soprintendenza* reports include the consolidation of walls, the restoration of external *intonaci*, stuccowork and stonework, the re-laying or repair of dilapidated roofing and the replacement of decayed or damaged *infissi* (jambs, lintels etc.), windows and casements.

The terminology of the reports still implies restoration focused on the recovery of original structures and forms, hidden or altered by subsequent interventions of one kind or another. The word *ripristino* is one that appears very frequently, not least because in the case of buildings in very poor condition, 'heavy' restoration, involving the substitution of large parts of the walls or the insertion of reinforced concrete into the thickness of the wall, required that the monument be stripped down to its structural components. Sometimes the procedure was a real and proper *smontaggio e rimontaggio* (dismantling and re-assembly) of parts of the building, which would begin with the removal (and sometimes total discard) of the 'skin' of the building – plasterwork, decorations, *infissi*, flooring etc. This was generally followed by consolidation, as a prelude to the succeeding reconstitution of the various parts of the building. Here the autopsy to which the building had effectively been subjected usually offered, inevitably, quite a large latitude for interpretation: arches, windows, cornices and stonework of all kinds that had been uncovered cried out to be 'repristinated', especially since what might have been the competing voices of former surfaces, layers or patinas on the building had been silenced. Whatever their right to existence, whatever their historical value, they had disappeared.

Among the most important operations conducted by the *Soprintendenza* following this procedure was the restoration of the former church of San Gregorio in 1967, which involved "the *ripristino* of the vault above the left apse, of the paving, of the plaster, of the *infissi* and other elements ... and the making good (*reintegrazione*) of the carved stonework of the apse windows". Similarly, the church of Santa Caterina de' Sacchi received "restitution to its former state" in 1967; Santa Marta "the restitution of apertures ... and the *ripristino* of large Gothic windows" in 1967; at the Madonna dell'Orto, already the arena of numerous restoration campaigns, "the fifteenth-century chapel was restored to its original forms" in 1969.

In general the practice was always to re-render totally, even though in Venetian tradition *intonaco marmorino* (plaster mixed with marble dust) was regarded as highly durable and expected to last a very long time, not as expendable or as requiring renewal. Notwithstanding, *intonaco marmorino* was removed and re-made at the churches of San Geremia (1965), San Sebastiano (1964), San Francesco di Paola (1967), Santa Maria della Salute (1968) and of the Patriarchal Seminary (1971) and of other buildings.

Even more common was the *ripristino* of ordinary traditional *intonaco* renderings, which brought with it a notable change of colour, as on the internal walls of the Ca' d'Oro, of San Lorenzo, San Giorgio Maggiore and Santo Stefano (1967), of San Moisè, San Sebastiano and Palazzo Pisani (1968), of Santa Maria del Giglio or Zobenigo (between 1970 and 1972), and of Sant'Andrea della Zirada (1971).

In other buildings again, a complete scraping down of the rendering was carried out in order to bring to light the original *marmorino* (at the Gesuati or Santa Maria del Rosario, 1971; Santa Maria del Giglio, 1972; and so on). Many decorative, painted and architectural elements were the subject of fairly radical restoration and making good (*reintegrazione*) (painting at Palazzo Pisani, 1965; plasterwork at San Nicolò da Tolentino, 1961, and the Caffè Florian, 1967; stucco cornices in the church of San Geremia, 1967; stonework in Santa Maria della Salute, 1967; and so forth).

More or less universally, repairs to brick walls were carried out using the *scuci-cuci* or 'unstitch-stitch' patching method (Ca' d'Oro, 1967; Santa Marta, 1967; Santo Stefano, 1970), and injections of liquid cement were also made (San Geremia, 1966; Santa Maria della Salute, 1967; etc.).

For the cleaning of plasterwork, stuccowork and stonework, for the most part ordinary tap water was used. Any making good was executed with traditional materials or materials with characteristics similar or analogous to those replaced or repaired. Many restorations were undertaken with effective conservation of the materials of the building: for example, at the *Istituto Manin*, plaster that had cracked and become detached from the supporting wall was consolidated and the painted surfaces were cleaned and stabilized, the missing parts being filled in with uniform neutral tones. Similarly, at Palazzo Pisani in 1968, the fine white stucco ornamentation was stabilized and cleaned, but the other *intonaci*, the flooring and the window glass were not given the same degree of consideration and were made good or replaced.

One other restoration merits a brief mention, that conducted between 1967 and 1978 at the Ca' d'Oro (figs. 50–52, pp. 90–91), already the site of unhappy operations in the past. Here, after the repairs to the brickwork mentioned above, "the marble claddings of the loggia were stabilized, and a complete overhaul of the marble facing was carried out, restoring with the absolute minimum of replacement the dentil borders of Verona marble round the apertures, consolidating the broken panels with adhesives and appropriate pastes, and after washing, treating the decaying Venetian-Byzantine friezes of Greek marble or similar and the Gothic capitals of the two loggias with a fluorosilicate solution applied by capillary absorption under vacuum". Unfortunately, one of the results of these operations, though there is little mention of it in the *Soprintendenza*'s report, was the complete loss of colouring on the loggia balusters, which have the colour today of dismal grey cement.

8.4 Restorations by the private sector; an overview

Institutions during these years acted on the basis of a completely different approach to that taken by the *Soprintendenza* or the *Comune* in the comparatively few projects they had undertaken in previous years: there was no longer any question of going in search of lost images of the former Serenissima. That was because Venetian identity had completely evaporated: the past was forgotten and unattainable, and the present seemed ever more bound into developments on the mainland. Never before had there been such a conspicuous renunciation of the entity of Venice, the abandonment of any attempt to keep alive its economic autonomy and its cultural and social vitality – worn down by Austrian rule in the nineteenth century, further weakened during the early twentieth century, but obliterated only in the 1960s. Venetians were being coaxed into exile, into emigration to the industrialized areas.

As a result there was no more of Venice to save than the physical remains of a phantom city that had been reduced to mere monuments, to an image that grew dimmer every day. Meanwhile the subsidence of the lagoon was growing ever more acute, bringing this problem

Fig. 87

In the typical Venetian *calle* of Piscina Venier in the parish of San Vio in Dorsoduro two kinds of plasterwork or *intonaco* are in stark contrast – in the foreground the yellows and reds that are becoming so prevalent in the city, even though there is no tradition for them, and the immemorial *marmorino*-style russet or plum pink of the building closing off the street. The much brighter colours, obtained in plaster that is no longer lime-based as it had always been, have transformed the city in the space of a decade. Is there some reaction against a sense of decay, a desire to scrub the picturesque, or Guardiesque, out of view?

Figs. 88, 89

How should Venice look? Should it be preserved with the peeling, run-down, faded, quietly decaying walls that until recently could be seen everywhere unrepainted, inherited, in many cases, from a surprisingly distant past, or should it be renovated, spruced up, cleaned up, replastered and freshened? Clearly historic *intonaco* should be preserved if it can be preserved; otherwise tact is required, but is increasingly less in evidence. Modern mixtures for plaster are no longer lime-based, and as a result they take on often shockingly bright colours that are alien to Venetian tradition and plainly unsuitable. All over the city, it seems, venerable houses are being daubed and decked out as if they were seaside cottages on a beach – they are being made to look, indeed, like the fishermen's dwellings on Burano or elsewhere in the lagoon, where the use of stronger colours has been established for some time.

Above left, houses near Campo San Barnaba (at Sotoportego del Casin dei Nobili) in Dorsoduro show contrasting *intonaci* – one bright, clean and full of colour, the other the older and muted. (Since the photograph was taken this house, too, has been replastered with a non-lime-based harshly coloured *intonaco*.) Above right, the traditional and the modern can blend harmoniously in Venice, as an iron bridge inserted in the late nineteenth century throws its shadow atmospherically on a peeling wall bounding the Rio Santa Margherita: the wall could be – should be – repaired and maintained without being obliterated by modern colours.

Figs. 90, 91
Despite its busy location, outside the entrance to the Accademia Galleries and beside the Accademia Bridge, the little inlet remaining of a canal by the Palazzo Querini in Dorsoduro had a peaceful, uniquely Venetian and surely befitting atmosphere in 1989 (above). The replastering of the wall has given way to a harsher, brighter colour scheme no longer recognizing its own antiquity in 2003 (below). Since the wall, bordering the former British consulate (hence the security camera), had been attacked with paint bombs, it undoubtedly needed recovering, but ideally it should have been done in such a way as to preserve the older colours and textures.

to the fore and eclipsing the many others; it began to take precedence, in terms of urgency, over anything else. Certainly the cry of alarm over Venice's sinking led to a serious under-estimation of the importance of using correct procedures in restoration.

It was predictable that the saving of a Venice that was sinking should be entrusted *a priori* to technology. Technology would be capable of radical intervention, technology would be able rapidly to halt the degradation of the lagoon. It was also not surprising that the legis-lation and the various Plans (if they can be called plans) should be interpreted with excessive, even arrogant, flexibility, in the face of new and urgent circumstances. Characteristic of this period are ambitious engineering schemes on a lagoon-wide scale on the one hand, and restorations dependent on the use of reinforced concrete on the other. If, for instance, we leaf through Eugenio Miozzi's voluminous work *Venezia nei secoli* (Venice through the ages), besides comparative photographs from the nineteenth century and the early 1960s that reveal strik-ingly the degree to which the city had sunk, we find a proposal to arrest the subsidence by the creation, underground, of counteracting pressurized air pockets. This scheme or another might indeed have a theoretical value, but none of them took into consideration the historical events that had led to the current situation and from which one might arrive at a deeper understanding of it. In fact almost all of them remained ideas on paper, partly because the suspension of indiscriminate draining of the water table through artesian wells was sufficient to reduce the subsidence of the city dramatically.

On the other hand, as far as the upkeep of the heritage of existing buildings was con-cerned, the use of reinforced concrete, in the pattern of the works undertaken on the Fondaco dei Tedeschi, the Ateneo Veneto and San Lorenzo, soon appeared to the private sector as the most economic and efficient solution to the deterioration of property. Reinforced concrete is undoubtedly inexpensive, it can be used with great flexibility, and it makes it possible to re-construct the structural frame of a building in a very short time; furthermore, when used in beams inserted in the thickness of the wall (*in rottura di muro*) it is without question capable of blocking rising damp caused by the capillary absorption of lagoon water. And so, even if it had considerable drawbacks, as has already been pointed out, the availability of concrete for building restoration had the effect of encouraging a considerable number of private landlords to undertake such work. Indeed never before, except when so many convents were converted in the early nineteenth century, had there been such a proliferation of worksites so techno-logically similar to one another.

Files kept in the archives of the *Magistrato alle Acque* (Water authority), relating to hundreds of works carried out over these years, bear eloquent witness to the volume and extent of the restorations conducted by private operators in the 1960s and 1970s. Sampling these, we dis-cover that three main procedures seem generally representative of the building work of the time: the use of beams and vertical partitions or other reinforced concrete structures inserted into the brickwork or in substitution of it; the partial or total rebuilding (not always justified)

Figs. 92, 93

Though it retains its attractive site in the back reaches of Dorsoduro and its magnificent windows, and, inside, its picturesque courtyard and outside staircase, the Palazzo Ariani (or Cicogna or Ariani-Cicogna) has suffered quite drastic restoration, as could be guessed from its scrubbed look, or from the corrected straightness of its horizontal and vertical members, or from the uneven colours of its exposed brickwork, betraying replacements by the *scuci-cuci* method. A nineteenth-century photograph shows the state of disrepair to which the palace had been reduced. Inevitably the palace has lost further patina having been turned to institutional use, being now part of the *Istituto Universitario di Architettura di Venezia*. What may look like a satellite dish bottom left is, however, a mirror for the use of boat traffic.

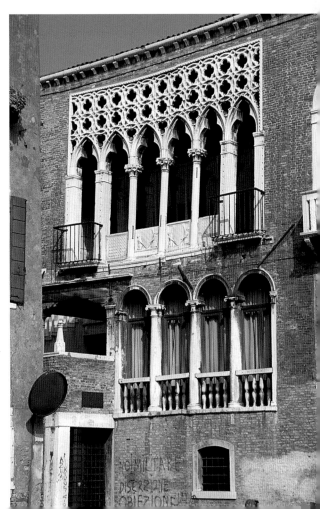

of brick walls using the *scuci-cuci* method; and the substitution of wooden floors with new tile-lintel floors or with other materials at odds with Venetian building traditions.

In some cases, these interventions were no more than piecemeal, as at Palazzo Ariani (figs. 92, 93) or in Campo Due Pozzi (a restoration project carried out by the *Soprintendenza*; figs. 94, 95), where the buildings were dismantled in sections and reassembled in order to correct sagging and misalignment. In other residential buildings, floors with 500 kg load-bearing capacity were laid (more than double what was necessary), wooden beams were replaced with steel ones; or entire floors were rebuilt, as in the Palazzo Vendramin on the Giudecca (figs. 96–100), where the roof, the top floor and the walls of the ground floor were completely demolished and rebuilt.

The most disturbing examples of a truly improper use of modern technology in Venice are to be found in three interventions, on buildings in San Polo (nos. 1808–11), in Campo Santa Maria del Giglio (San Marco no. 2467; fig. 101), and on Palazzo Morosini in Canaregio. In the first case, a four-storey building, foundations were laid measuring between 2.5 and 2.8 m in width and about 1.8 m in depth, imposing on ground that was already sinking a very considerable, unjustified load; in the other two cases, the buildings were completely gutted, retaining only their façades, and rebuilt with walls and partitions in reinforced concrete.

One could list dozens of similar cases throughout Venice, documented examples of a practice that continued at least until the approval of the *Norme tecniche d'attuazione* (Technical

Figs. 95, 96
A fourteenth-century house in campo Due Pozzi, Castello no. 2599, is interesting as a rare surviving example of more modest architecture from such a distant period; it is not, however, either as interesting or as pretty as it was before the late 1960s (see left), when it was demolished and rebuilt under the aegis of the *Soprintendenza*. Indeed nothing now is really medieval about the house except its abstract form, echoing, with straightened alignments and consolidated masonry, that of its vanished *doppelgänger* on the same spot. This unfortunate, even tragic, result is a reflection and consequence of the 'typological' approach that was at its height in the 1960s and is still enshrined in Italian heritage legislation: the entity of the house was deemed to consist in its dimensions, its spatial dispositions, its voids and solids and its use, rather than in the physical materials of which it was built. There is no reason to suppose that the medieval house, repaired rather than rebuilt, would not have been able to house inhabitants as happy and as well provided for as those presently in occupation.

Figs. 96–100

The Palazzo Vendramin (on the left), a fifteenth-century Gothic palace on the Giudecca, may appear still to be just that, but behind the façade and its characteristic four-light window there is little of the original. Every element of the palace, including the four-light windows and the arches of the courtyard (see right), was dismantled in the 1960s; the façades were retained or remounted, while the rest of the building was rebuilt, using new materials, which were regarded as superior, more economic and more convenient. Such an approach is undeniably destructive, however. Beside the Palazzo Vendramin is the late seventeenth-century stone-faced Palazzo Mocenigo.

guide to implementation) of 1979, which sanctioned such total make-overs only when carried out using traditional techniques and materials. It was only then that the indiscriminate and inappropriate use of reinforced concrete ceased, even if static exigencies have often since required relaxation of the ban. Reinforced concrete, to say it again, while useful in particular circumstances, so much so that it was recommended even in the Athens Charter of 1931, was completely out of place in Venice, where an age-old building tradition, unusual but entirely in keeping with the particular characteristics of its site, had always favoured the use of elastic structures, of which the various parts do not rigidly lock into each other, but are free to 'move' – as a principle apparently impossible, but in practice an effective and versatile

Fig. 101
Though one would not know it walking through the *campo* of Santa Maria del Giglio, the apparently fifteenth-century *palazzo* San Marco no. 2467 is a mere façade, behind which there is a building constructed entirely in reinforced concrete.

Fig. 102 (right)
The quite small cloister of Sant'Apollonia, tucked away inside a sixteenth-century building behind San Marco, is the only example of a 'mainland' Romanesque architecture in Venice – but what one sees today is the result of a very extensive restoration of 1967–70.

approach, if the building was properly maintained. Such technological mismatching is one more emblematic consequence of the break in Venetian autonomy and continuity occasioned by the Fall of the Republic nearly two centuries before.

One more illustrative example of the use of reinforced concrete, to very different effect, was an important restoration for which a private body engaged the services of *Soprintendente* Ferdinando Forlati. For its proprietor, the *Fabbriceria* of San Marco, Forlati undertook the restoration of the cloister of Sant'Apollonia (fig. 102) from 1967 until 1970. As mentioned above, this Romanesque cloister, one of the oldest in Venice, had been subject to works in the past, which had involved raising the level of the floor, erecting buttresses in the middle of the court to counteract movement in the east wall, and the occlusion of many of the arches of the arcade. Forlati's aim was to restore the building not to its original state but to the way it must have looked in 1492, when, according to historical records, it was ceded to the Republic.

To restore the building to "its former glory", Forlati rebuilt parts of the walls using the *scuci-cuci* or patching method and inserted reinforced concrete joists, injecting cement for consolidation. The floor of the cloister was to be restored to its original level, which would inevitably lead to flooding, given that through subsidence over time the cloister had sunk

almost to mean water level. So an impermeable tank was to be installed beneath the new floor level, anchored to the foundations of the building – except that the building did not actually have any foundations, and Forlati had to create them from scratch, by inserting piles of rein-forced concrete that were attached to the walls by means of girders and interlocking struts, all made of reinforced concrete.

These undoubtedly were decisions informed by good sense and professional expertise, and they demonstrate that the discriminating use of new technologies could help to resolve previously unsurmountable problems. The judiciousness of Forlati's restoration is also demonstrated by the very few concessions made to *ripristino* and replacement: a so-called accretion (*superfetazione*), an entire floor built in the nineteenth century, was retained, although its very large apertures were removed in order to restore the original small square windows. The nineteenth-century staircase was also preserved and so were the exposed beams, al-though the ceiling they had supported was replaced with a platform of reinforced concrete, thus relieving them of any load-bearing function.

Seemingly the times were ripe for change, and such model projects would now tilt the balance towards conservation rather than restoration in the old sense. In fact this change of outlook hardly took hold in Venice until 1980, and even then would be implemented on a limited scale. Until then, and also afterwards, one is faced with lost opportunities, with *immobilismo*, with funds made available but not properly used, with laws that were not applied and laws that were not applicable, with all the dishonesty and malpractice inevitable under an urban management that lacked all unity and coherence. Increasingly, the bias of this management would be linked to competing political interests.

NOTES

The dramatic events immediately consequent on the *acqua alta* of 1966 were reported and discussed in the media of the entire world. There followed a phase in which the problems of the lagoon and of the organization of recovery and restoration were studied, which culminated in a publication by UNESCO, *Report on Venice*, Milan 1979. Once the shock of the tragedy had been overcome criticisms made themselves heard, in particular regarding the provision for the emergency and its management; see the book by the investigative journalists Stephen Fay and Phillip Knightley, *The Death of Venice*, London 1977 (which was also published in Italian). There is, furthermore, a rich bibliography covering the activities of the committees for Venice and of the *Soprintendenza* in the twenty years after 1966, among which may be noted: UNESCO, *Venise restaurée*, Paris 1973; *Venezia restaurata: 1966–1968. La campagna dell'UNESCO e l'opera delle organizzazioni private*, Milan 1986; Soprintendenza ai Beni Ambientali e Architettonici, *Venti anni di restauri a Venezia*, Turin 1987, and, most recently, Italian National Committee of UNESCO, *UNESCO for Venice. International campaign for the safeguarding of Venice (1966–1992). Review of results*, Rome s.d. [1992].

The foreign and Italian committees active in Venice from 1966 are the following: America-Italy Society of Philadelphia (USA), Amici della Basilica dei SS. Giovanni e Paolo, Amis genevois de Venise (Switz), Arbeitskreis Venedig der Deutschen Unesco-Kommission, Association France-Italie, Associazione Amici dei Musei e Monumenti Veneziani, Associazione per la Conservazione del Patrimonio Culturale degli Armeni a Venezia, The Australian Committee for Venice, Comité belge pour la sauvegarde de Venise, Venise aux étangs de Bruxelles (B), Canadian National Commission for Unesco, Comitato dei Veneti per Venezia, Comitato internazionale per la conservazione e la tutela dell'antico Arsenale, Comitato Iraniano per Venezia, Comitato Italiano per Venezia, Comitato Italo-Bavarese per la Difesa della Gondola, Comitato per il Centro Storico Ebraico di Venezia, Comité Dante Alighieri de Aarau (Switz), Comité du Québec, Comité français pour la sauvegarde de Venise, Comité luxembourgois pour la sauvegarde de Venise, Comité national iranien d'entraide à la ville de Venise, Committee to Rescue Italian Art (USA), Comité San Marco (F), Dansk Venetia Komite, Deutscher Koordinierungs-rat Frankfurt, Deutsches Studienzentrum in Venedig, Fondation 'Pro-Venezia' (Switz), Fondation Singer-Polignac, Fondazione Ercole Varzi, Fondazione Venezia Nostra, Friends of Venice – Dallas (Texas), Gladys Krieble Delmas Foundation (USA), International Committee for the Safeguarding of Venice and the Great Wall of China (USA), International Fund for Monuments (USA), Italia Nostra, Italian Art and Archives Rescue Fund (GB), Italian Committee – Toronto, Rallye San Marco, Samuel Kress Foundation, Save Venice Inc. New York, Società Dante Alighieri, Stichting Nederlands Venetie Comité, Stifterverband für die Deutsche Wissenschaft, Swedish Committee 'Pro Venezia', 'Venedig lebt' (A), Venetian Heritage Inc., Venice European Centre for the Trades and Crafts of the Conservation of the Architectural Heritage, Venice in Peril Fund (GB), Venice International Foundation, World Monuments Fund (USA), Zonta International Venice. Many of these are still active, and still, together with local entities, raise funds for the restoration both of buildings and of works of art.

An important publication in English (much of it contributed by Italian authors) describing the 'present state' of Venice was a special number of *Architectural Review*, CXLIX, no. 891, May 1971, 'Venice: Problems and Possibilities'.

After years of debilitating controversy there is a definitive plan for the defence of the lagoon against excessive tides (for these see the website www.comune.venezia.it/maree). The direction, coordination and control of its implementation has been entrusted to a committee, known as the *Comitatone*, set up by the Special Law no. 798 of 1984, which is chaired by the *Presidente del Consiglio dei Ministri* and formed by various different bodies with different remits – including, of course, the *Magistrato alle Acque*. The defence of the lagoon is to be based on a system of floodgates known as MOSE (*MOdulo Sperimentale Elettromeccanico*) that has been developed since 1988 by the *Consorzio Venezia Nuova*, founded in 1982 and working with the *Magistrato alle Acque* since 1984; at that date the *Consorzio* was appointed the executive agent of the *Ministero delle Infrastrutture e dei Trasporti – Magistrato alle Acque di Venezia*, as provided by article 3 of the law of 1984, for the execution of operations for the protection of Venice and its lagoon (which by the same decree was made the responsibility of the State). The *Consorzio* is a joint venture of national companies, local enterprises and institutions. For further bibliography see Notes to chapter 11 below.

The reports on the restorations undertaken by the *Soprintendenza per i monumenti di Venezia* in 8.3 are taken from *Arte Veneta*, 1967 and 1968, in the section devoted to restorations, *s.v.*

9 | The Special Laws of 1973

9.1 The 'legislative arsenal'

The *acqua alta* of 1966 marked the beginning of a new cycle in Venice. The city's destiny acquired an international dimension, of which the first consequence, already mentioned, was the influx of extraordinary financial resources for the restoration of *palazzi*, works of art and the lagoon environment. The second consequence was a long and damaging power struggle to establish who was to control the funds and resources available, and how they should be used. Who is in charge in Venice is a question that has still not been settled. One notable recent battle revolved around the controversial threat of the *Soprintendenza*, following the promulgation of the Special Law of 1983, to invoke its power to place the entire built heritage of the historic centre under a protection order; another around the so-called *Decreto Galasso* (Galasso decree), which would have provided the authority to exercise very tight control over all building activity in the lagoon area through a protection order banning any building until it might be granted approval under an awaited *Piano paesistico* (Environmental plan).

A significant development, following the disaster of 1966, was the promulgation of the Special Law for Venice no. 171 of 1973, which was intended finally to settle the issue of the *Piani particolareggiati* (Detailed plans) and the *Norme tecniche di attuazione* (Technical guide to implementation) which had been dragging on for some ten years. It imposed, for the first time in Italy, building regulations that decisively shifted the balance of power towards the public sector. There was now a great deal of scope for far-reaching control over building operations in the city; on the other hand, it proved impossible to establish this control. There was a desperate attempt to establish regulations, parameters, frames of reference, justifications, authorities and powers. New laws, seemingly ever more paralysing, were added to old, and new powers were created alongside existing powers. There was nothing new about this: these Lampedusan overtones are one of the constant features of the Venetian story. We find them in all the various stages of evolution through which Venice has passed in its transformation from a city of commerce and canals to a city of streets and poverty, an evacuation zone, a suburb of Marghera, a village of displaced persons, an ailing city, a theme-park city for tourists.

By the 1970s, Venice, despite itself, had a new role, that of testing-ground for the application of laws and regulations produced by a new culture of town-planners (known in Italy as the *cultura degli urbanisti*). For years, this culture effectively denied Venice a modern existence. The city became marooned in bureaucracy, in which new and old, true and false, action and paralysis were issues that become meaningless in the face of meta-languages that seemed only to get lost in themselves, heedless of any practical, specific requirement. It was the *ars moriendi* of a city asphyxiated by the loss of its own role.

Never before had Venice been such a 'problem', but never before had there been such determination to turn the city into an object without a life of its own, regulated and sustained by legislation that might as well have come from outer space. The object of so many studies and analyses, it had imposed on it sterile, restrictive procedures when what it suffered from was not lack of regulation but lack of motivation, lack of purpose.

In the following chapter we will attempt to disentangle the complexities that gave rise to this state of affairs, and to make sense of the legislative material and the restorations carried out between 1973 and 1988, when this book first appeared. My theme will be, once again, the frequently culpable failure of the public authorities to exert any influence in the face of the widespread rape of the area, despite all these laws designed to prevent precisely that.

9.2 Legislation and planning:
the Comune's *'Detailed Plans'*
It was only with the promulgation of the Special Law no. 171 of 16 April 1973 that Venice received any satisfactory clarification of executive procedures governing works of restoration and construction or reconstruction in Venice. This fifth special measure for Venice was in fact the first that meaningfully addressed the preservation of its environment and of its built heritage. It was supplemented by a ratified decree, no. 791 of 20 October 1973, entitled 'Interventions for purposes of restoration and conservational repair in the island city of Venice, the islands of the Lagoon and the historic centre of Chioggia' – the sixth Special Law, intended to clarify particulars and specify operative procedures.

These laws raise important issues that deserve to be examined at greater length and in more detail, and can only be briefly stated here. The first point is that they reflect a structural anomaly inherent in Italian political history, the tendency to resort too readily to special legislation, regarding ordinary legislation as inadequate to deal with specific problems. It is true that urgent situations may arise requiring special action, especially to secure funding that otherwise would take too long to be allocated. Unfortunately, however, the Italian record in this sphere, not only as regards Venice, but also for natural disasters such as earthquakes and floods, has long been one of failure to follow up the special intervention with an effective distribution and management of resources and engagement of the political and bureaucratic machine – with perhaps one memorable exception, the reconstruction that followed the terrible earthquake in Friuli in 1976.

In Venice this syndrome has recurred chronically, undermining the constitutional operation of the local administration. So much was observed notably by Edoardo Salzano, *Assessore all'urbanistica* (Councillor for town planning) for the *Comune* of Venice, in a debate that took place in the pages of *Casabella*, the leading Italian architectural magazine, in 1978. He denounced as "... perverse, reactionary and historically outdated both in its approach and in its practical consequences the requirement of creating for Venice a proper 'special regime', characterized not only by the massive intrusion of the central authorities in matters generally entrusted to the independent decision-making of the local body, but also – which is less serious in principle, but more deleterious in practice – by a confused and paralysing overlap of power between the central bodies of the State and the more local levels of administration, the Region and the *Comune*".

Secondly, the political class that resorted to special laws at the same time often included in their rigid and paralysing regulations provision for exceptions, interpretations, waivers and respites of the kind precisely that the laws were meant to prevent, which meant that resources and funding were squandered or were not used, with consequent implications of corruption and complicity. Thirdly, Italian laws, which are nearly always issued as decrees, as decisions made by the government, as such are seldom the outcome of proper political and social debate, and they have consistently delegated to subsequent laws yet to be drafted the task of specifying exactly how they are to be applied. This gives rise, as we have seen, to delays and legislative vacuums destined to drag on for years, if not for ever. Needless to say, these situations have been exploited by those who stand to benefit from the absence of controls or the failure to implement them. Worse than that, they have engendered in Italian society such a generalized lack of faith in the legislature that there have frequently been calls for deregulation or for hybrid and inappropriate forms of decentralization or devolution. Apparent liberalism of this kind has been skilfully exploited by the country's economically emergent and dynamic groups on terms that would have been unacceptable in any other Western country. These are quintessentially Italian anomalies. As Stephen Fay and Phillip Knightley, investigative reporters for *The Sunday Times*, wrote in a ground-breaking exposé of 1966, published as *The Death of Venice* in 1976: "Politics in Italy *are* different, and politics in Venice ... are unusual even by Italian standards".

Even from this brief outline it is evident that an analysis of recent legislation in Venice is driven by the question of the relation between the central goverment and local government. While intervention from above, in Venice, has often proved disproportionate, mistimed, paralysing or simply useless, it is nevertheless significant that one of the primary, fundamental aims of the Special Law of 1973 was to try to remedy the culpable failure of a local administration that had perpetuated the chronic lack or inadequacy of measures that would allow the efficient planning of building operations. Indeed, it was due to the Special Law that the thirteen Detailed Plans for the historic centre were finally adopted on 31 December 1974. Until this date, as we have seen, Venice did not have any Detailed Plans, and this meant in effect that it was impossible to carry out any works through the usual procedural channels that set out guidelines and ensure respect for the regulations. What served in place of the Detailed Plans were in fact the old *Piano di risanamento* (Sanitary improvement plan), dating from as long ago as 1939, and the obsolete *Piano di ricostruzione* as defined by Law 1402 of 27 October 1951.

However, the main effect of the forcing through of the Detailed Plans by the Special Law of 1973 was to reveal the inadequacy of both the General Plan and the Detailed Plans to provide a legislative basis for the regulation of building and restoration in the historic centre. Seeing this, those responsible were confronted with two alternatives – either to make a considerable number of amendments to the apparatus at their disposal or to overcome the limitations of the Detailed Plans by creating a further apparatus, whether *ex novo* or on the basis of existing regulations. The choice fell on the second option, which therefore allowed (after deferment under Regional laws no. 13 of 1972 and no. 3 of 1974) the reasonably prompt adoption of the thirteen Detailed Plans, on 31 December 1974, although approval by the Regional administration would be delayed until 1979. But what did the Detailed Plans do? Nothing more than divide the area of Venice into zones, following the General Plan and the old *Piano di risanamento*. Certainly the Special Law confirmed the inviolability of the Detailed Plans, but in doing so it effectively made projects for restoration and redevelopment subject to the *Comune*'s programmes relating to them (article 13); and, partly with the intention of expediting their compilation, it did not insist that any clear indications be given in them to determine what exactly might or might not be done, for the *Piano di comparto* (Plan for designated building units) envisaged by the general Law no. 1150 of 1942 was assigned to deal with specific projects. Law no. 1150 of 1942, however, refers to the *Piano di comparto* in these terms: "... a municipality may proceed, on approval of Detailed Plans, to the formation of sectors consisting of building units including areas not yet built on and constructions to be converted with special constructions" (*sic*).

In the legislation of 1942 the designation of building units was an exceptional instrument, whereas in Venice it became generally applicable, without ceasing to be an executive measure, which made it entirely dependent on further definitions in other instruments. These were, again, the Detailed Plans and also the *Piani di coordinamento dei comparti edificatori* (Plans for the co-ordination of the building units), which were drawn up by the *Comune* precisely in order to render more specific the very vague and general provisions of the Detailed Plans. Having begun life as the *Progetto di coordinamento dei comparti edificatori*, the *Progetto* became the *Piano di coordinamento*, at the suggestion of the *Comune* of Venice, under the terms of Regional Law no. 55 of 9 September 1977. It was hardly more incisive than the Detailed Plans. The city was subdivided into 405 zones, each with its own *Piano di coordinamento*, within which the minimum units, in other words the *comparti*, or building units, were to be identified, as envisaged by article 13 of the Special Law: these *comparti* corresponded more or less to every component part of the city, and therefore numbered several thousand.

Behind the tortuous procedures outlined above, described by Salzano as "the production of plans by means of plans", lay the fundamental vacancy of the Detailed Plans. What Venice ended up with, as Feliciano Benvenuti observed, was the creation of "two planning measures, the General Plan and the Detailed Plans, and two executive project measures, the *Piano di coordinamento* and the *Piano di comparto*", existing side by side; however, none of these measures embodied the necessary independent power to modify the terms of the measure from which it derived, and once again this led to a process that served more to hinder building operations than to programme their implementation.

There was a clear contradiction in the *Comune*'s position: on the one hand it deplored the inadequacy of statutory measures and the unwelcome meddling of central government, while on the other hand it consciously tolerated or contributed to the proliferation of such measures, driving a process by which all building operations became subject if not to its control then certainly to its bureaucracy.

The basic sequence was as follows: State law, of which provisions are generalized and difficult to apply; development by the local administration of new measures (not alternative measures – that is no longer possible) intended to make the situation workable (this is the stage of regulatory gridlock, which becomes an excuse, and of recourse to measures no longer involving planning as such but improvising); the election of left-wing administrations, with a consequent emphasis on programmes and therefore of plans; the inevitable reaffirmation of the impracticability of the legislative apparatus, whence the impossibility of carrying out the programmes; finally, extensive recourse to compromise or to radical action (such as the *Decreto Galasso*, the proposed general conservation order).

In this complex scenario, many of the politicians' actions and declarations take on a decidedly ambiguous complexion, because they never cease to be involved in an unresolved conflict between a woeful Italian tradition, in this sphere, of non-government and non-laws, and a moral position that opposes this tradition – but does not have the strength or the means to distance itself from it completely, and ends up dissipating itself, producing weak and indeterminate results.

9.3 Restorations under the Special Laws of 1973

Having briefly surveyed the premises of Special Laws nos. 171 and 791 of 1973, let us summarize their contents, or at least their pertinent aspects. Excepting those relating to buildings of monumental, historic or artistic interest or for public use, restoration and conservational repair in Venice and the lagoon area were subject to the *Piani particolareggiati* (Detailed Plans) and the *Piani di coordinamento*, which the *Norme tecniche d'attuazione* (Technical guide to implementation) of the Detailed Plans specified as "the exclusive initiative of the municipality" (no. 171, article 19, paragraph 1). For monuments, *"restauro conservativo"* or conservational restoration (as defined in no. 791, article 4, paragraph 2) was always permitted; this extraordinary oxymoron derived from the conflation of two mutually exclusive definitions given in the *Norme tecniche*, *restauro* and *risanamento conservativo* (conservational repair).

Works were to be organized according to the *comparti edificatori* (building units); they were to be of a unitary nature and tend towards "the conservation of the structural and typological characteristics of the buildings within [the unit]" (no. 171, article 13, paragraph 3).

A scheduled programme was to establish the path of the works and the necessary funding over a period not exceeding three years, setting the priorities to be observed in the compiling of the *Piani di coordinamento* (no. 171, article 21, paragraph 1, and no. 791, article 3, paragraph 1). The law also required the compilation of a *Piano comprensoriale* (District plan) (no. 171, article 2) and the establishment of a supervisory commission, the *Commissione di Salvaguardia* (Commission for the protection of Venice), consisting of eighteen members, including the chief medical officer of the *Provincia*, the *Magistrato alle Acque* (Head of the Water authority) and the *Soprintendente ai monumenti*, who each had a power of veto; their task was to rule on the merit of projects proposed by the *Comune* or as modified to comply with the *Piano comprensoriale* (no. 171, article 6).

Within sixty days of the law coming into force, a list was to be drawn up by the *Soprintendenza* of "buildings of monumental, historic and artistic interest" that had not been registered under Law no. 1089 of 1 June 1939.

Provision was made for the public or public/private management of operations conducted on the *comparti* or building units (no. 171, article 13, paragraph 6) through a publically controlled company, *Edilvenezia*, or, alternatively, subject to approval, by the proprietors, acting either individually or as a group.

The Special Laws no. 171 and 791 were intended to bring a greater level of prescription to the definition of practices and techniques permitted in works involving the built heritage. As such, they developed Italian legislation for the protection of the built heritage from Law no. 765 of 1967 and the corresponding ratificatory circular no. 3210 of 1967 towards Law no. 457 of 1978 and its offshoots. They drew directly from ratificatory circular no. 3210 of 1967 the concept of restoration as the "*ripristino di parti alterate*" (renewal of damaged or falsified parts) (no. 791, article 2, paragraph 2) and as the "*eliminazione delle superfetazioni*" (removal of accretions) (no. 791, article 2, paragraph 7), and they conceived conservation of the built heritage primarily in terms of structure and typology – preserving the inherited fabric and nature of the building. Thus renovation or restoration was to be directed towards "the integral conservation of surviving historic structures, the *ripristino* of parts that have been destroyed but are necessary to the integrity of the building, the removal of accretions and additions at odds with their surroundings, restoring the system of internal and external open spaces" (no. 791, article 3, paragraph 3), and towards securing "the conservation of the external architectural vestment", with particular regard to frames and casements, plaster renderings, floors, roofs, external staircases and doors, "which should, if necessary, be replaced or repaired with traditional materials" (no. 791, article 2).

In paragraph after paragraph the terms *ripristino, demolizione, risarcimento* (repair) keep recurring, implying the complete equation of the concepts of renewal and of protection. This is an attitude, in the early 1970s, still echoing earlier positions based on a conceptual rather than an empirical approach, and as a consequence seeking rather the preservation of an image of Venice than of the material in which its history was inscribed. In any case, there was a need to act, under the pressure of national and international public opinion, which by now was keenly aware of the Venetian problem and naturally interested in knowing the final destination of funds that had been raised all over the world for its sake. The *Comune* faithfully applied the reasoning of the Special Laws in their *Norme tecniche*, once again linking the idea of protection with that of producing something new (in the report presented to the Council by Edoardo Salzano, *Assessore all'urbanistica*, on the occasion of a debate on the Detailed Plans).

In essence, Special Laws nos. 171 and 791 preserved intact an age-old disregard for the conservation of the physical context of the built heritage; they went no further than uniting in a single document the entire body of current formulations on conservation issues. They represented a real novelty, however, in treating all restoration projects as part of a single overall programme, even if it might be extended over time, which it was the responsibility of the local authority to draft and implement.

There was no lack of criticism of this approach: a whole series of protests and demands made themselves heard, from an extremely diverse cultural spectrum. Among the most significant positions were those adopted by *Italia Nostra*, which favoured a protection order on the whole of Venice, and by UNESCO, which expressed a highly critical view of government action in its *Reports on Venice* of June 1969, September 1970 and January 1973. Also worthy of note is the *Rapporto sulla pianificazione urbana a Venezia* (Report on town planning in Venice) compiled in 1975 by Leonardo Benevolo and others; they re-stated and expanded on their position a few months later in a second report, and there were many international conferences on 'The Problem of Venice'. Indeed a law was drafted (4 February 1970) for a comprehensive protection order on the lagoon, and alternative Special Law proposals were presented to the Senate by the Italian Communist Party on 9 November 1971.

Criticism was also directed against the contents of the Plans, in particular against what was considered the harmful division of the historic centre into zones A and B, which, according to the critics, represented "a subdivision into different zones of protection and non-regulation". During this period there was debate (both sterile and fertile) on the future of historic city centres all over Italy, and undoubtedly it seemed criminal "to make demolitions, reconstructions and new construction enforceable" in some cases and not others on an arbitrary basis of zoning.

But the debate did not address, other than marginally, actual practice when restorations were carried out, that is to say, techniques, materials and specifications. It was confined to the problem of "method" of operation, seeking to identify theoretical parameters that would apply to every case, thereby guaranteeing sure results, tested in advance. Above all there was a call for "scientific criteria", criteria that were indeed worked out and specified in the *Norme tecniche di attuazione dei Piani particolareggiati* (Technical guide to the implementation of the Detailed Plans), which were approved in July 1976.

It was, however, extremely difficult to determine restoration programmes relying on criteria that were essentially little more than aphoristic generalizations. One unfortunate consequence was that the distribution of public funds to the private sector for restoration and conservational repair, provided for by article 13, paragraphs 7 and 8 of Law no. 171, came about only after an extremely long bureaucratic process. The following hurdles needed to be cleared: approval by the *Provincia*; positive vetting by the *Commissione edilizia comunale* (Municipal building commission); positive vetting by the *Commissione di Salvaguardia*; the issue of a municipal building licence; the certification of an agreement between the *Comune* and the *Provincia*; further approval from the *Provincia*; a decree from the *Magistrato alle Acque* (Water authority); positive vetting by the *Corte dei Conti* (National audit office), which authorized access to funding. This procedure took an average of some thirty months, and, given a context of high inflation, incurred an increase of about 45 per cent in the project budget during that time. In the same way, Law no. 457 of 1978, though requiring a different procedure, provided for the distribution of funding to the private sector (envisaged by article 33) only "on completion of inspection", thereby, in many cases, paralysing the "widespread" action the law sought to foster, and compelling administrations to perform financial and legislative acrobatics in order to incentivize otherwise uneconomic restorations.

9.4 The Special Laws and private initiative

The possibility of carrying out restoration in Venice without setting in motion the cumbersome apparatus created by the Special Laws was, however, offered by some vague but important definitions to be found within Special Law no. 171, which were interpreted and taken to their logical conclusion by Special Law no. 791 and the *Norme tecniche*. These provisions relate to building works of *"ordinaria e straordinaria manutenzione"* (ordinary and extraordinary maintenance), which might be carried out even in areas under a protection order if they were restricted to *"restauro"* and *"risanamento conservativo"* (restoration and conservational repair), as long as there was no *Piano di coordinamento* (in other words, as long as the *Comune* had not yet drawn one up) and consequently no *Piano di comparto*. Article 13, paragraph 4 of Special Law no. 171 authorizes "urgent" works on "minor buildings", during such time as the Detailed Plans undergo the process of approval; article 4, paragraph 3 of Law no. 791 adds clarification, defining urgent works as interventions "intended to deal with situations of danger and imminent collapse, though alteration of the internal and external structures of the buildings is not permitted, and also for ordinary and extraordinary maintenance". Article 24 of the *Norme tecniche* includes among operations for "ordinary maintenance" the renewal of plaster and facings in general, and among those for "extraordinary maintenance" "if need be, the opening-up or closing of window apertures and internal doorways … the partial or total substitution of horizontal structures … the demolition of non load-bearing walls … the renewal of external architectural features". Similar definitions are to be found in other instruments, for example article 31, 'Definition of interventions', of Law no. 457 of 1978. Furthermore, according to article 8 of Law no. 791, besides ordinary and extraordinary maintenance works, individual proprietors could also carry out "limited internal modifications, as part of alterations intended to improve sanitary conditions in dwellings, and the re-laying of roofs". This produced the paradoxical situation that the more derelict and dilapidated a building became (of course, it might deliberately be left to fall into decay), the more extensive were the works allowed.

What was not so clearly defined was a diagnostic parameter that would serve to evaluate when a building might need work. Indeed there was no means of checking the true state of a building, because no mechanism obliged or encouraged either those directing operations or those carrying them out to provide a survey of the building on which works were to be conducted.

NOTES

On the context and contents of the Special Law of 1973 see above all W. Dorigo, *Una legge contro Venezia. Natura storia interessi nella questione della città e della laguna*, Rome 1973, but also the seminars organized by Italia Nostra (in particular that held in Rome on 7 March 1976) and U. Carraro et al., *Il problema di Venezia: oltre la legge speciale per un diverso sviluppo*, Venice 1979. The debate was aired at length in the local and national press, and numerous architects, *urbanisti*, politicians and environmentalists made their views known.

On the problems of the use in practice of the Detailed Plans see the contributions to the *Comune*'s own publication, Comune di Venezia (Assessorato all'Urbanistica), *I piani particolareggiati del centro storico di Venezia, 1974–1976: atti delle controdeduzioni ai piani particolareggiati del centro storico*, Venice 1977, and, more generally, to *Riuso e riqualificazione edilizia negli anni '80*, Milan 1981; also F. Benvenuti, 'La legislazione per i centri storici: l'esperienza veneziana', and E. Salzano, 'Produzione di piani a mezzo di piani', both in *Casabella*, 436, 1978, pp. 14–15 and 18–22, and the *Rapporti sulla pianificazione urbana a Venezia* presented by Benevolo, Calcagni, Cervellati, D'Agostino and Malisz.

The quotation in 9.2 is from E. Salzano, 'Produzione di piani a mezzo di piani', in *Casabella* as cited.

10 | Restoration Methods, Policy and Procedures, 1973–87

10.1 Additional laws

The Special Laws of 1973 conferred on the Venetian local administration considerable and onerous powers of control over building and planning activity. Its officers were required to prepare *Piani particolareggiati* (Detailed Plans) and a *Piano comprensoriale-territoriale* (Plan for the regional territory), while the *Provincia* (Provincial authority), the *Comune* (Municipality) and the various *Soprintendenze* (State supervisors) were called on to assess and decide upon practically every initiative affecting the city.

These powers were further increased with the promulgation of the *Norme tecniche di attuazione* (Technical guide to implementation) and the creation of the *Piano di coordinamento* (Plan for the co-ordination [of building units]), by which every project, excluding those concerned with "ordinary maintenance" and those in Zone B (outside the historic centre), was strictly tied by the administration's bureaucratic procedures.

As we have to some extent seen, the origins of this tendency towards central control can be traced to three different developments in Italian society over the course of the 1960s: the election of left-wing local administrations, which sought to impart dynamism and credibility to public programmes; excessive confidence in the opportunities presented by the *Piano regolatore generale* (General Plan); and the moral and practical need for conservational activity to take account not only of environmental, monumental and picturesque values, but also of socio-economic issues. This last concern was echoed at international level, the Amsterdam Charter (1975) having clearly advocated the principle of "integrated conservation" – the conservation not only of the appearance, but also of the social configuration of historic centres.

Accordingly we find in Italy during this period a change of direction in developments involving the existing building stock, a change towards large-scale works, directed and pushed through rapidly by the public authorities in order to combat social decay in historic centres and their indiscriminate assimilation to tertiary-sector use. This obviously brought with it a need for a scientific, positivist methodology that could be applied widely to meet various requirements, on various scales. The need was answered by the almost unanimous adoption of the principle of *ripristino tipologico* (renovation in conformity with original classification), which is invoked and elaborated in particular in the Venetian *Norme tecniche* of 1976. Essentially it meant the adoption of an abstract 'typological' model (which might never be carried out in every particular) as a main reference for projected operations, entailing the elimination of

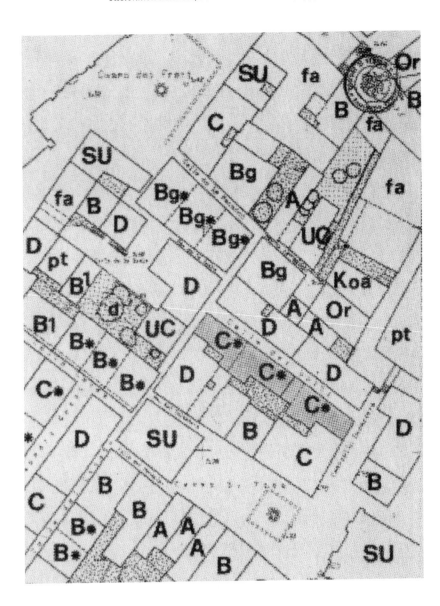

Fig. 103

The detail is taken from the map accompanying the 1992 *Variante per la città antica al Piano regolatore di Venezia* (Variant for the historic city to the General Plan for Venice): the building units and open spaces are labelled with letters and numbers corresponding to an index that details the kind of operations permissible on each type of unit. The classification is purely 'typological', and fails to register the material reality of the building units, the layers and parts of which they may be made up, the way or ways in which each has been built, their architectural or formal characteristics, or the effect of these in all. Yet abstract 'typology' was not only a guiding principle of the 1970s and 1980s but is still dominant in the current Italian approach to conservation and is enshrined in Italian legislation(see further pp. 212ff.).

elements that did not fit and the addition of new elements necessary for its fulfilment, especially as regards the disposition of spaces within the building.

The choice of 'typology' as a means of building classification, in Venice, Bologna and other Italian cities, was not only dictated by the need to act rapidly but also, in part, to the general currency of the concept – in disciplines such as geography, linguistics and structuralist theory. The work of theorists such as Saverio Muratori, Aldo Rossi, Carlo Aymonino and Gianfranco Caniggia was influential in architectural and urban studies; so also were the writings of the so-called Venice School (from the University Institute of Architecture of Venice, or IUAV) and the guidelines to the redevelopment of parts of the city of Bologna undertaken by the *Comune* of Bologna under the direction of Pier Luigi Cervellati.

In Venice the typological approach to restoration became, with few exceptions, the standard approach to all works involving such of the built heritage as was not evidently monumental. This remains the case today, and it makes Venice rather an unusual case in the wider context of the predominant trends in the major Italian historic centres.

Generally, during the 1970s and 1980s, which for Italy (despite grave social problems) were years of economic boom, the historic centres, hitherto under-used and inhabited by the poorest levels of society, became the new frontier of building investment, previously channelled into the construction of suburbs. It is no accident that within a few years there was passed a national law of major impact, still in force, Law no. 457 of 5 August 1978, 'Regulations for residential building'. The new law defined and controlled building works by intentionally generic criteria, establishing extremely flexible regulations for large-scale operations as well as encouraging their funding.

This was a revolution, for which the price is still being paid today. The Law established a *Piano di recupero* (Redevelopment plan), which granted partial exemption from the protection extended by the General Plan, at least within individual dwellings and while Detailed Plans were not yet forthcoming. In some cases the Law was actually used to set aside restrictions imposed by existing protective legislation. It was drafted in such a way as to introduce considerable freedom of interpretation, and indeed paved the way to more deregulation.

Article 31 of Law no. 457 established five categories embracing all interventions on existing buildings: ordinary maintenance, extraordinary maintenance, conservational restoration and repair, building restructuring and urbanistic restructuring. Ordinary maintenance (*ordinaria manutenzione*) included, among other things, all "repair, renewal and replacement of finishings", and did not need permission. Extraordinary maintenance (*straordinaria manutenzione*) included works "to renew and replace structural parts of the building" and "to install and make good utilities", and was subject to authorization on the principle of consensual silence (authorization had to be sought, but was deemed to have been granted if not explicitly refused). Conservational restoration and repair (*restauro e risanamento conservativo*) included all *ripristino*, renewal and consolidation not covered by the previous categories, and had to be carried out "with respect for the typological, formal and structural elements" of the building. Building restructuring involved radical transformation, and urbanistic restructuring affected the urban environment.

Operations on the built heritage are still administered by means of these instruments in Venice and all Italian centres. As they have come into effect, they have generated more and more friction with the earlier regulatory framework, including the Special Laws of 1973, bringing heritage control and town planning to a crisis. To summarize very briefly, since 1973 the *Comune* of Venice has produced fewer than a dozen of the 405 *Piani di coordinamento* originally envisaged. After the Detailed Plans had been approved they were to have been produced at the rate of a dozen a year, or one a month. Consequently, operations directly administered by the *Comune* have been very few, there has been paralysis of the anticipated procedure, and private-sector operators have sought more flexible solutions by resort to the more ambiguous or more permissive parts of the 1973 Special Laws, of Law no. 457 of 1978 and of the 1976 *Norme tecniche*.

In an attempt to circumvent the standstill, the central government passed another, seventh Special Law, no. 798 of 29 November 1984 ('New interventions for the safeguarding of Venice'). This re-presented what had already been set out in the Laws of 1973, and allocated new funds for works of conservational restoration and repair, as defined by Law no. 457, and for operations serving to re-establish the hydro-geological equilibrium of the lagoon. The law also greatly reduced the scope and the effectiveness of a very important controlling body, the *Commissione di Salvaguardia* established by the 1973 Special Law no. 171, revoking in article 14 the commission's control over all operations defined under article 31 of Law no. 457 except those involving urbanistic restructuring.

The State therefore continued to make available considerable contributions (from 50 per cent to 80 per cent of capital expenses and up to 100 per cent of interest payments) on works over which it was gradually losing any power of control – in particular, in island Venice, over replacement of external facings and roof claddings and methods of tackling rising damp.

In article 9 the Special Law of 1984 required once again a complete listing of monuments to be made subject to the protection order envisaged by Law no. 1089 of 1939. It was to be drawn up under the auspices of the *Ministero per i Beni Culturali ed Ambientali* (Ministry for the culture and environmental heritage), that is to say, by the *Soprintendenze*. Notoriously, this provision inspired a controversial initiative by the Venice *Soprintendente*, Margherita Asso, who listed the entire built heritage of Venice. Those who immediately protested saw this tactic as an attack on individual freedom and a calculated attempt to mothball the city. That was not in fact the *Soprintendente*'s intention, since in Italy listing a building does not make it untouchable, far from it; it only makes any work on it subject to prior authorization. She sought, however, to extend the control of the *Soprintendenza* over all Venice. However, it was clear that the Ministry and its dependent bodies did not possess (and do not possess) the means to inspect or enforce any such control, and that is the reason why, after all the controversy, nothing in fact was done.

Another, still bigger row developed over the so-called *Decreto Galasso*. This decree, which subsequently became Law no. 431 of 8 August 1985, imposed on the administrations of the Regions an obligation to draw up, by 31 December 1986, *Piani paesistici* (Environmental plans) for areas or zones under protection orders, or about to be placed under such orders. In effect, or so it seemed, this enabled the State, or its agencies the *Soprintendenze*, to make new protection orders (so-called *galassini*), and indeed the Venice *Soprintendente* issued such protection orders for the whole lagoon.

The immediate consequence was the cessation of all building activity in the lagoon area, because of the impossibility of obtaining a building licence; not only that, but in many cases operators in possession of a valid licence, granted before the protection order decrees were issued, decided not to begin works in the fear that the licence would be revoked once work got under way. However, in July 1986 the constitutional court declared the *galassini* illegal because they were published at a later date than Law no. 431, which had assigned to the Regions alone the power to grant protected status.

This affair, which only touched in passing on the question of restoration, nevertheless brought about a considerable worsening in relations between the private sector and the *Soprintendenza* – relations already damaged by Asso's blanket protection attempt. Whether true or false, the notion gained ground of a 'hostile' *Soprintendenza*, little disposed to dialogue with the private sector, intent on protecting its monopoly, on exercising complete control.

A second consequence of the Galasso decree was that the *Regione* of the Veneto, unable to meet the deadlines that had been set, accumulated the usual mountain of Russian-doll plans, adopting in 1986 an unnamed *Piano territoriale regionale di coordinamento* (Regional territorial plan of co-ordination). This referred to subsequent *Piani d'area* (Area plans), which in their turn were supposed to refer to *Piani territoriali paesistici* (Territorial environmental plans), which at this point might not anyway have been binding, the *galassini* having been declared illegal in the meantime.

Thus the *Comune*, incapable, as we have seen, of carrying out the exemplary, methodologically correct restorations envisaged, gradually ceased to be able to set a lead. Meanwhile the *Soprintendenza*, the body most qualified to take on this role, had alienated much of the public, and in addition was only able to act, mainly, by recourse to the funds raised by the international Venice committees. Venice was very far away from a comprehensive public policy of conservational maintenance.

It is only more recently that the *Soprintendenza* has been able to rid itself of a concept of restoration bound to 'typology', and to replace theoretical or iconographical analysis with precise reading of the material reality as the sole and proper frame of reference. However, *ripristino tipologico* remains the frame of reference in the *Norme tecniche di attuazione*.

The Special Laws with all their apparatuses have probably had little impact on the ability of private-sector contractors to conduct works on the built heritage of Venice with practices close to the margin or outside the regulations. It would be difficult to make a proper quantitative and qualitative analysis of these works in the absence of documentary evidence, but, given the margin that private interventions are in any case allowed by the law, one may imagine the worst.

10.2 Public restorations, 1973–87

By contrast, details of restorations and other works carried out by the public bodies in Venice are, naturally, available, though not complete, and enable us to trace a development in their methodology from 'integrated conservation' to mere 'building recovery'. In 1973, 1974 and 1975 *Programmi di attuazione della Legge Speciale* (Programmes for the implementation of the Special Law) were drawn up by the *Comune*, which, in identifying nine zones for which there should immediately be drawn up a *Progetto di coordinamento*, intended to get public-sector redevelopment of the housing stock off the ground. The programmes had no practical effect, however, as a consequence, it has been cogently argued, of "too many obstacles of a procedural nature, resulting either from the infinite range of individual demands of residents in accommodation or of displaced residents unable to find sufficient temporary accommodation nearby, or from the uncertainty of contractors about costs and about the consequences for the resident population …".

As it turned out, therefore, the first effective redevelopment programme dates from 1978, obviously much later than the Special Law had anticipated. The works were supposed to be "concentrated and integrated", and included the conservation of the social elements *in situ*; drawing on funds from the *Comune*'s budget of 1978–79 and others made available under Law no. 513 of 8 September 1977 ('Extraordinary programme for the creation of temporary housing'), the authorities were able to undertake works on a total of eighteen residential buildings, divided into six building sites, with a final result of thirty-two dwellings created after sanitary improvements and "cleaning up [*ripuliture*] to restore the internal distribution of space closer to the building's original typology". Of the six sites, four were deemed to be works for "conservational restoration", while the others were of "extraordinary maintenance". During the course of 1980 the *Comune* was able to extend its field of action to two cases of works of extraordinary maintenance and five of conservational restoration.

In these projects, even though the procedures adopted were essentially cautious, the consequences of applying the principles laid down in the *Norme tecniche* are apparent in the descriptions by those responsible: "… *ripristino* of the original character of the façade; *ripristino* of the two original typological units, which had been treated as one in terms of usage" (Castello no. 2221, conservational restoration); "The roof was completely taken down and reconstructed, and the fine chimney stack was rebuilt strictly in accordance with the original design" (Castello no. 2954, conservational restoration); "The project envisages the *ripristino* of the original typology ... attic windows were introduced through the *ripristino* of the original attic windows ... the roof was completely redone ... the interventions were determined on the basis of an analysis of typological characteristics and significance of the building unit" (Castello, Calle delle Ole, conservational restoration, in conformity to the *Progetto di comparto*). Who decides, and how, what possesses "significance"? "The intervention restored (*ripristinato*) the traditional division of the elevations by reinstating the hoods on the external chimneys on the façades, in accordance with the original design, established on the basis of an historic print" (Berchet, too, had operated in this manner); "the intervention, moreover, allowed for the recovery of two units that in the existing state appeared almost destroyed, extending to these also their historic typologies" (Dorsoduro, Fondamenta delle Burchielle, conservational restoration, in conformity with the *Progetto di comparto*).

It was the intention of the *Comune* that the dwellings gained by this initiative should become the first temporary 'housing park' for residents about to be displaced from buildings on which work would soon commence. However, the emergency of the *acqua alta* of December 1979 created an urgent demand for housing. As a consequence the restored dwellings were let on a permanent basis, while a programme of new building was initiated – a result which no-one wanted, either in Venice or at the national level, since the point of re-habilitating historic centres was precisely to provide an alternative to continuous new build-ing. New works were carried out to provide forty dwellings on Murano, seventy-two on the Lido, twenty-six on Pellestrina and ninety-four on the Giudecca, on the site of the disused Trevisan shipyard, deemed to be "of no environmental value, and destined for 'building re-structuring and urban restructuring'" in the terms of Law no. 457 of 1978. The project for this last area was entrusted to Gino Valle, and was completed at the end of the 1980s. In addition, there were dwellings acquired on the mainland with funds made available by Law no. 25 of 1980. Altogether, of course, these initiatives made no appreciable impact on housing needs.

It was clear by the beginning of the 1980s that an extensive programme of rehabilitation was too costly and too demanding to be achieved without private-sector involvement, and that Italian local administrations were unequal to the onerous, utopian task they had taken on. Meanwhile, they had been overtaken by events, or the complexities of economics and politics: concern about the decontextualization of historic centres had weakened, and so had aspirations for rapid and widespread redevelopment by the public sector. Decontextualization had effectively happened: the pressure of the tertiary sector had had its way. The priority had shifted rather to the institutional and bureaucratic management of the *status quo*, for which the best hope seemed regulation – the prevention of evictions or the (misguided) application of the *equo canone*, a system for fixing rents.

Thus Venice's complicated problems were exacerbated and, worse, their discussion was re-duced to ideology, slogans, to programmes and plans that played to the political arena rather than possessing any real practical potential. In the political activity of the late 1970s there seems to have been a kind of missing link between the fashionable solutions being proposed and a practical understanding of the modifications required to the legal situation in order to achieve them. There was no revolution that might have allowed things to be seen as they were rather than under the excessively synthetic, or actually distorted, aspect they took on when part of a programme. The typological basis of restoration law helped to create a skewed, displaced image of the reality being considered, managing, by force of law, to project on things an image that was not only spurious but obliterated all others.

Surveying the results of the *Comune*'s redevelopment programmes of the 1970s we can only concur with Marco Dezzi Bardeschi, who has maintained: "As though by a kind of historical paradox, every time we are funded to take action in favour of a monumental complex (as in the case of State-sponsored or other public restoration) or a building complex (in accordance, for instance, of Law no. 457), the legitimate intention at the outset – that is, to carry out an effective conservation of the degraded physical fabric that prompted the intervention – ends up forgotten, and everything turns into more or less casual renovation".

After 1980, given the failure to get very far with the rehabilitation of the older building stock, and the stalemate that prevailed, it was decided to extend the competence of the *Commissione di Salvaguardia* to projects relating to 'minor' or domestic buildings subject to extraordinary maintenance (as defined by article 31 of Law no. 457 of 1978). But, at the same time, the *Comune* put forward an informal proposal for a *legge di raccordo* (bridging law), by which the *Piani di coordinamento* would have acquired equal status with the *Piani di recupero* under Law no. 457: the new law would have overturned the statutory requirement for Detailed Plans in the historic centres, provided that buildings were classified typologically as integral units and their important features differentiated. Its purpose was supposed to be to allow works to be carried out on the basis of ordinary building permits, ostensibly to introduce more flexibility and pragmatism. Indeed its proposal marked the end of any aspiration to large-scale programmes by the public authorities. In practice it would have been dangerous, however: it would have partly invalidated the measures in force and thereby created a power vacuum, which would have forced greater liberalization. It would have been liable to encourage a repeat of the situation consequent on the passing of Law no. 765 of 6 August 1967, which was followed by a year's moratorium allowing speculators to accumulate a great number of building permits that enabled them to continue for almost a decade building in areas that Law no. 765 placed under protection order, without retrospective effect.

While things stood like this, the *Comune* undertook a study of five pilot schemes, funded under the terms of Law no. 94 of 1982 ('Programmes for experimental building'): the redevelopment of the former Dreher brewery and the Magazzini della Repubblica ('the Republic's warehouses') on the Giudecca; of the Casa dei Sette Camini in Dorsoduro; of Palazzo Gradenigo in Castello; and of the convent of Santi Cosma e Damiano.

The interest this initiative raised was considerable, to the point that Oikos, or the *Centro studio ricerca e documentazione dell'abitare* (Centre for the study, research and documentation of habitation) presented a 'Coordinated programme of experimental building interventions in the municipalities of Bologna, Brescia, Sasso Marconi, Turin and Venice', while new consideration was given to the idea of *Laboratori di quartiere* (Neighbourhood workshops), for which in 1980 Renzo Piano had already conducted a feasibility study with reference to Burano. The declared objectives of the initiative were "a quest for quality of intervention on an urban scale ... in parallel with organizational and management procedures, experimentation of methodologies of project design and technologies of intervention, with the aim of building a parametric framework to compare the relation between cost sustained and performance achieved", as well as "examination of the role of the public-sector operator" (which was a bit of a joke).

Chief among the reasons for the decline of ambitious rehabilitation projects by the public sector at the end of the 1970s was surely the inability of administrations to deliver either the necessary flexibility or rapid execution to a high standard. Thus the leadership and example that was to have been set to the private sector failed to materialize. This was surely more from lack of political resolution than from any problem with national or local legislation. It would have been easy enough to exploit the drafting deficiencies of the relevant laws, and thus to encourage modest renovation for "ordinary" or "extraordinary" maintenance. Indeed the laws, as we have seen, allowed too generous scope, permitting radical reconstruction and improvement and not making adequate provision for real control over possible abuses. There were now two very distinct spheres of action, on a quite different scale. One was concerned with the monumental heritage, isolated, sporadic, but relatively conspicuous, though limited to a small, privileged group of buildings, which were restored using the most advanced techniques and with a high level of control and transparency. The other, the general heritage, the building stock, the urban environment, the connective tissue of the city, operated to quite different standards, dominated more by criteria applicable to modern, new building than to old – by market considerations, by fashion and the media, and by self-interest.

There was indeed a popular, collective rejection of the old and an unconditional embrace of the new, fuelled by media advertising, but more profoundly perhaps constituting a cathartic rite of passage signifying the end of the hardship, poverty and migration that had so long prevailed before the post-war economic boom. As the Italian urban and rural working class came to experience a previously unknown prosperity, they renovated their old houses and their inferior old materials with the ferocity with which one might tear off a humiliating uniform. Wooden floors which always shook were replaced with solid ones of concrete; traditional doors and windows were replaced with new ones in bronze-coloured PVC or plastic, to grotesque effect in most cases; without and within, floorings and claddings were replaced with new cheap materials – with marble and coloured tiles instead of fired brick and *terrazzo*, with toxic plastic paints incompatible with traditional materials instead of less durable but more reliable lime-based distempers; for staircases and steps granite and machine-squared and -polished stone from Brazil, Spain and Africa was preferred to the traditional Istrian stone. These and other such were totems of the modern taste, the status symbols of change, the new look that celebrated the definitive end of a continuity going back centuries.

Once that continuity in materials and practice was gone, what was left was a building measured in square and cubic metres, with an identity no more than volumetric: in theory and in 'typology' it retained its past or its kinship to the past, but otherwise it had been stripped and reclothed in alien garb, gutted and refashioned according to the myths of the new progress, false to its very core.

This revolution, this remarkable display of popular self-determination, took place quietly, day after day, month after month. One immediate consequence was, too, the disappearance of a highly specialized skilled labour force that until only a few years earlier had been capable of working expertly with traditional materials, of carrying out small but valuable jobs of maintenance, repairing instead of replacing.

The pressure from below driving these irreversible and substantial changes, and an ever greater willingness to uphold the free market, reached a critical point in the early 1980s, when the demand for greater 'deregulation' became alarmingly strong. In 1983 even the *Assessore ai lavori pubblici* (councillor for public works) in Venice, the future mayor Nereo Laroni, declared the need "to adopt an approach with regard to the rules that apply to Venice similar to that typical of highly developed modern societies, an approach which is summed up by a term that is ugly, no doubt, but telling: deregulation, that is, the simplification of legislation, of rulings, controls. That there is a need for this is clearly evident from the fact of private-sector use of the funds made available by the Special Law."

In the meantime, alongside the 'pilot schemes' in progress, the *Comune* continued its "diffuse" activity of urban rehabilitation, setting aside funds for this purpose in 1982, and benefiting from additional funds on the basis of article 11, section (f) of Special Law no. 171 of 1973. It was therefore able to carry out another twenty-seven projects: in 1982, ten contracts of "conservational restoration" on thirty-two dwellings and five of "extraordinary maintenance" on another thirty-two dwellings; in 1983, seven contracts for "conservational restoration" on fourteen dwellings, two of "extraordinary maintenance" on six dwellings, and three of "ordinary maintenance". The kind of work involved was the same as for that in 1980–82, in so far as it was directed at "a genuine *ripristino* of the original typology ... that had been distorted by recent unauthorized works .... The extent and the nature of the building work envisaged were in direct proportion to the level of degradation and 'violation' of the building in question, and the dimensions and compactness of the same".

The works envisaged and carried out consisted mainly of the re-laying of roofs, the *ripristino* of the internal walls, of the original apertures in the façade, the repairing and *ripristino* of staircases, the reconstruction of chimneys on canal-facing walls ... in compliance with the provisions laid down in articles 23 and 24 of the *Norme tecniche* and in articles 2 and 15 of Special Law no. 791 of 1973 – or so much one reads in the report for the *Progetto di coordinamento* no. 378. The 'new' philosophy underlying these and other operations is well summarized in these remarks by Edgarda Feletti: "The watchword is and remains 'extend'. Extend action to extend experimentation, and, in turn, extend the area of diffusion; extend interventions from isolated instances and buildings to whole series of urban areas; extend them from ordinary maintenance that changes the façades of houses and the 'face of the city' to redevelopments, restorations, functional conversions or reconversions". The "experimentation" quoted is that of operations licensed under law no. 94 of 1982 or programmed by the *Comune* in the period 1980–82, and was limited in reality to changing the use of the building undergoing rehabilitation, therefore once again involving only 'typological' issues and the arrangement of internal spaces. Quite surprising is the generalized desire to change the 'face' of the city: it suggests an element of play, an interest in the ephemeral, as if to re-create Venice as a city of Carnival, a city for tourists – a sensibility that took architectural form in certain entries in the competition at the time for a new Accademia Bridge. Venice seems conceived as a 'theatre of the world'; one recalls the vein of iconoclasm in some of Aldo Rossi's watercolours of 1975, and in the 'ruin of architecture' as read out of Rossi by Manfredo Tafuri.

At the end of 1983 the *Comune* launched a new programme of construction in the areas it had purchased on the Giudecca and in Canaregio (the site of the former Saffa match factory), and at the same time attempted the environmental rehabilitation of an area that had suffered badly, the island of Mazzorbo, where there had been illegal building and a dubious reclamation scheme dating from the early 1900s. Here the entire project was entrusted to Giancarlo De Carlo, an independent professional rather than an officer of the Comune (fig. 105); likewise, Vittorio Gregotti was given responsibility for the Saffa site (fig. 104). The project was initially, in early 1985, blocked by the *Soprintendenza*, but effectively its fate had been sealed, despite the heated debate that followed, nearly ten years earlier, when it was included in the 133,890 m² defined as "urban fabric located on the fringes of the historic fabric and unsuitable for conservation in its physical characteristics or use".

The two schemes marked a retreat by the *Comune*: the attempt to manage redevelopment entirely from within the public sector was finally relinquished, owing partly to the difficulty of acquiring suitable sites, but chiefly to the failure to plan, let alone realise, the general and definitive response to Venetian problems that it had once confidently expected to achieve.

In any case there was a shift in the balance of power in the coalition that ruled the administration, which reverted to a more traditional relationship with the private sector and the city as a whole. In the great scope, or slack, now offered to private operators there was an increase in the number of works undertaken in the historic centre, not all of which were subject to proper control or compliant with conservational principles. In the later 1980s private operators at Corte del Remer or Campo Santo Stefano cloaked under the misleading term of "extraordinary maintenance" the reconstruction of floors and the "dismantling" (and then no doubt substitution) of the structure of these buildings. No-one was able to check what went on in such restorations except the inspectors of the *Soprintendenza*, and they were in no position to take over the direction of the work, as would probably have been desirable in certain cases. That in any case would have carried the risk of instigating new conflicts with the local authority, which was tending increasingly to indulge the private sector – it gave the proprietors of the Palazzo Grassi (fig. 49, p. 89) virtually a free hand in its refurbishment in 1985 – or itself to set a bad example – a blatant case of 'façadism' was that of the former Dreher brewery on the Giudecca (fig. 106), which was practically razed to the ground, leaving only the outside walls, behind which residential flats were built. The *Soprintendenza*, while technically advanced in conservation, was active in its own right in relatively few worksites, and elsewhere, beside the *Comune* and the private sector, was forced to play the role of gooseberry – more of a rival than a partner.

The *Soprintendenza* was itself affected by the stalemate of those years: apart from works it carried out with funds raised by the Venice committees, it did very little in the period 1973–80, under Renato Padoan. It undertook mainly consolidation and maintenance of buildings (notably Santo Stefano, the Gesuiti, Santa Maria dei Miracoli, the Scuola Grande di San Marco) that were still in a precarious condition after the flood of 1966, though it embarked on more major operations at San Stae, the Pietà and the Ghetto synagogues. A significant novelty of the period was the growing use of protective, strengthening, neutralizing or detersive agents that would not alter the appearance of materials. Although there were mistakes made in the 1972 cleaning of Sansovino's Loggetta (in the use of airjet abrasives and an epoxyresin coating which gave it an unnatural colour and a 'wet' look), the new techniques made possible very sensitive and precise restorations. In 1978, for example, cleaning was conducted by means of biological compresses (applications of substances that support colonies of bacteria capable of attacking carbon-black incrustations) on the Porta della Carta of the Doge's Palace, the well-head in Campo Santi Giovanni e Paolo, and the Lombardo frieze of the Scuola Grande di San Giovanni Evangelista (figs. 107, 108). Even so, genuinely conservational techniques did not everywhere gain acceptance, and at the self-same Scuola di San Giovanni Evangelista there was recourse to ultrasonic drilling, in order "to make possible the perfect restitution of the formal characteristics of the sixteenth-century decoration". Not all the new products turned out to be reliable: while the strengthening of the base of the statue of Bartolomeo Colleoni (fig. 64, p. 110) with acrylic resin gave good results, the same cannot be said of acrylic-silicone resins, reversible though they were: these in many cases markedly changed the colour of the stone, so much so that there were numerous calls for the removal of the protective coatings.

After Margherita Asso had replaced *Soprintendente* Padoan in 1980, the *Soprintendenza*, not surprisingly, attempted to tackle the worsening regulatory situation by extending its range of

Figs. 104, 105, 106

In Canaregio, the Saffa project (above; 1981–94) by Vittorio Gregotti, on the site of a former match factory, incorporates references to Venetian vernacular (such as the arch over the *calle* seen above, which recalls similar arches bearing the proprietor's coat of arms erected between pairs of tenement blocks constructed during the Republic) but otherwise has little Venetian about it in its overall disposition – nothing resembling either a canal or a *campo* – and might be an estate anywhere.

By contrast to the Saffa factory, the former Dreher brewery on the Giudecca (below right) was not razed and built over; on the other hand only the outer shell of the former building was retained for the entirely façadist 'conversion' into flats (1981–88) by Giuseppe Gambirasio.

The modern housing estate on the island of Mazzorbo, near Burano (above right), shows considerable feeling for traditional forms and masses and spatial dispositions (1980–89; by Giancarlo De Carlo). Its rendering was intended to reflect the tradition in the outlying islands for greater colour than in Venice proper, although it now seems rather closer to the city tradition than much of the plasterwork than has recently appeared there.

action into the arena regarded as 'political' – with proposals, as we have seen, for a comprehensive protection order, and with a stream of rejections of projects submitted by private operators. But there is little sign that it impeded property speculators: advertisements in the newspapers continued to offer, to the tune of hundreds of millions of the *lire* of the time, "completely restructured" sixteenth-century 'lofts' and the like. Nor were they deterred by such dubious tactics, on the fringe of legality, as unofficially discouraging private-sector operators from submitting projects to the *Comune* before approval of the proposed *Piano paesistico* (Environmental plan).

While the proposal for a protection order covering the entire city might have appeared rather whimsical, or – as some said – quite possibly unconstitutional, the *Soprintendenza* has since that time been very practical in its approach. What it has undertaken has not been of major proportions, but that does not lessen its importance or value, because there is evidence of greater consideration for the built fabric in its entire historic complexity, including all the vicissitudes that have contributed to its appearance and form, and for its materials. Restoration is based solely on what is known of what is there, and that knowledge, historical and technical, is the "scientific foundation for subsequent decisions". As was declared by the *Soprintendente* in 1986, it was a question of carrying out "a comparative assessment of the building and external data, with due recognition of the materials, of the craftsmanship of the artisans that worked on them, and of earlier restorations ... checking everything at first hand ... using non-destructive procedures ... establishing a 'continuous' study of the monument not limited to the moment of analysis or operation". What effectively was required was "the identification of the figure of the historian with that of the restorer", which needed a very high degree of specialization.

Leaving behind *ripristino tipologico*, we have perhaps carried conservation to extremes. State-of-the-art technology is now expected at worksites; reversible resins are used as a matter of course, with other products offering protection to materials while maintaining the appearance and colour with which these have so far survived; not least, traditional techniques are also being used or re-used. The terms *ripristino* and *eliminazione delle superfetazioni* (removal of accretions) have finally disappeared from *Soprintendenza* reports; scrupulous concern for the preservation of materials is a constant preoccupation. Even on major operations a totally conservational methodology has been adopted: at the Ca' d'Oro, the survey and consolidation of the flooring was carried out with painstaking care; at St Mark's Basilica, the main arch of the central vault was consolidated with acrylic-silicone resins (with the collaboration of one of the greatest experts in the field, Ottorino Nonfarmale); at the Scuola Grande di San Giovanni Evangelista the *intonaco marmorino* was very carefully consolidated (although the fact that the treatment did not entirely arrest deterioration is evidence that the science of conservation is by no means yet perfect); and the delicate stuccowork at Casino Venier and Palazzo Pisani was consolidated.

Figs. 107, 108

At the Scuola Grande di San Giovanni Evangelista, near the Frari in San Polo, the entrance courtyard had been adorned in the late 1480s with exceptionally rich carvings, attributed to the Lombardo workshop. Though sheltered to some extent by their situation, these carvings were subject to aggregations of carbon deposit of the kind that afflicted stone throughout the city acutely as a result of emissions from domestic heating and from industry in Porto Marghera. The ultrasonic drilling technique used achieved a very crisp, precise finish.

Once a skin of carbon deposit or of incrusted salts has formed on carved stone there is no choice but to attempt to remove it in good time, for such deposits are not static: they continue to eat into the stone and to grow, until such time as they fall away, taking the surface of the stone with them. New desposits form on the new, exposed surface, which is weaker, and the process continues with irreversible results.

To conclude this part of our account (though the issues and debates are far from having reached a conclusion), one may reflect on the fact that, after one hundred and fifty years of restoration, it is perhaps only very recently, for the first time, that the various positions and trends of thought have been clearly marshalled, both operatively and politically. For a long time conservation was merely proposed, urged, but not applied; now it has begun to be applied systematically, though still within a limited sphere. Conservation certainly started at a disadvantage, owing to the conflict between the demands of the private sector and those of the administration; and, while it is true that the private sector was considerably encouraged towards conservation by finance made available under Law no. 798 of 1984, it is also true that obtaining such financial aid, which requires procedures similar to those established by Law no. 457 of 1978, has proved difficult if not disadvantageous. It is true again that the research that the *Soprintendenza* regards – quite rightly – as an indispensable prerequisite before any work on a building can be undertaken inevitably carries further costs.

It has been a feature of the postwar situation that many have identified conservation with extreme or reactionary positions, exacerbating relations between the parties involved. Others have challenged the whole principle of conservation, claiming it to be an obstacle to getting anything done, as leading to *immobilismo*. As a result it has been necessary more recently to avoid espousing any kind of unrealistic idealism (except on a theoretical level), but instead to take full account of the priorities of the disciplines and sectors involved, though without prejudice to the principles of the conservational imperative. This, too, one can call analysis and knowledge of the reality of the monument, and it has been, and can be, of help in understanding the characteristics and 'calling' of historic buildings.

NOTES

Among the best studies of the characteristic structures and 'typologies' of the city of Venice are those by S. Muratori, *Studi per un'operante storia urbana di Venezia*, Rome 1959, and P. Maretto, *L'edilizia gotica veneziana*, Rome 1960.

For an outline of the activities of the *Istituto Universitario di Architettura di Venezia* in these years see *Aspetti e problemi della tipologia edilizia*, Venice 1964; *La formazione del concetto di tipologia edilizia*, Venice 1965; and *Rapporti tra la morfologia urbana e la tipologia edilizia*, Venice 1966, all with essays by various contributors.

Important contributions to the study of urban structures have been made by Carlo Aymonimo, for example *Lo studio dei fenomeni urbani*, Rome 1977, and Gianfranco Caniggia, in *Strutture dello spazio antropico*, Florence 1978; see also the writings by Aldo Rossi collected in his *Scritti scelti sull'architettura e la città*, Milan 1975.

On the work of the *Comune* of Bologna in the historic centre see the special issue on the subject of *Casabella*, 422, 1978.

The criteria for the planning of its activities by the *Comune* are also set out in Comune di Venezia (Assessorato all'Urbanistica), *I piani particolareggiati del centro storico di Venezia, 1974–1976: atti delle controdeduzioni ai piani particolareggiati del centro storico*, Venice 1977.

For a brief survey of economic trends of the era see B. Secchi, 'Immagini della città', in A. Bellini, *Tecniche della conservazione*, Milan 1986.

In 10.2 the quotations are as follows: G. Lombardi, 'Gli interventi di risanamento', *Casabella*, 436, 1978, p. 23; E. Feletti, 'La politica di recupero del Comune di Venezia: tra l'emergenza e la strategia', *Edilizia Popolare*, 176, 1984, p. 16; F. Costa, F. Grazzani, C. Pepe, 'Gli interventi di recupero del Comune di Venezia', *Edilizia Popolare*, 176, 1984, *passim*; M. Dezzi Bardeschi, 'Saper conservare per poter innovare', *Recuperare*, 2, 1982, p. 92; E. Feletti, *ibid.*, p. 20; M. Dezzi Bardeschi, 'La materia e il tempo, ovvero: la permanenza e la mutazione', *Recuperare*, 2, 1982, p. 131; and N. Laroni, 'Salvaguardia e/o sviluppo?', *Edilizia Popolare*, 175, 1983, p. 51. Margherita Asso made her remarks at a round-table meeting of 14 February 1986 in the Ateneo Veneto on the subject of 'Restauro, conservazione, manutenzione. Realtà e tendenze della tutela degli anni Ottanta'.

Fig. 109
At Calle delle Beccarie, in
Canaregio behind San Giobbe, a
house that had long since been
in *Comune* possession and had
fallen into ruin was chosen for
restoration in a joint project
between the *Comune* and the
Venice in Peril Fund, under the
guidance of Mario Piana. It was
intended to demonstrate that
such older houses could be
adapted for modern living
without the costs involved
being necessarily any greater
than building from new or
completely restructuring with
modern materials. Work finally
started in 2004 (photograph
2001). Although it is to be
provided with an underground
vasca or tank to protect the
ground floor against the effects
of flooding and is to be divided
into flats, as many original
elements of the building as
possible will be preserved (even
though it is not of venerable
antiquity). In particular its
brickwork will be rid of its
corrosive salt deposits by
prolonged washing in fresh
water, rather than being
replaced in the more destructive
scuci-cuci method. It is hoped
that the project will
demonstrate that the path of
conservation is no more
expensive or time-consuming
than complete renovation.

11 | A Resumé of Developments to Date

11.1 The destruction of La Fenice

The Italian edition of this book was published in the autumn of 1988. This new edition in English is appearing some sixteen years later, and the reader needs to be brought up to date, however briefly, on developments and events.

These years have been marked by one event that, once again, after the *acqua alta* of 1966, dramatically made known to the whole world Venice's fragility, and the difficulty of safeguarding the city surely and effectively – the fire that destroyed La Fenice theatre. Its fate was written in its name and its history: the theatre was first built by Giannantonio Selva when the San Benedetto theatre was destroyed by fire. In 1836 it almost completely burned down and was rebuilt to a design by the Meduna brothers, subsequently undergoing numerous alterations, modernizations and restorations.

On the night of 26 January 1996, a devastating fire broke out while restructuring works were being carried out on the building, as a result of arson, for which so far two electricians who were working on the site have been found guilty at two levels of jurisdiction. The fire did not destroy the whole building, but affected the entire roof area, the fittings, the boxes and the foyer. The rest of the building was mostly demolished afterwards, for fear of its collapse and further damage.

In the months following the tragic event, which only by good fortune caused no casualties, a debate began on how and when to rebuild the theatre. The mayor, Massimo Cacciari, pledged on behalf of the city administration to give the Fenice back to the people of Venice within the space of two years. A few days after the disaster, he said, among other things, in an interview given to the Venetian daily *Il Gazzettino*, "The Fenice could become the symbol of the city's rehabilitation, if we have rebuilt it within two years", or else "it could become the death sentence for Venice. The Fenice has a symbolic value as never before. This is clear to everyone. Either we shall be able to rise again remarkably in the eyes of the world, in which case it will turn out to have been a 'providential misfortune', or the Fenice fire will become our tomb."

In short order, the work was put out for bidding and contracts were issued. The consortium headed by Gae Aulenti was selected and works rapidly got under way. For a few months Venice seemed indeed to have broken with an unhappy tradition of inertia and incapability. However, after little more than a year, the appeal lodged with the administrative tribunal by one of the losing consortia, which argued that the winning project had not been taken into consideration the restoration of the theatre's so-called Sale Apollinee, which had survived the

Fig. 110
A view taken in February 1996 of the north side of the burnt-out *Teatro La Fenice* reveals the gutted building made safe by further demolition and the instalment of scaffolding.

fire, was finally upheld by the State council. It was in fact the case that this omission made the winning project and the quoted costs of implementing it incomplete.

Although the work was already in progress, not only did the company that won the contract change, but even the project itself: the plan submitted by Aldo Rossi's studio, which comprised the restoration of the Sale Apollinee and the entrance, the rebuilding *com'era, dov'era* of the auditorium (with some modifications to allow an increase in the number of the audience), and a new element, the big scenery tower, replaced that of Gae Aulenti. Both this and the change of construction company caused delays. The most optimistic forecast for the inauguration of the newly restored and rebuilt theatre was the autumn of 2003. The theatre was at last re-opened (for concerts) on 14 December 2003.

11.2 New planning strategies and
defence of the lagoon

The evident impossibility of dealing with the problem of interventions on the built heritage by means of the provisions of the 1972 General Plan and the 1974 Detailed Plans – and the anticipated enabling legislation that never came to fruition (*Piani di coordinamento* and *Piani di comparto*) – compelled the local administration from the end of the 1980s seriously to reconsider its urban planning and city management policies. It was by now widely accepted that the destiny of the island city of Venice could no longer be considered solely in local terms, but had to be seen in a broader, if not regional, context.

Thus, in 1986, the *Regione Veneto* passed a *Piano territoriale regionale di coordinamento* (Regional territorial plan of coordination; PTRC), approved in 1991, that was very mindful of the environmental issue and the metropolitan reality of Venice, regarded as part of a more extended, interconnected system including the cities of Vicenza, Padova and Treviso. This *Piano territoriale* was broken down into a series of *Piani d'area* (Area plans), including the *Piano d'area della laguna e dell'area veneziana* (Area plan for the lagoon and Venice area; PALAV), approved in 1995, which was born from the ashes of the *Piano comprensoriale* envisaged by the Special Law of 1973 but never enacted. The PTRC and PALAV, along with preparatory and related documents, outlined, albeit in very general terms, strategic choices confirmed in subsequent planning laws (*Atti di pianificazione*) passed by the *Comune* of Venice. At the same time the *Provincia* passed its own *Progetto preliminare del Piano territoriale Provinciale* (Preliminary scheme for the Provincial territory plan; PTP).

The intention behind all these measures was primarily to restore Venice and Mestre to a central position within a broader context, with Mestre re-cast as a public- and private-sector administrative centre and Venice more than ever a museum and tourist destination, research centre and university town.

Within this relatively new perspective, the plan was to construct and put into operation a new polycentric order, based initially on the reorganization of transport facilities and new infrastructures, to involve also the lagoonside that was common to both and that until now had been the area to which both cities banished their most chaotic activities (railway station and parking for Venice) or those least acceptable to the urban environment (industries and warehouses for Mestre). Naturally, within this framework, of central concern was the problem of restoring the balance of the lagoon's eco-system, by encouraging anti-pollution initiatives and also by moving the petrol-tanker traffic elsewhere and re-converting the industrial areas of Porto Marghera (where the 30,000-strong workforce of the 1970s had fallen to 14,500 by 1995) to a scientific and technological park (in Marghera's industrial zone I). To this end, there was to be a reorganization of port operations, of access routes to the historic centre and of transport facilities, with rapid new trans-lagoon (and sub-lagoon) links envisaged between Marco Polo airport at Tessera, Murano and the Arsenal.

The *Comune* of Venice immediately embraced these guidelines emerging from a more general level of planning, adopting an approach to city management in some respects diametrically opposed to previous policy, yet in other respects substantially along the same lines. Among the most innovative aspects was undoubtedly a new acceptance of urban planning, which was no longer regarded as a mere regulatory measure, but as a set of guidelines and proposals for managing change. With this new vision the hope was to break free of old arguments and of old measures that had become unworkable.

It is, however, important to reflect on the intrinsic reason for this move towards rethinking. It certainly did not come from any reassessment in theoretical or procedural terms, but rather from the need to control new dynamics that had been encouraged by national legislation (in particular Law no. 457 of 1978) and by deregulation, necessitated at local level by poor drafting of the legislation. Of these the *Variante per la città antica* (Variant for the historic city), passed in 1992, is the clearest example. It is discussed in detail shortly below. Its intention was to facilitate works on existing buildings by replacing the old measures with a new system of regulation, directed towards individual building units, though still based on typology. It was no accident that it should have been adopted almost word for word in the new instrument for city management put forward in 1997 by the *Comune* of Venice, the *Progetto preliminare di piano regolatore* (Preliminary project for a general plan), co-ordinated by Leonardo Benevolo, which became the final *Piano regolatore* in 2002.

Far from tackling a situation in which laws and 'variants' had removed any control over restoration (with the exception of buildings subject to protection orders), the plan effectively has given its blessing to it. It has fostered the recovery already under way in the property sector (in the last few years the price of houses in northern Italy has risen by 300–500 per cent) and in the building sector, for which conditions have been almost ideal. Contractors have systematically made renewals and replacements with modern technology and materials, for these, above all else, bring companies the greatest economic return. Building companies (and architects) have therefore been able to draw the maximum economic benefits from the creation of a large volume of business requiring unskilled labour with only limited need of technical supervision, often indeed working unnoticed, without formal notification, or in violation of the building regulations. They have systematically paid these workers illegal wages, for they do not have the necessary papers – this being a typically Italian scourge, encouraged by successive governments, which, except during the 1990s, have periodically passed more or less total amnesties for such violations. Recently (2004) this habit has culminated in the damaging, shameful and immoral total annulment of tax liability, christened, with rare aptness, a *condono tombale*, an annulment that buries the tax liability.

The newly approved plan for Venice resumes, stitches together and co-ordinates all the acts and provisions so far brought into effect or still being ratified. It has thus determined strategic choices for some sectors (housing, Porto Marghera, economic activity, the historic

heritage, the environment, urban organization, services, welfare and transport), laying down general guidelines. Directive measures have also been drawn up (a *Piano strategico* or strategic plan, a *Carta delle trasformazioni urbane* or Charter for urban change), which in turn are intended to generate *Progetti urbani*, *Sub progetti*, *Interventi puntuali* and *Strumenti urbanistici* (Urban plans, Sub-plans, Individual operations, Planning tools). This apparatus has itself been endowered with new cognitive instruments, in particular a cumbersome 'GeoDatabase' set up in three different formats to process and present data – a GIS format for cartographic representation, spatial processing and the creation of thematic tables; a Database report format, for the maintenance and development of the area data bank; and a web format, for the internet.

One of the foundations of the plan and of its execution is that strategic choices must be defined and modified after due consultation with representatives playing an active role in Venice and its surrounding area, with the guidance also and coordination of a 'Venice District for Innovation' (*sic*), a service structure set up by the *Comune* to support investors in the area, both Italian and non-Italian. In conjunction, two major projects, modifying proposals put forward in the past, have been prepared, destined, should they be realised, radically to transform the condition and maybe even the equilibrium of Venice and the lagoon.

The first is a plan new in form and name, but not in terms of the thinking that underlies it. This is PRUSST, a suggestive acronym – in Italian, as in English, it sounds like the name of the author of *A la recherche du temps perdu* – which stands for *Programma di riqualificazione urbana e sviluppo sostenibile del territorio* (Programme for urban redevelopment and sustainable development of the territory). At its heart is a sublagoon link, a technologically advanced railway under the lagoon bed, between the airport at Tessera and the Arsenale, stopping also at Murano. This 'metro' is intended to complement the rail and road links to Venice with a more practical one between the airport area, for which there is an ambitious master-plan of still greater growth in the future, and the great complex of the Arsenale, at present underexploited, but soon to be the site of all sorts of productive research and cultural activities as well as residual military functions. PRUSST incorporates not only some ideas from earlier district and regional plans but also those made in 1986 by a consortium of private individuals and companies known as *Consorzio Venezia 2000* (Venice consortium 2000). Formed originally with the aim of bringing a millennial *Expo 2000* to the lagoon, this project had strong political support, but ended in swift and inglorious failure. During the same period the architect Renzo Piano was commissioned to develop a project for a huge multi-function centre to be

Figs. 111, 112 (previous pages and following pages)
Venice is not only a city but a city within a setting, which recently has required and will in the future require much more care and attention than it received in the twentieth century. By such far-reaching and heedless acts as the foundation of the industrial complex at Marghera, the draining of the water-table with artesian wells and the annexation of much of the lagoon to fish farms, the twentieth century has wrought more, and more lasting, damage on the lagoon than any previous period in its ecologically short and precarious history.

built near the airport: known as the 'Magnet', it consisted, on paper, of an artificial round hill, one kilometre in diameter, with a central 'crater' 480 m wide. From this structure, two thirds of the extent of which would have been underground, trips to Venice (and *Expo 2000*) were to have been run.

Both *Expo 2000* and Renzo Piano's 'Magnet' came to nothing after encountering vehement criticism and opposition, especially to its expected environmental impact. The revival of a projected airport–Arsenal link, though it appears today it may meet with greater support, has also not failed to give rise to vigorous new protest over the effect that it might have on the lagoon bed. This, at the point of contact with the water, consists of a layer of *caranto*, a clay and lime mix the characteristics of which are little known. But, besides these quite reasonable and justified (until proved otherwise) worries about the effect such a great intrusion may have on the integrity of the lagoon environment, it is difficult not to feel another kind of reservation, of a cultural kind. Does Venice really need to be reached more quickly? Does the city need to be engrossed within the general modern contraction of time? Is there not a risk it may be deprived of one of its main characteristics, that of being sited at a distance from the mainland, in a unique environment, to reach which one must necessarily, like a pilgrim, undergo a rite, that of overcoming the defences constituted by the waters? Venice is now a global icon of well-heeled and leisured lay pilgrimage: let it at least preserve the peculiar dimension of its own time, in which its history and myth are inscribed. This is not an argument dictated by residual romanticism – how could it be, given that present access to Venice from Mestre first imposes the spectacle of the chimneys of Marghera and then that of Piazzale Roma and the Tronchetto car-parks? – but by recognition that apart from its population, which is small, and its palaces, which have been 'restored', Venice possesses another true and original pecularity, its time. This is well known to anyone who, like the author of this book, does not live in Venice, but goes there to pursue their studies or to work: travelling times, which in any other city can, in case of necessity, be shortened by taking a ratrun, a taxi, the Underground, or perhaps by resorting to bicycle or scooter, in Venice are immutable. Even running is hindered by the number of people crowded into the main streets.

The other side of the coin is that the lagoon is not just some irksome obstacle to getting from place to place; rather, it is an indispensable complementary aspect of the city. City and lagoon need to be experienced as one, which involves a passage, which cannot be instantaneous, from the rhythm, time, sounds and images of any ordinary city or countryside to those of the water and canals and *campi* and *calli* of Venice. To deny these considerations is perhaps to deny the very uniqueness of Venice, to implant it once and for all with the chromosomes of the consumerist ethic – with the corollary that it can be technically reproduced.

The second proposal hanging over the lagoon is the latest version of the project to construct mobile barriers to close the inlets of the sea in the event of very high tides, initially proposed in 1988. At first MOSE (*MOdulo Sperimentale Elettromeccanico*; Experimental electro-

mechanical device) was favourably received, internationally and at home, and then during the 1990s the *Magistrato alle Acque*, in charge of the development of the project, set up a *Studio di impatto ambientale* (Study of environmental impact), in which there also participated, among others, a panel of professors from the Massachusetts Institute of Technology in Boston. However, the response of both the *Ministero per l'Ambiente* (Ministry for the environment) and the *Ministero per i Beni e le Attività Culturali* (Ministry for the cultural heritage and cultural activities), set out in their *Valutazione di impatto ambientale* (Assessment of environmental impact), a document required by Italian and European law, was negative. Their verdict, published as a special decree in December 1998, called the project into question, despite the renewed support for it immediately expressed by the *Comuni* of Venice and Chioggia and by the *Regione Veneto* (Regional administration of the Veneto).

In the face of great inertia on the part of the Italian administrations, on 29 October 1999 more than one hundred deputies of the European Parliament signed an 'Appeal for Venice', calling on the Italian government to make a decision before the end of 1999 on proceeding to the executive planning phase of the project. On 31 December 1999 the *Magistrato alle Acque* completed its study of the project, in some 10,000 pages organized in several volumes. On 14 July 2000 the *Tribunale Amministrativo Regionale per il Veneto* (Regional administrative tribunal for the Veneto) issued a ruling annulling the negative decree issued in December 1998, on the grounds of its procedural and material shortcomings.

On 15 March 2001 the Council of Ministers requested three further specific studies and additional plans for protective measures, in view of the new forecasts of a dramatic worldwide rise in sea levels over the coming decades as a consequence of global warming. The additional measures for which plans were requested mainly concerned devices to increase resistance to the water entering through the channels connecting with the open sea. These measures could, it was estimated, reduce the height of exceptional tides by up to a further 4 cm, which would make a considerable difference to the volume of water exchanged between the sea and the lagoon.

Four centimetres are not, of course, very much. Yet there has been growing apprehension that the mobile barriers may prove insufficient and not easy to use. Therefore a quite different approach has also been taken, one which inevitably arouses misgivings – provision to raise the *difesa locale dei centri storici* (the local defence of the historic centres) to a height of 120 cm. At issue is the ground level of public and private spaces in the islands and the houses of the lagoon, and of Venice in particular. Venetian streets and squares, which at their highest are about 100 cm above mean sea-level, are to be raised to 120 cm, and ground-floor levels inside houses are to be raised as well, wherever possible. This has been sanctioned and required by the national government, but the *Magistrato alle Acque* and the *Comune* have already been at work on raising these "local defences" for some years.

Indeed Special Law no. 139 of 5 February 1992 ('Interventions for the safeguarding of

Venice and the lagoon') not only strengthened and financed various aspects of the Special Laws of 1973 and 1984, but also repeated the provisions of the *Piano regionale per la prevenzione dell'inquinamento e il risanamento delle acque del bacino idrografico immediatamente sversante nella laguna di Venezia* (Regional plan for the prevention of pollution and the improvement of the waters of the catchment area emptying directly into the Venice lagoon), which had been approved in 1991, giving new impetus to urban maintenance and establishing a single, integrated system for its management. Much of this involves "local defences".

On 3 August 1993, the *Comune* of Venice, the *Magistrato alle Acque* and the *Regione Veneto* signed an accord to work together, and in 1994 the *Comune* drew up a *Piano di programma degli interventi integrati per il risanamento igienico ed edilizio della città di Venezia* (Programme of integrated interventions for the improvement of hygiene and buildings in the city of Venice), which envisages the carrying-out of a series of works – dredging canals, stabilizing and cleaning canal-side walls and the water frontages of private buildings, restoring bridges, rationalizing underground or underwater utilities (cables, drainage), maintaining and replacing paving, and, while anticipating the eventual erection of mobile barriers at the mouths of the lagoon, raising the ground level to a height capable of providing defence against normal high tides.

To this end Venice was divided into forty zones or *insulae*, and in 1997 *Insula Spa* was founded, a public/private company (52 per cent controlled by the *Comune*) for urban maintenance. *Insula Spa* launched an enormous programme to raise ground levels in the historic city and the islands, called the *Progetto integrato rii* (Integrated canals project). The programme also envisaged the development, realisation and management of a *Sistema informativo per la manutenzione urbana* (Computer system for urban maintenance) and a *Sistema di monitoraggio ambientale* (System of environmental monitoring), monitoring the degrees and dynamics of the city's sinking, the speed and direction of currents, the quality of the water, the wash created by motorized water traffic and its effects, but also the state of buildings fronting on canals, the stratigraphy of the subsoil and the history and behaviour of building structures. Participating in these programmes are UNESCO, the US Environmental Protection Agency of Athens (Georgia) and the Worcester Polytechnic Institute (specifically on fire risk).

The intention to resume the maintenance of this aspect of the city, which for centuries had been its duty, its pride and the very guarantee of its existence, but which had long been neglected, is of course commendable. But the nature of the works envisaged brings with them the intrinsic risk of uncontrolled replacement and definitive alteration of those parts of the Venetian built fabric that are least visible but perhaps the most precious, and the least studied, those under or close to the water.

The *Progetto rii* establishes that the height to which street levels in the historic centre are to be raised should be 100–120 cm above mean sea-level, which is calculated to reduce the number of *acque alte* by up to 80 per cent. However, the ground-floor level of dwellings giving on to streets are to be raised to the level of +150 cm, if they are to be certified as habitable. A number of the larger *insulae* in the centre have already been subject to these works, as have extensive areas along the banks of the main canals, including those on the Zattere and the Giudecca, carried out by the *Magistrato alle Acque* in partnership with the *Consorzio Venezia Nuova*. While there is a need to limit disruption to circulation in the city, the profile of *calli* and *fondamenta* flanking canals has been considerably altered, some of them having been raised 40–50 cm. We shall soon have a Venice with lower houses!

And conservation of the paving stones, the traditional *masegni* of trachyte from the nearby Euganean hills? *Insula Spa* admits that at least 30 per cent of existing stones are regularly being replaced by its contractors, partly owing to damage caused by removing the stones from their original position, partly because the laying of such stones, which is not always easy, requires great expertise and takes time.

To return to the MOSE project, it remains to be added that on 29 November 2001 the *Comitato interministeriale per la programmazione economica* (CIPE; Interministerial committee for economic planning) allocated funds totalling 455 million euro for the first tranche of the system (for the three-year period 2002–04). On 28 November 2002 the *Comitato tecnico di magistratura* (Judicial technical committee) approved the executive project for the barrier of the Malamocco mouth of the port, on which work could begin immediately. The entire defence project could be completed within eight years, for a total estimated cost of €2,400 million.

But in February 2003 the local bodies involved, headed by the *Comune* of Venice, announced their desire to seek an amendment to the project on the basis of a new study by the *Magistrato alle Acque* and *Consorzio Venezia Nuova* regarding the possibility of reducing tides by raising the seabed in the lagoon mouths.

11.3 An "at least credible" Venice

The consequences of the basis of building regulations in 'typology' have become clearer in recent years, following movement towards a new General Plan and a radical re-definition of the policy for managing building works in the city, only partially facilitated by the new regulations of Law no. 457 of 1978.

In December 1992, as noted above, a partial variant to the General Plan was adopted, entitled *Variante per la città antica* (Variant for the historic city; see fig. 103, p. 183). It was approved together with its preparatory materials and supplementary notes, which included a monumental planimetric map of the entire island centre to a scale of 1:500, on the basis of which every building was classified according to its typology – or, rather, in terms of its most obvious or dominant typological characteristics, or of those considered to be original. Yet we know that most of the buildings that constitute the Venetian fabric, as in all historic centres, consist of many strata, reflecting sometimes radical changes to their nature and appearance in the course of history (usually regarded at the time as improvements), involving additions and the removal of parts and materials and changes of use. Many buildings have been hybrid from the outset, or have been split up when an estate was divided, or absorbed into a neighbour, or been built over. And how can one distinguish between alterations introduced by proprietors in 'normal' circumstances and those of the 'restorer'? Surely the many works of gutting and internal reconstruction carried out in the second half of the twentieth century could be considered abusive of the original typology of these buildings?

These are not the only objections that might be raised to typological definition, practically or theoretically. Nevertheless a classification of all the buildings in the historic centre into typological families was carried out, based on the "mental models" that governed their design in ages past. Authorization to undertake works (except where any other protection order prevailed) was then made dependent on an architect's project, judged not on its own nature and the merits of the plans but on its adhesion to the building's typological characteristics. This made it possible to start work very quickly, but encouraged a kind of architectural planning concerned principally, if not solely, with abstract, conceptual paradigms. Reference only to the typological categories identified, based on a few, mostly structural, variables (spatial disposition, lines of walls and their relative thickness, some technical and stylistic properties) obviously relegate to secondary importance what seem to our eyes the most vital characteristics of a building's identity. They are also the most fragile. Important are not only the variations and individuality of materials, of techniques and of appearance, but also weathering, patina and signs of change. Effectively, the preservation of these is left to the judgement of the individual proprietor or architect. All in all, typology is utterly inimical and completely blind to the historical strata of a building, which make up its identity and which are imprinted by its former inhabitants.

Apart from opening the way to corrective interventions of dubious value to say the least, the presumption that the features of an 'original' state can be determined is not very convincing. Still greater concerns arise when we find that a great number of buildings have been placed in the categories UI or NC, or *Unità incoerenti con l'organizzazione morfologica del tessuto urbano* (Units inconsistent with the morphological organization of the urban fabric) and *Non coerenti* (Incongruous [units]). These are destined, all of them, to be demolished.

Be that as it may, units have been identified on the map as residential and non-residential, and subdivided by period (pre-nineteenth-century, nineteenth-century, twentieth-century), by organization of 'cells' and frontages (mono-cellular, bi-cellular, tri-cellular, in a block, serial or otherwise, and so on), by level of alterations that have been carried out (original, rebuilt, of architectural or artistic merit, "integrated with the addition of spatial elements", and so on), as well as by level of "coherence" (congruence or consistency) with the surrounding fabric. Thus every building is designated by a letter of the alphabet that specifies its typology (see fig. 103, p. 183). This indicator cross-references with the *Norme di attuazione della Variante* (Guide to the implementation of the Variant), consisting mainly of a kind of check-list that identifies the chief characteristics of every typology: height and depth of the construction, number and

Figs. 113, 114, 115

The two views (left) of the Corte Seconda del Milion near the Rialto show that the four-light window once admired by Ruskin has hardly changed in the hundred years or so that separates the two photographs, the latter taken in 1999. In the view above, taken in 2002, the demands of a modern heating system have forced themselves through the lower arch of the leftmost of the four windows. However, although the result is hardly desirable, it is at least an adaptation of the fabric of the city to changing needs that one can only expect and that is not entirely different from the kind of botching that the windows have already undergone in the course of a long history – Marco Polo was born in a house in the neighbouring courtyard. Though insensitive, it is certainly not so bad as would be a complete *ripristino* of the row of windows, which, in 'rescuing' the building from the ravages of time, would tend to sever it, sometimes brutally, from its context and history. One may compare it with the restoration that has recently refurbished a house near San Silvestro (fig. 118), which has virtually killed off its material continuity and patina, whilst flagging its antiquity. This was a private initiative, but the recent restoration of the façade of the church of Angelo Raffaele (figs. 116, 117) demonstrates that authorities are at least as capable of insensitivity as private individuals. One can only call not only for greater control, but also for greater education about such damaging abuse of the city's fabric.

position of internal staircases, chimneys, open prospects, windows and doors, articulation of the main façade, the presence or otherwise of internal courtyards and canal frontages, modes of combination (simple or multiple) with other similar buildings or 'cells'. The list is used to check which of these characteristics actually exist and in the majority of cases to determine what action is taken.

On the basis of this profiling, the regulations establish for each of the categories the level of interventions permissible. The mode of categorization and description in general allows almost total freedom of action as far as materials and construction techniques are concerned, and it provides no more than very general guidelines as to what may or may not be altered, added or removed in the spatial disposition. The guidelines specify, for instance, that the front of the building must be maintained as it is, permitting alterations only when these can be justified by reference to the original typology; or that the existing structural, spatial and compositional characteristics must be maintained, unless a total or partial reconstruction is made of elements that have been altered by changes made more recently. What does this mean in practice? It means referring to the basic characteristics of the identified typology, as codified in the *Norme tecniche*, and showing that the survival of original elements makes such a reversion to 'type' "at least credible" (to quote the *Norme*).

So this is the Venice that typological renewal (*ripristino tipologico*) is preparing for us – a Venice that is "at least credible", where the boundaries between true and false are no longer distinguishable, but where falsification is considered, under law, acceptable and reasonable.

The Variant was re-submitted, with few corrections, by the drafters of the recent *Progetto preliminare del nuovo Piano regolatore* (Preliminary project for the new General Plan), approved in 2002 in its final version. Indeed the December 1992 Variant is there endorsed as "the only coherent product of the past management regime fit to be incorporated in the new General Plan".

The *Progetto preliminare* has partly corrected the approach of the Variant by introducing procedures for ascertaining the states of alteration of the building compared with the typological model according to which they are classified, but has simplified the regulations on destined use, which are to be established mainly on the basis of compatibility with the physical facts. It was meant, as well, to lay the foundations for a classification of twentieth-century buildings, correcting the guidelines in the 1992 regulations, but only to identify those "of recognized value, to be individually safeguarded", permitting "the transformation of other buildings depending on the requirements of the context". Overall, the *Progetto preliminare* retains the chronological and typological classification of the 1992 Variant, thus subdividing the built heritage into residential building units (ten categories for pre-nineteenth-century and ten for nineteenth-century), special building units (four categories for pre-nineteenth-century and four for nineteenth-century) and other building units (pre-nineteenth-century, nineteenth-century and twentieth-century). There is also categorization by building lot (*lotto di pertinenza*),

Figs. 116, 117
Restoration of the church of Angelo Raffaele in Dorsoduro, completed in 2004, involved the complete replastering of the façade, in the course of which the statue of Tobias and the Angel Raphael over the portal (attributed to Sebastiano Mariani da Lugano, died 1518) has become almost indistinguishable from its backdrop, in a blanket-white effect that eliminates not only the dirt, but much of the character of its five-hundred-year-old architecture. The former photograph (left) dates from 1998.

which may be monocellular, bicellular or tricellular (residential building) or unitary, modular or singular (special building). On the basis of these categories and types, one may carry out different kinds of works – *ripristino*, new construction, restructuring for a new use.

What then has happened to Venetian buildings in the last fifteen years? Or what may have happened, since it is difficult to assess the situation in quantitative terms, given the enormous mass of projects carried out that fall into the apparently least radical categories of "ordinary" and "extraordinary" maintenance, as described by Law no. 457 of 1978, and often exploit such legal and regulatory slackness. Here there are investigations under way, still in progress, examining the permissions given by the *Commissione di Salvaguardia*, the *Commissione edilizia comunale* (Municipal building commission), the *Soprintendenza per i beni architettonici e ambientali di Venezia*

Fig. 118
A visit in 2004 to the house near San Silvestro illustrated on page 1 (photograph *ca.* 1995) reveals further 'restoration' and the rediscovery of columns to accompany the medieval arch segments that had previously been isolated within the *intonaco*. Unfortunately these valuable relics of the past are rather unpleasantly and unnaturally exposed, and the new yellow plasterwork is garishly bright and out of character with the former patina of the city streets. This recent act of *ripristino* seems as brutal and misguided as many another of the more distant past.

and the *Ufficio contributi Legge Speciale* (Office for Special Law subsidies). Even from the uncoordinated data a worrying picture has emerged, because the only voice defending the principles and needs of conservation seems to be that of the *Soprintendenza*, affecting a very limited number of buildings, those covered by a protection order. It is true that a representative of the *Soprintendenza* is also on the *Commissione di Salvaguardia*, but it is also true that that representative is often in a crushed minority when it comes to the vote. Considering the more than 12,000 judgements that *Commissione di Salvaguardia* has delivered over the last ten years, one can only be struck by the very few occasions – in a very high number of cases – on which the conservationist position has prevailed, and this despite attempts at regular intervals to illegitimize the commission and remove its powers.

Building works, one may deduce from the terminology of the reports, from their references to the regulations and the typological categories, and from comments accompanying the votes and verdicts, are almost invariably blind to conservational issues, to the preservation of old materials and former techniques. Often one finds that they are associated with initiatives by the local authorities aimed at stimulating productivity or encouraging entrepreneurs or creating jobs for faltering businesses. For example, from 1996 the *Comune* of Venice allocated a share of the funds made available by the Special Laws to private citizens who carried out works on the common parts of buildings used for productive activities. Up to 80 per cent of the costs were covered, even though such works involved the complete replacement of the finishings (external rendering, inside staircases, floors, internal plastering and ceilings), the instalment of tanks or other devices to stop rising damp in the walls, and the repair or replacement of roofs.

To set against this onslaught, one can count only the few operations conducted by the *Soprintendenze* and the Venice committees (which, unfortunately, have not always been perfect, mainly owing to economic and logistical difficulties and the many different contractors involved). Which is not very much, when all is said and done, and little better can be said of new building, often neither proportionate nor suitable – though the city has, of course, turned down projects from Le Corbusier, Frank Lloyd Wright and Louis Kahn.

The struggle for an authentic Venice, for a genuine life for Venice, for an appropriate programme for Venice, seems a hopeless quest.

NOTES

The fire at the Teatro La Fenice occasioned a great deal of press, not only in Italy. For contemporary discussion of the options and means available for its reconstruction see the survey of opinions and reports compiled in the dedicated issue of the journal *ANANKE*, 13, March 1996. On the broader questions see G. Mencini, *Venezia acqua e fuoco: la politica della salvaguardia dall'alluvione del 1966 al rogo della Fenice*, Venice 1996. For debate on the nature and course of the restoration see V. Pastor, *Il Teatro La Fenice a Venezia: studi per la ricostruzione dov'era ma non necessariamente com'era*, Venice 1999, and M. Galofaro, *Riscatto virtuale: una nuova Fenice a Venezia*, Turin 2000.

Giorgio Gianighian has for many years conducted research into the incidence and destructive effect of 'minor' restorations and maintenance even when carried out in accordance with national legislation and local regulations, research which he has published in numerous conference papers and in specialist periodicals, such as 'Venezia invariata. Sulla sopravvivenza del restauro tipologico' and, with L. Cliselli, 'Quattro schede su Venezia', *ANANKE*, 14, 1996, pp. 43–56; 'Le façadisme à Venise', in *Façadisme et identité urbaine/ Façadism and urban identity, Papers from the ICOMOS International Conference (Paris 28–30 January 1999)*, Paris 2001, pp. 242–45; 'Venice, Italy', in R. Pickard (ed.), *Conservation of the European Built Heritage Series (Volume 2): Management of Historic Centres*, London and New York 2001, pp. 162–86. It may also be remarked how, in the last few years, there has gained ground a new vogue, against which hardly a voice has been raised, for dividing up larger dwelling units into small flats, which can be rented out by the week or the month at considerable profit. The local regulations once stipulated that residences could not be divided into units smaller than 200 m^2; the minimum has been lowered more recently to 120 m^2.

Regarding vernacular, non-monumental architecture, the Venice in Peril Fund, in co-operation with Gianighian, Mario Piana and others, organized a symposium entitled 'The Other Ninety Per Cent: The "Minor" Architecture of Venice/L'altro novanta per cento: l'architettura minore a Venezia', held in Venice on 17 May 2000: the *atti* were published (in Italian) in *ANANKE*, no. 37, March 2003, pp. 20–137. Also devoted to minor architecture is G. Gianighian and P. Pavanini (ed.), *Dietro i palazzi: Tre secoli di architettura minore a Venezia, 1492–1802*, exh. cat., Venice, 1984.

An outline of the new plans for Venice over recent years is well presented in L. Benevolo (ed.), *Venezia: il nuovo piano urbanistico*, Rome 1996.

On the activity of the *Consorzio Venezia Nuova* see its own publication, *L'attività per la salvaguardia di Venezia e della sua laguna*, Venice 1997. The Venice in Peril Fund sponsored a Fellow, Caroline Fletcher, at Churchill College, Cambridge, to gather together over three years the science literature and scientists involved in relevant coastal studies, organize a conference on the subject and provide a layman's summary (*The Science of Saving Venice*, ed. C. Fletcher and J. Da Mosto, Turin, London, Venice and New York 2004; also in Italian); the papers of the conference, held at Churchill College, are due to be published in summer 2005 (*Flooding and the Environmental Challenge for Venice and its Lagoon*, ed. T. Spencer and C. Fletcher, Cambridge University Press, forthcoming).

The projects by Le Corbusier, Wright and Kahn mentioned were, respectively, for a hospital in Venice (1964–66; see A. Petrilli, *Il testamento di Le Corbusier: il progetto per l'ospedale di Venezia*, Venice 1999), for the Masieri Memorial (1959), and for a convention centre at the Arsenale (1968–74).

The reflections of *sindaco* Cacciari are taken from an interview that appeared in *Il Gazzettino di Venezia*, 1 February 1996.

Introduction to the 1988 Italian edition, *Venezia 'restaurata'*

Marco Dezzi Bardeschi

Perhaps the elusive secret of Venice, unique city of art and monuments – enigmatic arabesque, drifting through time, on the quivering mirror of water in which it is reflected – lies after all in the spectacle of its slow, protracted death.

It is Venice's all too fragile appearance that every day renews amazement and passion in those who come to it, unprepared or not, and that provokes two opposed, contradictory reactions to its stones, which, under the sign of time, seem to convey to us all their (and therefore our) waiting for death – on the one hand the splendid contemplation of the good death of all things ("ruin is more beautiful than beauty", in Gabriele D'Annunzio's words) or on the other the overwhelming desire to scotch from these unquiet marbles every symptom of their bespoken end by pursuing the delusion of returning them to their former glory.

Confronted with the perennial myth of a dying Venice, it is difficult, in short, to remain solidly attached to the reality of the present, and much easier to succumb to the treacherous insinuations of ideology: either one plays Cassandra or one plays Viollet-le-Duc. Both are kinds of escapism, whether anticipation of a final collapse it is impossible to avoid, which the different approaches and interpretations of Camillo Boito in architecture or Mahler, Mann and Visconti in the arts have in common, or re-creation, *ripristino*, restitution, 'restoration' at all costs and in all senses of what might have been and is no longer. These two conflicting approaches, or narratives, or aesthetic dispositions, both operate at a figurative level, but with literal results, and costs, to the fabric that sustains them.

The former, involving the dreamy enjoyment of the 'picturesque ruin' has, for instance, inspired pages such as this (by Boito) that retain their descriptive charm today:

"When, as at Altino, Jesolo, Torcello, the mud carried down by the rivers has silted up the lagoons, and fevers have driven away the last wretched inhabitants, and the houses have all collapsed ... nevertheless, when the sun sets, the remains of some ancient buildings will still rise beneath the gilded clouds. The church of the Frari will display its exposed colossal naves .... The temple of Santi Giovanni e Paolo will be a pile of ruins, apart from the five apses, and Colleoni will remain intact on his shapeless pedestal, but the ornaments of the Ospedale [Scuola di San Marco] – so fine, so delicate – you will have to search for among the rubble and debris. And Piazza San Marco, what a marvel! The glistening gold of the mosaics of the internal vaults will be visible from outside, through the breaches in the collapsed walls, and the marbles and porphyries and alabasters of the broken columns will cast strange glimmers in the sepulchral gloom ...."

Boito, claiming that Venice "is a city not of this earth; it is a divine mirage", cannot content himself with what he sees: he needs to imagine it even more beautiful, as if, in some refined drawing-room game, he were cultivating a hyperbolic literary model based on the fascinating destructive power of time. By contrast, Viollet-le-Duc, deeply disturbed by "the most poetic city in Italy", complained in a letter of 1837 to his father of Venice's unbearable "frightful *tristesse*", manifest in "boarded-up windows" and "plaster covering the rose windows", and inveighed against its "dreadful hovels, dilipidated, without tables, without firedogs". Confronted with what he would not or could not accept of the past, he would claim instead that he could reproduce *com'era* (as it was) whatever he felt had been lost.

Whether held in the grip of an apocalyptic vision or consumed by sentimental dreams of the resurrection of an archetypal image, too many who approach this magnificent urban palimpsest end up losing sight of the present day. It becomes too difficult to focus on the everyday here and now, which is far too transparent and impalpable. It was the great achievement of that exceptional observer John Ruskin, by contrast, to have trained his eye, both captivated and perturbed, on the inimitable drama of the fleeting moment, the shadow of which passes like a subtle shiver over its stones.

It was surely no accident that the great realisation contained in *The Seven Lamps of Architecture* (1849) and *The Stones of Venice* (1851–53), the realisation that constituted the theoretical turning-point from so-called 'restoration' – involving alteration, not to say violation, of the existing object – to conservation – respect for the authenticity of the work – should be consequent on a real personal drama for the young Ruskin, which he experienced as a kind of luminous dark malaise (the 'spleen' of the sensitive intellectual who will not or cannot resign himself to a fateful loss). On returning to a city he had imagined to be a sublime and timeless invariable, he found instead that it was changing irreversibly, and recognized that his primary duty, if he was to be involved at all, was to 'fix' it on paper – since he could not, of course, fix it in time – by means of a detailed survey, in every particular, of the accretions of so many cultures, the fragile traces of so many generations, that have built and experienced at first hand the city with all its contradictions.

The singular and unprecedented journey that Gianfranco Pertot offers us, his expedition in search of those persons who have counterfeited our patrimony in their misguided understanding of 'restoration', in a sense begins at this point, with the amazement and indignation of Ruskin on 10 September 1845, on his third visit to the lagoon – he expressed his shock in an immediate account to his father:

"We turned the corner of the bastion, where Venice *once* appeared, & behold – the Greenwich railway, only with less arches and more dead wall, entirely cutting off the whole open sea & half the city, which now looks as nearly as possible like Liverpool at the end of the dockyard wall .... When we entered the Grand Canal, I was yet more struck, if possible, by the fearful dilapidation which it has suffered in these last five years. Not only are two thirds of the palaces under *repair* – we know what that means – but they could not stand without it – they are mouldering down as if they were all leaves & autumn had come suddenly .... Danieli's is peculiarly remarkable in this respect – he has done the thing thoroughly. All its rich red marble front is covered with a smooth, polished, bright white stucco, painted in stripes .... Add to this, that they are repairing the front of St. Mark's, and appear to be destroying its mosaics ...."

The devastation and the sacking of the sacred setting was total, and just four days later, on 14 September 1845, Ruskin wrote again to his father:

"I am tired of writing, as doubtless you are of receiving, accounts of calamities – how painful it is to be in Venice now I cannot tell you. There is no single spot, east or west, up or down, where her spirit remains – the modern work has set its plague spot everywhere .... I am but barely in time to see the last of dear old St. Mark's. They have ordered him to be 'pulito' and after whitewashing the Doge's palace ... they are scraping St. Mark's clean. Off go all the glorious old weather stains, the rich hues of the marble which nature, mighty as she is, has taken ten centuries to bestow – and already the noble corner farthest from the sea, that on which the sixth part of the age of the generations of man was dyed in gold, is reduced to the colour of magnesia, the old marbles displaced & torn down – what is coming in their stead I know not ...."

Now as never before, I am firmly convinced, it is indispensable and urgent to compile a painstaking account of the violations carried out in the name of 'restoration' in over a hundred and fifty years of uninhibited, utterly uncaring intervention, in order to prevent confusion between conservation and reproduction (of materials, of a supposed original, of a 'type', etc) from continuing to wreak havoc. Many authoritative voices, beginning with Ruskin, have of course been raised against this casual way of proceeding (Zorzi, Boni and others). And yet all these occasional protests and denunciations have not brought about any general radical and conscious change in the treatment of the Venetian heritage.

Pertot has risen to the challenge, starting with the degree thesis he discussed with me at the *Politecnico di Milano* in 1986, overcoming all sorts of difficulties (from the blocking of archives belonging to institutional bodies, to every kind of suspicion and hostility towards anyone seeking information that ought to be in the public domain and which instead is carefully not divulged, as if it were secret knowledge available only to the 'authorized'). His patient investigation has taken calm but implacable form, like a kind of 'white paper' that puts a finger on the historic – but still open – wound and exposes the colossal lie that is 'restoration'.

Finally the previously untold story has emerged, naming those responsible – and their accomplices, whether cultural or institutional – for the high price the city has paid in the waste of its resources, pointlessly, over the course of nearly two centuries.

Obviously this book presents only a preliminary chronological outline, still somewhat summary and partial, but it can serve to encourage more detailed research by others. Even the list of works undertaken provides very instructive pointers. One might start with its information on what we may describe as perpetual restoration sites (the record for works undertaken – not, of course, for maintenance – is held by the San Marco complex and the Doge's Palace). No one would have believed the number of times the restorers, with a maniacal persistence surely worthy of a better cause, have revisited monuments (and continue to do so) to interfere, substitute, reproduce (particularly targeted are roofs and unassuming surfaces), while often wilfully neglecting to devote even minimal attention to the timely and sensitive care of all those 'other' buildings that by contrast have serious problems of maintenance.

These restorers, pursuing a personal mythology of identification with the monument and with the city, the city, for instance, as depicted in the aerial view of 1500 by Jacopo de' Barbari, have operated, like sculptors, by a process of removal. Their noble objective of renovating deteriorated materials has paradoxically manifested a preference for the copy over the embarassingly authentic original. They wage war on stucco facings and ordinary surfaces (the systematic stripping of plaster is the order of the day), and apply themselves assiduously to the removal of 'accretions', which are invariably regarded as unwelcome and to be got rid of without the least compunction.

The issue of 'accretions' would alone take us far. A particularly good illustration is the case of the Fondaco dei Turchi, the object of a very detailed survey by Berchet that might have seemed to promise scrupulous respect for its materials, but which instead resulted in one of the most sensational cases of distortion: Berchet resorted to Jacopo de' Barbari's view "as if it were a plan to be followed" (above, p. 52) and in the firm conviction (which in itself is symptomatic) "of not having added anything, not even the smallest moulding profile of his own".

In this instance, just as badly as in the horrific case of the Ca' d'Oro, 'restored' by Meduna in 1845, pursuit of a supposed original form ends up, as Ruskin protested, in taking the original work to pieces in order to introduce, clandestinely, the most awful imitations.

Retracing what happened in Venice also means having to recognize the negative results of the persistent ambivalence of such as Camillo Boito, who always allowed too much interpretive leeway "between saying and doing" (to use one of his favourite phrases) and had a constant inclination to compromise. It also means being confronted with the interminable Penelope's web that successive restorations (always destructive, unfortunately) have given rise to, with the result that Meduna's creative interventions, for instance, were inevitably followed, with inescapable logic, by those of the equally intolerant anti-neo-Gothic de-restorers of the 1920s.

In Venice, more perhaps than anywhere else, so-called restoration and renovation (from Meduna at the Ca' d'Oro to Boito at Palazzo Franchetti, from Saverio Muratori to Gianfranco

Caniggia) have been locked in a deadly fusion, a *liaison dangereuse* that, even theoretically, has never been properly untangled or confronted with the necessary discipline.

Even today there are those who, seriously, think of "restoration as a work of taste" – the title of a book that relates the experiences during his career in the not very distant past of a *Soprintendente* of the Veneto – or advocate operations to "make good the image" of a monument (or of the entire city) with a particular date in mind. Caniggia proposed something similar in 1986 in the context of the competition to 'redesign Venice' (*Ridisegnare Venezia*) .

The ways in which we deal with this ever more elusive city that attracts ever greater crowds of tourists are certainly changing. Without doubt there have been special laws (Pertot unravels this unedifying story), and there is certainly no lack of funding or of projects (these being equally 'special', that is to say, consistently presented in promotional terms). And yet a strange and embarrassing situation of operative paralysis persists. It does not take a great deal of investigation to establish that in recent years, despite three special laws in force, very, very little has been done, and that has been badly done, for want of the famous *Piani di coordinamento* (only seven out of the envisaged 405 have been adopted!).

Officially, there is simply a passive 'conservation' of the *status quo*, but in reality there is rampant a clandestine, undisclosed makeover of the built environment, together with widespread abuse of the 'grey' area of the law. Thus an ever greater divergence between two co-existing cities is developing: below is the 'functional' city of day-to-day survival that exists in a present without quality or substance, totally indifferent to accumulated values and devoid of history or memory; above is the stage-set city, a surface structure, an outer membrane, almost immaterial, an empty mask undergoing perpetual modification because of *restauro in corso*, increasingly bereft of its basis and its ultimate reference. In this now systemic dissociation between the low-profile city for general use and the elevated city of iconic representation, the former is subject to the unscrupulous abuse of the market, while the latter, just like Nero in Ettore Petrolini's characterization, seems ironically destined to keep presenting itself, come what may, as 'greater and more beautiful than ever before'.

Our hope is that this gem of book will make a tangible contribution to the cause of the conservation of the wider architectural heritage, launching the necessary and long overdue process of the rediscovery of what Venice is today – mired in compromise and confusion between economic liberty and the principle of safeguard and control. Recovering the city's lost identity requires above all, after the great betrayal of *ripristino*, that we consciously face up to the distinctiveness of its present, and start operating in a correct, respectful and scrupulous manner in order to be able to transmit that precious history that the present bears to the future.

QUOTATIONS
C. Boito, *Questioni Pratiche di Belle Arti*, Milan (Hoepli) 1983, p. 9; *Le Voyage en Italie d'Eugène Viollet Le Duc, 1836–37*, exh. cat., ed. Ecole Nationale des Beaux Arts, Florence (Centro Di) 1980, p. 22; *Ruskin in Italy: Letters to his Parents, 1845*, ed. H.I. Shapiro, Oxford 1972, pp. 198 and 201–02; Federico Berchet, 'Sui restauri del Fondaco dei Turchi' , in *L'ingegneria a Venezia nell'ultimo ventennio*, Venice (Naratovich) 1887.

BIOGRAPHICAL INDEX OF PERSONS